Dec. /82.

Dear Verna -

MERRY XMAS!

And all the very best for 1983!

xxx....,

Barbara.

P.S. Reservations for 2 at the George V for '84?

[signature]

January 1990

A Different World

A DIFFERENT WORLD

STORIES OF
GREAT HOTELS BY
CHRISTOPHER MATTHEW

PHOTOGRAPHS BY
BEN MARTIN

THIS BOOK WOULD not have been possible without the kind co-operation of the proprietors and general managers not only of the hotels included in this collection but of many others which, for various reasons, I was not able to include.

Particular thanks are due to John Iversen, general manager of the Hotel Lancaster in Paris; James Nassikas, managing director of the Stanford Court Hotel in San Francisco; and Susan Orde of the Savoy Hotel Group in London.

I should also like to express my thanks to all those kind and patient souls whose help and experience I sought in my efforts to decide which hotels should go into the book, especially Mr. Anthony Hayes of Hayes & Jarvis (Travel) Ltd., London, and Mr. Richard Joseph, travel editor of *Esquire* Magazine.

Library of Congress Cataloging in Publication Data

Matthew, Christopher, 1939–
A different world.

1. Hotels, taverns, etc.—History. I. Title.
TX908.M37 647'.9409 76–3802
ISBN 0–8467–0135–9

Photoset by Tradespools Ltd., Frome, England
Printed in the USA.
Designed by Richard Browner
Assisted by Richard Johnson

IN THE UNITED STATES
PADDINGTON PRESS LTD.
Distributed by
GROSSET & DUNLAP

IN THE UNITED KINGDOM
PADDINGTON PRESS LTD.

IN CANADA
Distributed by
RANDOM HOUSE OF CANADA LTD.

IN AUSTRALIA
Distributed by
ANGUS & ROBERTSON PTY. LTD.

Table Of Contents

A Note from Robert Morley

MY FRIEND CHRISTOPHER Matthew is markedly starry-eyed where hotels are concerned, and when the assistant manager of the Beverly Wilshire Hotel correctly hazarded the number of his bedroom, he was pleasurably surprised even though we learned later he was occupying the honeymoon suite named after the Prince and Princess de Bourbon, in which the decorations were inspired by the Hindu God of Love. Cynics might imagine that there are not so very many honeymoon suites in the Beverly Wilshire occupied on any given evening by single gentlemen, and for all we know the entire floor might have been entirely empty. But Mr. Matthew is not, thank heavens, a cynic. Nor is his book, as he explains in his preface, intended only for the rich and the powerful and the famous who are used to the best, but also for those who have not yet arrived or indeed may never arrive at the Grand Hotel to occupy the Imperial Suite. Sometimes it is better to travel hopefully or even to stay by one's own gas fire and just read all about it. You may not, once you have managed to recognize Gary Cooper's daughter, Jennifer Jones and Pierre Salinger as fellow guests at the Plaza–Athenée in Paris, care to explain to Monsieur Roland, the restaurant manager, that you are eating alone by choice and not because you are unable to find anyone who wishes to eat with you; or be confronted by Monsieur le Bail, the sommelier, who covers the table with Armagnac bottles, defying you to choose a dud. However, where hotel decorators dream up headboards painted in antique gold and decorated with extremely rare Majorcan floral designs, and where furniture consists of hand-carved sixteenth-century reproductions, and lamps are made out of hand-painted ceramic vases from Talavera, and where a successful racehorse owner will have his messages delivered to him by a page-boy dressed as a jockey and wearing his colors, there you will find Mr. Matthew, who never tires of the pantomime and the transformation scene, and not only recognizes a palace when he sees one but describes it eloquently to the Cinderellas among his readers. I immensely enjoy reading the travels of this enthusiastic Sinbad, comforted by the thought that if he should ever get trapped in the cave by his wicked uncle, he would merely pick up the magic lamp and demand room service.

OPPOSITE The staircase of the Beverly Wing of the Beverly Wilshire Hotel, Beverly Hills.

AMSTEL HOTEL

PREFACE

SINCE I STARTED writing this book, I doubt if I have met a single person who does not hold passionate views on which are the best hotels in the world. For one well-traveled friend it is the Gritti Palace in Venice every time; for a London banker I know, the Savoy; for the man I sat next to at a wine weekend in Portmeirion, the Store Kro at Fredensborg in Denmark; for an American couple I spoke to in Vail, Colorado, the Inverlochy Castle in the Highlands of Scotland.

But what do we mean when we describe a hotel as being "the best"? Do we mean it has the most delicious food? The most comfortable bed? The manager who offers the most advantageous rate? The wittiest head waiter? The staircase that shows off an evening dress to its best advantage? Or do we simply mean the best known and the most expensive? All of these factors obviously play a part in helping us to judge the quality of a hotel. And yet, when you come right down to it, isn't the reason we acquire a fondness for a particular hotel far more fundamental and sometimes a good deal more indefinable than that?

Take the sort of people who travel constantly around the world. For them, a great hotel is the one where they are best known, where the hall porter calls them by name as they walk through the front door and the assistant manager shows them up to the same room they have always had; and where the housekeeper, as well as arranging the furniture the way they like it, has remembered their wife has a weakness for blue flowers.

For the less peripatetic, and the less rich, the great hotel is the one where they went for their honeymoon, or spent a holiday they'd been saving up for all their lives, or fell in love; where they played the greatest rounds of golf ever, swam in the clearest waters they'd ever seen, got the deepest tan they had ever had, and one way and another were pampered and fed and looked after in a style they had hitherto thought of as existing only on the cinema screen or between the covers of some glossy travel brochure.

For them, a night or two at a hotel like the Grand Hotel du Cap at Antibes, or Claridge's in Mayfair, or the Beverly Wilshire in Beverly Hills is like stepping into a different world. For a brief while they are

OPPOSITE The main staircase of the Amstel Hotel, Amsterdam.

really somebody, staying under the same roof—perhaps even in the same bed—where film stars, statesmen, financiers and kings have stayed before them. They are eating food that has been prepared by the greatest chefs alive, and drinking the finest wines. They sit reading in chairs that are over 200 years old and rub shoulders in the elevator with people whose families go back even further. They are served at table by a man who was taught his job by someone who learned from César Ritz himself, and the table itself may be the very one at which Aly Khan planned his speech of proposal to Rita Hayworth.

The rich and powerful and the famous will return again and again to such places, as they have done for years, and they will continue to take things for granted.

For everyone else . . . well, some too may get the chance to go back and for them it will be like that first time all over again; the others must settle for their memories.

For those who have had the luck to stay in one of the world's great hotels, if only once in their lives, I hope that this collection will bring back a few fond memories. For the ones who will never have the chance to aim so high, I hope it will allow them to dream a little anyway; while for those who even now are toying with the thought of a trip, who knows, it may give them a few ideas. . . .

This is not, let me hasten to add, a guide book. Inevitably it will be used as such, if for no other reason than that any book that describes fifty or so hotels is bound to help travelers make up their minds which ones they would be happiest to stay in. But it is certainly not a guide book in the sense that it lists all the choices in a given place, or how much they cost, or whether one is better than another, or any of the information to be found in guides like Fielding's. This is a personal anthology of a number of great hotels in Europe and the United States that I consider, by virtue of their high standards of comfort, service and food, location, architecture and furnishings, historical associations and type of clientele, to be genuinely outstanding.

It includes famous old city hotels like the Ritz in Paris and Le Grand in Rome; splendid new ones like the Berkeley in London and the Stanford Court in San Francisco; charming country hotels like the Bas-Bréau in Barbizon and Tresanton in St. Mawes; fabulous resorts like The Greenbrier in White Sulphur Springs and Gleneagles in Scotland, as well as one or two that do not quite fit into any of these categories. And while most books about hotels make judgments on the quality of the service provided, the comfort of the rooms, the standard of the food, the speed at which it is possible to put through an inter-continental telephone call, the aim of this one is rather to try and explain how these hotels succeeded in achieving the distinction they did, and how, in this ungracious age of supersonic travel, they are managing to retain their distinction.

Hence it is a book not of criticism but of stories—stories of how the hotels came to be built in the first place, and by whom; of the extraordinary people who have stayed in them and the strange events that have taken place within their walls; of the great managers who have run them, the great chefs who have cooked in them, and the great concierges whose constant gaze nothing and no one ever escapes; of the heights of success they have reached as well as the depths of despair; of how they fared in times of war, in times of plenty; and, perhaps most important of all, how they are coping in these times of economic change and uncertainty.

Like anyone else who has had the good luck over the last year or so to stay in some of the most splendid hotels in the world, I have many fond memories—of people I met, of things I saw, of meals that I ate and wine that I drank, of beaches that I lay on and views that greeted me through my bedroom window when I woke up in the morning. And by including some of my own experiences among the stories that I heard from other people, I hope to be able to give some impression of what it is like to stay in the Gritti Palace or the Imperial in Vienna, and at the same time to offer to the knowledgeable and well-traveled reader the chance to compare notes and agree or disagree.

Some of you may feel that the proportion of European to American hotels shows an unreasonable bias against the hotel industry in the United States. Let me explain that, since the art of hotel-keeping originated in Europe toward the end of the nineteenth century and practically all the great hoteliers of the world since have been Europeans by training if not by birth, it is almost inevitable that most of the finest examples of that art should still be found on this side of the Atlantic. At the same time of course there are many marvelous hotels all over America, of which several notable examples are included in this collection.

There are omissions from both sides of the Atlantic, some of them glaring, and people failing to find the hotel where they once spent the best two weeks of their life will doubtless be convinced that I have missed one of the best hotels in the world. They may well be right. However, let me repeat: this is in no way intended to be a definitive list. It is a personal choice of hotels that I know and like and believe to be, for one reason or other, particularly outstanding and charming. There are many hotels, both in Europe and the United States, about which I have heard marvelous reports from friends and colleagues and only wish I had had the time to visit myself. Among them are: Reyes Catolicos in Santiago de Compostela in Spain, the Villas La Massa and Medici in Florence, the Villa Cipriani in Asolo, the Schloss Fuschl just outside Salzburg and the Schloss Pichlarn at Irdning in Austria, the Castle Hotel Kronberg in the Taunus Mountains near Frankfurt and the Krone at Assmanshausen on the Rhine, the Auberge des Templiers at Les Bezards and the Mont d'Arbois in Megève, Inverlochy Castle in the Highlands of Scotland and the Mauna Kea in Hawaii—not to mention the Ritz in Lisbon which, until the revolution of 1974, was considered by many to be the finest new hotel in Europe.

Of the ones that I do know, some have been omitted because I felt they lacked the charm and warmth that is to be found in the world's greatest hotels. Everything worked, the staff were most efficient, and it took only thirty-two seconds to make a telephone call to New York. But somehow I just never believed that I was in the hands of a host with impeccable manners who was genuinely delighted that I had come, and took it upon himself personally to see that I felt thoroughly happy and at home. I never really felt I was in a different world. Others I left out for the simple reason that I did not like them. I am perfectly prepared to believe that there are thousands of people who did, but I did not. And over that there is simply no arguing.

Christopher Matthew
London, 1976

OPPOSITE A light switch in a room of the Hotel Ritz, Paris.

FAMOUS OLD ONES

AMSTEL
AMSTERDAM, NETHERLANDS

I HAVE SAID elsewhere that people's fondnesses for hotels are strange and totally unaccountable. Can it really be true that a man always returns to a certain hotel simply because he enjoys swapping lines from Pope's *Rape of the Lock* with the barman? Why not? As reasons go, it is no more bizarre than that claimed by the woman who announced that whenever she went to Amsterdam she always stayed at the Amstel largely because it had one of the few staircases in Europe that enabled her to show off her clothes to their best advantage. Well, all I can say is that she is in very good company. Queen Juliana of the Netherlands always uses the Amstel as her unofficial Royal Palace whenever she comes to Amsterdam, and when she and Prince Bernhard celebrated their Silver Wedding anniversary in 1962, not only did she choose the hotel's staircase as the setting for the official photograph of herself and all her friends and relations, but the hotel actually had the entire staircase altered and widened to show off the ninety-nine distinguished guests to their best advantage. The occasion was, as the Dutch would say, *"een hoogtepunt in de annalen van het Amstel Hotel"*—a high point in the annals of the Amstel Hotel.

Not that the Amstel has ever been unused to welcoming guests of the highest distinction. In 1867, the same year the hotel opened, the Dutch Royal Family honored it with a visit. And scattered throughout the VIP guest book we find the names of the Empress Eugénie, wife of Napoleon III; the Empress Elizabeth of Austria, wife of Franz-Joseph; the kings of Belgium, Sweden, Saxony and Bulgaria; the Grand Dukes Nicholas, Vladimir and Sergius of Russia, the King of Siam and the Shah of Persia.

On the occasion of Queen Juliana's investiture, the hotel's staircase provided a handsome setting for a group of royal guests that included the King and Queen of Sweden, Crown Prince (now King) Olav of Norway and his wife, Prince Jean of Luxembourg, Princess Margaret of England, the Earl and Countess of Athlone, Crown Prince Axel and Crown Princess Margarethe of Denmark, and Prince George of Greece. Again, the Amstel was chosen by Queen Juliana and Prince Bernhard for the pre-wedding party for Crown Princess Beatrix and Prince Claus—an event so successful that it was

OPPOSITE The ceiling of the entrance hall.

not until four o'clock in the morning that the royal party finally retired to their rooms. It is also a long-standing tradition that whenever a State visit takes place in Holland, the visitor always throws a big dinner at the Amstel in honor of the Dutch Royal Family and the Dutch government.

No, the Amstel Hotel has never been unused to the royal occasion.

But never before or since have quite so many important people come together beneath its roof as on the occasion of the Silver Wedding.

To name all ninety-nine subjects of that famous Silver Wedding photograph would require a separate book for itself. However, when I tell you that the Queen of England and the Duke of Edinburgh were there, and the King of Norway, and the Shah of Persia and Queen Farah Diba, and the Prince Michael of Greece, and Princess Marina, Duchess of Kent, and Prince Bertil of Sweden, plus nearly fifty assorted princes and princesses, dukes, barons, graafs and gravins, meurows and heers, you will begin to see just how high a high point it was in the Amstel's history.

Although completed in 1866 and ready to welcome its first guests in the same year, the hotel never actually opened at all—for the simple reason that not enough people wanted to stay there. The owner, one Dr. Sarphati, apparently quite undismayed by this setback, conceived the brilliant idea of throwing the place open for the public to look around. Within a matter of weeks the bookings began to come in, and the following year the Amstel opened its doors at last.

If the visit of the Dutch Royal Family in the same year did not assure the hotel of a good (i.e. rich) clientele, the appearance three years later of the celebrated physician, Dr. Johan Mezger, certainly did. To what precise skills his enormous success and fame can be attributed is not quite clear. But one thing is certain: his presence in the hotel, where he took up more or less permanent residence in the early 1870's, put the Amstel well and truly on its feet.

Even so, another twenty years were to pass before the hotel began to make a profit, and when one considers that a room on the first floor cost only two guilders, a room on the second or third floors only one guilder, and dinner only two guilders, one begins to understand why.

At all events, by 1899 the business was doing well enough to be able to afford the addition of a fourth floor, with a wonderful view across the Amstel River. More and more famous names began to appear in the guest book: William Gladstone, Paul Kruger, Ferdinand de Lesseps, Isadora Duncan; and later, after the First World War, Sergei Rachmaninoff, Richard Strauss, Paul Hindemith, Vladimir Horowitz, Leopold Stokowski, Bruno Walter; and later still, Winston Churchill, Harry Truman, Henry Moore, Marc Chagall, and always, of course, the royal guests of Queen Juliana and Prince Bernhard.

In 1942 the Amstel suffered a fate similar to that suffered by so many great European hotels: it became a headquarters for the German High Command. After the war the Canadians moved in and took it over. Up to 1962, when Amsterdam was very short of good hotel beds, the Amstel had things all its own way. And then suddenly, in the year of the Queen's Silver Wedding celebrations, work began on the construction of a number of new hotels. Within two years, no fewer than 4,000 new beds were available in a city that was fast becoming one of the great tourist centers of the world. One or two of the larger hotels suffered, even the Amstel. Even so, when a big meeting had to be held—as for example when the Dutch Bank of Hoogevens and the German Bank of Hoesch met to discuss their eventual merger—it nearly always took place at the Amstel.

One can see why. The situation—just a little out of the center, away from the traffic and staring crowds, with easy access to the front door and marvelous long views of the river in both directions—is both impressive and convenient. Since the British-owned Grand Metropolitan Hotel group took over the hotel in 1970 (along with the American Hotel in the middle of town), they have added a charming little dining room downstairs and completely redecorated the rather gloomy old bar overlooking the river, giving it a nice summery feeling with its rattan chairs and its gaily striped, tent-like ceiling.

But most important of all, the Amstel is one of those grand old European hotels that automatically exude an air of enormous reassurance—and nowhere more than in the splendid entrance hall: the moment you step into it, you are aware that you have arrived somewhere rather special. And of course, if you are the sort of person who enjoys making entrances, you won't find a better place to make them in all Europe than down that staircase.

PRECEDING PAGE The hotel is set on an island of tranquillity beside the Amstel River. THIS PAGE *Clockwise from upper left-hand corner:* The old landing stage; a ground-floor corridor leading off the main entrance hall; the restaurant downstairs, overlooking the river, has been designed to give the impression of an old library—the books may be false, but the silver is real; the bar, recently re-designed with views of the river in both directions; one of the main banqueting rooms; the staircase was specially widened in 1962 for the Silver Wedding phograph of Queen Juliana and Prince Bernhard; a stone tablet beside the main entrance commemorates the hotel's abortive first opening in 1866.

ANGLETERRE COPENHAGEN, DENMARK

A COUPLE OF hours earlier and we would have been lunching with the Queen. As it was, we were struggling back through torrential rain and seething traffic from Fredensborg where we had gone to look at the royal palace and eat smoked salmon and tiny shrimps at an old country hotel called the Store Kro.

Back at last in Copenhagen we had a brisk row with the people at the hotel where we had been staying, marched out in a huff and packed up the car. Five minutes later we swung into the pretty little square called Kongens Nytorv (or "King's New Square") and drew up outside the most famous hotel in the city and the one we should have gone to in the first place—the Hotel d'Angleterre.

Looking back on it, I don't suppose the welcome we received from the staff of the Angleterre was any more effusive than might be expected at any other hotel of that standard. Indeed, in some ways it was a good deal less so: the Danish appear not to go in for all that fancy stuff of accompanying you to your room when you arrive, and making small talk as you march along the corridor.

The bedrooms of the Angleterre (with the exception of the Royal Suite on the first floor), though large, are not particularly distinguished. The entrance hall has been almost completely ruined by the substitution (at the insistence of the city fire department) of an ugly elevator for the famous old staircase; the bar is cosy but dark, the dining room is much the same; the splendid old Palm Court, once the hub of the hotel, is now nothing more than a huge banqueting and conference room, with only a small palm motif in the carpet to remind one of its erstwhile Victorian splendor.

On the other hand, the Angleterre is, from the outside, one of the best-looking buildings in Copenhagen, as well as one of the most pleasantly and centrally situated. It is well run along old-fashioned lines by an excellent staff headed by one of the most efficient and charming managers I have met anywhere in Europe. It also enjoys a long and distinguished history.

Some time around the middle of the eighteenth century, a French hairdresser by the name of Jean Maréchal, who had originally come to Copenhagen with a group of actors, married the daughter of King Frederick V's *chef de cuisine*. Before long he had opened his own restaurant, which, thanks to his father-in-law's connections, soon became highly fashionable—so much so that in 1755 he was able to move his establishment to a house in the King's New Square, where he carried on a successful business until his death at the age of forty-four. For eleven years following his death the establishment continued to flourish under the ownership of his second wife. In 1787 she sold the hotel to a Berliner by the name of Gottfried Rau. Four years later disaster struck: fire broke out in the city and many of the buildings, including Rau's hotel, were totally destroyed. One house that survived the holocaust was Gramsgaard, the town mansion of the Grams family. Fortunately, Rau was able to purchase this splendid residence and in 1795 he not only moved in but also took

OPPOSITE An elephant was part of the crest of the Grams family, whose house the Angleterre originally was.

over the Grams family's coat of arms, which the hotel still uses (minus one small elephant) to this day. It was shortly after this that Rau, who had for some time been acting as host of the English Club in Copenhagen, decided to name his establishment the Hotel d'Angleterre.

Was it perhaps on the strength of the name alone that Mary Wollstonecraft, the mother-in-law of Percy Bysshe Shelley, decided to put up there? Anyway, to judge by the letter she wrote to her daughter from the hotel, her choice appears to have been a happy one. "I lodged in a hotel situated in a big open square where the troops exercise and there is a market. My rooms are very good. Because of the fire I was told that the bill would be enormous, but as I just have paid it I found it considerably less than in Norway, even though the dinner was in every way better."

Clearly, at the beginning of the nineteenth century, the Angleterre was beginning to make something of a name for itself among international travelers.

By the second half of the century, however, the feeling was beginning to be expressed—in the Copenhagen press and elsewhere—that the Angleterre, although unarguably an important international hotel, was just not grand enough compared with the leading hotels of, say, Hamburg or Stockholm. The problem was the side streets, which ran down either side of the hotel and thus prevented any large-scale expansion. But in 1875 the city fathers produced a report announcing a "drastic reorganization of an urban sector, which, although a central area of living and traffic, until now has been allowed to remain in an entirely unsatisfactory condition." The offending side streets were rerouted and work could at last begin on the rebuilding of the Hotel d'Angleterre.

The owner, Alexander Vincent, called in Wilhelm Dahlerup, one of the leading architects of the day. Dahlerup had been responsible for, among other things, the Royal Theatre, the Opera House, and the Chinese Pantomime building in the Tivoli Gardens. He altered the place beyond all recognition. Perhaps the outstanding new feature of the re-designed building was the hall in which carriages could deliver and pick up guests. The local press described the innovation in glowing terms: "A lofty and spacious crystal hall. . . . This is certain to become one of the hotel's fairest ornaments and assets, and, more than any other, contributes to the general impression of elegance."

Sadly, the Crystal Hall has long since gone, as for that matter have most of the hotels from which Dahlerup derived much of his inspiration. Yet to this day waiters in the main dining room of the Angleterre will sometimes refer to a certain part of the room as the gateway, often without really knowing why.

On April 29, 1875, Mr. Vincent inserted the following advertisement in the local newspaper:

The Hotel d'Angleterre, Copenhagen, will be open to

Left: The Lion and the Unicorn of England dominate the King's New Square. *Top:* The entrance hall—Queen Victoria by Winterhalter. *Bottom:* The hotel orchestra in the great days of the Palm Court.

travelers from Wednesday, 5th May. This new hotel—which in every manner is in accordance with present-day demands for comfort and elegance—has 150 salons and rooms on four floors, all of them stylishly furnished. The hotel's magnificent covered courtyard is on the ground floor, bordered by the restaurant, the table d'hôte salon, writing rooms, café and salons for smaller parties. All rooms have cold and hot baths and douches. For the convenience of our public, an hydraulic elevator, connecting with all floors, has been installed. Similarly, the elegant carriages of the hotel are at the continuous disposal of our guests.

A photograph of the hotel taken in 1860 shows a plain two-story building set in an open cobblestoned square. A few lampposts and a tiny clump of trees sprout where now stands the Krins, or Ring, and the statue of Christian V round which university students still dance in their white caps at the end of the academic year. By 1897, however, the Kongens Nytorv and the Angleterre had obviously become the social center of the city. A photograph of the time shows that the façade is now splendidly ornate, and the sidewalk fairly bustles with men in frock coats and ladies in long summer dresses enjoying the warm summer sun.

In 1902 the hotel was bought by the Anglo-Danish Company. It was at some point during their ownership that the astonishing figure of King (or, as it is inscribed on the foot, Kong) Arthur of England (and Round Table fame) first put in an appearance. No one seems to know quite where the statue came from, although there is a theory that it dates from the sixteenth century and was made, of all places, in Germany. Not so very long ago this impressive figure had pride of place on the grand staircase, and guests would salute him as they passed by. Today he is compelled to stand in a small corner staring rather crossly at the doors of the recently installed metal elevator.

Queen Victoria, on the other hand, whose portrait by Winterhalter hangs over the fireplace in the entrance hall, has fortunately escaped such indignity.

The photographic gallery in the long corridor bears witness to some of the glorious days the hotel enjoyed in the early part of this century: King Christian IX in a top hat and big moustache walking through admiring crowds in front of the hotel; a big party in the Palm Court to honor the distinguished Polar explorer, Roald

KONG ARTHUR
AF
ENGLAND

OPPOSITE *Top:* The Royal Suite. *Bottom:* The White Lady of Copenhagen. THIS PAGE ". . . staring rather crossly, at the elevator doors."

Amundsen; another big gathering, called to discuss humanity to animals and the preservation of wild life, which also took place in the Palm Court—a worthy successor to the Crystal Hall.

Hardly a social event took place in those days unless it was at the Hotel d'Angleterre, and hardly an important visitor came to Copenhagen who did not stay there: Sarah Bernhardt, Ibsen, Conan Doyle, Somerset Maugham, Charles Lindbergh, Toscanini, Grace Moore, Paul Robeson, Eisenhower, Ironside, Earl Warren, Andrei Gromyko . . . the list is endless.

But of all the distinguished guests the hotel has received over the past hundred years or so, never has it had to cope with quite so many in one go as it did in 1972, on the occasion of the funeral of the late King Frederick X. For Mr. Eigil Hummelgaard, the hotel's managing director, they were two of the most hair-raising, and at the same time most satisfying, days of his life. They began with a telephone call from the Royal Castle, requesting accommodation for the 144 members of royal families from all over the world, including the Queen of Holland, the King and Queen of Belgium, the King of Norway, the Grand Duke and Duchess of Luxembourg, Prince Rainier and Princess Grace of Monaco, ex-King Umberto of Italy, the heads of state of Germany, Ireland and Finland, and numberless princes and princesses. Only the Swedish Royal Family were invited to stay at the Royal Castle.

Of all the guests Mr. Hummergaard has had staying at one time under his roof, none have been so individually and collectively undemanding and charming as were the members of that august company.

Queen Juliana of the Netherlands was given the Royal Suite. ("Is this all for me?" she exclaimed as she was shown in.); The King of Belgium, upon hearing that his room was next door, rushed straight in to greet Her Majesty with a shout of "Hello, neighbors!" Only the Prime Minister of one Eastern Bloc country caused some concern by demanding, for security reasons, that the rooms on either side of his own should remain unoccupied. The King of Norway said that he was so glad to have had the chance to stay there at last, since he had previously only seen it from the outside. Queen Fabiola of Belgium told Mr. Hummelgaard it was the nicest hotel she had ever stayed in.

There is obviously no knowing why a guest, regal or otherwise, develops an instant fondness for a certain hotel; but I suspect that the thing that appealed to the members of that distinguished gathering was that gay and at the same time cosy atmosphere that the Danes enjoy at home and expect to find in hotels and restaurants whenever they go out. Plenty of flowers, and lighted candles, and good nourishing food. . . .

Of course, as Mr. Hummelgaard knows only too well, such food is often not fine enough for the clientele of an international hotel of that standing. He has to take great care to serve enough to attract the Danish businessman out for lunch, but not so much that the

international traveler takes to eating at the Sheraton. Gradually, however, he is beginning to find that many foreign guests enjoy typical Danish dishes, like duck with red cabbage, boiled and salted duck served with vegetables, cold boiled calf's head, stew made from chopped meat from the previous day's roast, fried with onions and potatoes, and especially plain fried plaice, which I had for dinner one evening, and was quite different from any plaice I have ever come across before. On the luncheon menu you can always be sure of finding such delicious Danish specialties as fried herring with a sweet and sour dressing, or *gravad laks*—the marinated salmon that everyone adores, or sensational hand-cut open sandwiches.

No one could tell me exactly what Queen Margarethe and her friends had eaten for lunch.

The important thing was that of all the places in Copenhagen she could have picked to meet her friends for lunch, she had chosen to sit in a small corner in the bar of the Angleterre, surrounded by businessmen, hotel guests, and, had we not at that moment been driving back through the rain from Fredensborg, two slightly disreputable journalists. Very democratic, Denmark.

Anne Morrow Lindbergh

Charles A. Lindbergh - Aug 28, 1933

Arturo Toscanini

6 - 12 - 933

Left: A small reception room. *Above:* A leaf of the distinguished guests' book.

Breakfast card

BAUR AU LAC
ZURICH, SWITZERLAND

OPPOSITE A mild sensation.

BREAKFAST AT THE Baur au Lac in Zurich is something of a mild sensation. Not because the food served is in any way extraordinary or exotic. On the contrary. But simply because it is one of the best proofs I have found in any hotel that it isn't so much what you give the customer as the way you give it.

Actually of course, the Baur au Lac being the great hotel it is and having in charge a fine hotelier like Georges Rey (César Ritz's nephew, by the way), one really should not be surprised to discover that the service is as impeccable today as it was fifty years ago. Even so, one is rather taken aback when one rings one's bell for room service at eight in the morning and within two minutes a floor waiter is knocking at the door ready to take one's order. Mr. Rey believes firmly that his clients do not care for disembodied voices at the other end of a telephone that might, and quite often do, get the order or the room number wrong; and that they are reassured when they see the same man every morning, who, when you suggest a slight increase in the strength of the coffee, knows how you had it the first time. It seems only moments later that the breakfast arrives, wheeled in on a silent trolley. The actual ingredients are not, as I say, out of the ordinary. Yet there are few hotels in the world that would bother to serve up, on a white linen tablecloth, croissants, two types of rolls, biscottes, Ryvita, two types of brown bread, butter in a dish on ice, individual dishes of jam, honey and marmalade, each with its own spoon, and as much coffee as I could drink. Generosity is halfway to luxury, and it was with deep contentment that I set off for the Bahnhof to catch the TEE Gottardo to Italy.

Anyone who is not lucky enough to be able to stay a night at the Baur au Lac and who just visits during the day might be forgiven for thinking it rather a dull place and wondering why sophisticated travelers rate it so highly.

On the other hand, it is a very welcoming hotel. I remember that when I first strolled in one balmy Sunday afternoon in early May in search of a good up of tea. I had the distinct feeling of being very much at home.

Tea is served in the garden, on a patio in the middle of which stands an umbrella for rainy days large enough to provide cover for the hosts of Gideon. A deserted bandstand bears witness to more exuberant days when tea-drinkers would suddenly break off in the middle of a piece of *apfelstrudel* and hoof it to the strains of "Edelweiss." Mind you, the cakes and the tea I had were far too good to be abandoned in favor of terpsichory. Apart from anything else, the setting is so very charming. On one side is the cool white airy shape of the summer Pavilion Restaurant, like a long conservatory with its bright red chairs, white tablecloths, red check lampshades and red flowers, where I was later to enjoy an impeccably served *emincé de veau Zurichoise*; to the other side is the garden that runs alongside the canal, its bright green lawn shaded by huge trees (including a giant Sequoia planted in 1844) and its vistas beyond of the lake and

Boite aux Lettres

mountains. It is hard to believe one is in the middle of a big town.

The entrance hall and public rooms of the hotel exude an air of quiet distinction, the marble floor leading through to polished parquet, rather good carpets and a lot of pale wood paneling, Louis XVI and Empire furniture and the occasional pretty little Swiss clock. Nothing gaudy, nothing extraordinary, but all in very quiet, very good taste. But then, as Monsieur Rey pointed out to me, with the money the Kracht family, who own the hotel, have spent on renovation and refurbishing over the last twenty years they could have built a whole new hotel!

On the other hand, the Kracht family have scrupulously avoided introducing the sort of features that are taken for granted in hotels of the very highest standing nowadays—things like mini-refrigerators in the bedrooms ("They always seem to me to be a confession of bad floor service," says Monsieur Rey); groups and incentive tours ("The only business meetings that take place here are between individuals. Walk into the salon any morning of the week and you will see some of the most powerful bankers and financiers of the world talking together over coffee, and you probably won't recognize one of them"). Nor are there television sets in the rooms ("We'd rather guests had a good bed than a good television. Of course both are possible, but we like to give people sets only when they ask for them") or a swimming pool ("It would only be used by the staff").

All of which says a lot about the sort of people who stay at the Baur au Lac, not least about their age. And yet try as he might, Monsieur Rey is only too aware of the difficulties of maintaining the high standards that will please both him and his clients equally. "Things have changed. Once upon a time it was the clients who taught the staff how things should be done. But that's all finished now—either because they themselves don't know or else they don't like to appear to be grumbling."

But then Monsieur Rey, like all perfectionists, will never achieve the perfection he seeks. The most self-satisfied thing I ever heard him say was, "Well, if we are able to continue to give the same service we have always given, I believe we shall always have the clientele for it."

PRECEDING PAGES *Top left:* The main entrance from the garden. *Bottom left:* The lake from the bottom of the garden. *Top center:* The entrance hall *Middle center:* One of the suites.

PRECEDING PAGES *Bottom center, far right and* OPPOSITE "Nothing gaudy . . . all in very good, very quiet taste."

HOTEL BAYERISCHER HOF
BLUMEN
TAXI
M·SE 1206

BAYERISCHER HOF
MUNICH, GERMANY

I UNDERSTAND THAT they are working on a German sequel to that famous American film comedy, *Weekend in the Waldorf.* It will be called *Bedlam at the Bayerischer Hof,* and it will be shot in and around the famous hotel of that name in Munich. The script is only in its preparatory stages at present but I gather that the opening sequence will show the hotel lobby in the middle of any normal week-day morning. To anyone who does not know the hotel it will seem incredible that so many different activities can be encompassed at one time in such a modest area. Porters staggering beneath the weight of a dozen matching suitcases; hard-faced men pacing up and down in expensive fur-collared overcoats, looking anxiously at their watches; receptionists darting back and forth at one end of the long main desk while at the other a small team of uniformed concierges perform prodigious feats of juggling telephones, keys, messages and enquiries; elegant women in berets carrying Christian Dior shopping bags and trailing perky little dachshunds; waiters scuttling past beneath silver trays of coffee. Wherever you look there is someone doing something—either gesticulating, or grimacing, or barking orders, or sighing, or clapping his hand to his forehead or talking or laughing. The noise produced by all this to-ing and fro-ing and up-ing and down-ing is prodigious, especially when added to it you have the muttering from the people waiting outside to buy seats at the Kleine Komödie theater, the constant *whump whump whump* of the swing door being swung, and the endless jangle of telephones behind the reception desk.

Having lovingly explored this positively Swiftian slice of life, the camera pans up and away to reveal, standing on the balcony that surrounds the hall, the paternal figure of the man who, with his father, was responsible for putting the hotel back on its feet after the war, and is today the figure upon whom the continuing success of the Bayerischer Hof ultimately depends: Mr. Falk Volkhard. Barely has he had time to survey the scene below than someone—perhaps Mr. Politis, the reception manager, or his right-hand woman Frau Flossman—approaches with yet another problem and he turns and marches away with them into his office.

The camera now pans down and tracks into the lounge where businessmen sit huddled in armchairs around small, low tables, bandying figures and ordering coffee from a splendidly full-busted waitress in Bavarian costume. Up a couple of steps to the right, and we are face to face with a huge log fire where great mugs of Fürstenberg Brau are dispensed from a nearby bar.

Drawing away from this scene of Bavarian *gemütlichkeit,* the camera takes us back into the noisy, bustling hall, turns sharp right and moves slowly past elegant shops and Trader Vic's into an altogether airier, loftier, more elegant and infinitely quieter world of glass and shining brass and clean white walls, where a sweeping staircase leads up past fine Belgian wall carpets, portraits in gilt frames, and antique side tables onto a succession of landings, huge

OPPOSITE The main entrance on Promenadeplatz.

ornate banqueting halls, small wood-paneled dining rooms and some of the smartest bedrooms and suites to be found anywhere in Munich.

This haven of peace is the Palais Montgelas, a fine eighteenth-century town house that Mr. Volkhard bought from the state in 1968, worked on for three years, and finally opened as part of the Bayerischer Hof in August, 1972, thus lifting his establishment at a stroke into the front rank of world hotels.

The Palais was named after a certain Count Montgelas, a minister under the Elector Maximilian III of Bavaria (a portrait of whom is to be found in the room that was once his study, now known as the Minister Zimmer). Originally, the house belonged to an electoral councillor by the name of Karl Friedrich Reichsgraf von Perusa. In 1803, however, Montgelas, by then Royal Secretary of State, bought the whole of No. 2, Promenadplatz. After a certain amount of remodeling work, the property was sold in 1817 to the State of Bavaria, in whose hands it remained until Volkhard bought it from them 150 years later.

During that time the Palais played a significant part in the public and political life of Bavaria. For a while it housed the Bavarian State Chancellery, and it was in the great white-and-gold Königssaal that in 1926 the papal nuncio, Pacelli, later Pope Pius XII, signed an important treaty with the Prime Minister of Bavaria, Dr. Held.

No one is more aware of the historical importance of the house than Mr. Volkhard; indeed, so conscientious has he been in his efforts to maintain the style and dignity such a building deserves, that any guest wandering in there for the first time might well suppose that he had stumbled by mistake into the private residence of some very rich Munich businessman. For Volkhard, like his father before him, is a passionate collector of antique furniture, good paintings and fine porcelain, and his taste is reflected in every one of the half a dozen or so exquisite salons that lead off from the various landings and corridors.

The Louis XV carved oak panels in the Gelber Salon are superb, as in the *boisserie* in the Kleine Bibliothek. The four carved panels in the Fürstensalon were acquired by Volkhard from a château in the Loire Valley, and the painted woodwork in the Watteau Salon is quite exquisite.

But for me the most fascinating feature of the Palais Montgelas is its cellar—or rather, its succession of cellars of different shapes and sizes, leading one into another. The largest room, known as the Refektorium, is suitably monastic in design, with its red-tiled floor and austere, low, white-vaulted ceiling. Of course we could as easily have decided to eat in the sauna-like Tiroler Stube which Mr. Volkhard

bought complete—chairs, tables and all—from a house in the Sud-Tirol in Austria and reconstructed in the cellar precisely as he had found it.

The Palais Keller, as the whole place is known, has been there, to the best of anyone's knowledge, since the beginning of the fifteenth century—although in fact it is probably even older than that. In 1443 the Munich Register of Localities mentions a salt cellar that was built in 1406 at the corner of Promenadplatz No. 2, and from then on references to its occur frequently in all sort of documents. Between 1753 and 1770 it was referred to as "Haeringsstadel," probably after the brewing family of Haering who owned the house next door from 1603 to 1683. In 1778 two of the salt warehouses were demolished, and only the Haeringsstadel remained as it was. Shortly after that, a search was ordered by the Elector of Bavaria for more storage space for salt. However, when it was discovered that the Haeringsstadel was not large enough to accommodate anything like the 15,000 barrels that needed storing, the cellar was left empty, and when the Portuguese architect, Emanuel Joseph von Herigoyen, began drawing up his plans for the reconstruction of the house for Count Montgelas, he quickly discovered that, so strong were the cellar walls, he would be unable to demolish them as he had hoped, and consequently that he would have to build on top of them. For years after that the cellars were more or less abandoned (or used for storing coal), and it was not until the Second World War, during a search for sites for air raid

shelters, that their full extent was discovered. Munich, like so many other large German cities, suffered terrible damage from Allied bombing during the war. The Cathedral, the twin onion domes of which can be viewed to splendid advantage from the top floor of the hotel, virtually lost its roof; in the Promenadplatz alone, every single building was destroyed except for two: the Bayerischer Hof and a house opposite called the Gunetztrainer Palais. Today, looking out across the roofs of the city from the pretty green breakfast room on the top floor, it is hard to believe there was any damage at all.

But of course it was not just the old buildings that were destroyed by the war; with them disappeared a whole way of life for Munich and for the hotel. In the old days Munich was very much a seasonal center for opera, leisure, enjoying the Bavarian countryside. Today it is a greater cultural and financial center than ever it was forty years ago. But where once it took fifteen hours to travel by train from Hamburg to Munich, it now takes an hour or so on a Lufthansa jet. Today the hall of the Bayerischer Hof no longer hums with the sound of dignified travelers discussing the previous night's performance at the Opera, but roars with the clamor of businessmen coming, going, bargaining, complaining, booking airline flights and signing chitties, often without really knowing where they are—or, I imagine, much caring.

PRECEDING PAGES *Left:* The green breakfast room on the top floor. *Center:* The staircase in the Palais Montgelas. *Right:* A detail from the *boisserie* in the Kleine Bibliothek.

OPPOSITE Part of the suites in the Palais Mongelas. *Top left:* The bar beside the huge log fire. *Center left:* A suite in the Palais Montgelas. *Top right:* The swimming pool on the top floor. *Bottom right:* Bavarian *Gemütlichkeit* in the Palais Keller.

LE BEAU RIVAGE
LAUSANNE, SWITZERLAND

OPPOSITE The Palace entrance.

IF THE BEAU Rivage-Palace Hotel in Ouchy-Lausanne is remembered for nothing else in years to come it will be remembered for providing Noël Coward with the setting for his play, *Private Lives*.

Needless to say, the Beau Rivage, being the great hotel that it is, has provided the setting for matters even more grave than the private lives of Elyot and Amanda and Victor and Sibyl. On the wall by the underground entrance by the lake is a marble tablet commemorating four important conferences that took place at the Beau Rivage: The Italian-Turkish Conference in 1912, the Conference of Lausanne, 1922–3 (at which the peace treaty between the Allies and Turkey was signed), the Fifth Treaty of Lausanne, 1923, between USA and Turkey, and the Conference of Reparations of 1932. Underneath are the names of some of the distinguished delegates—for Britain, Lord Curzon, Sir Horace Rumbold, Sir John Simon, Neville Chamberlain, and Ramsay MacDonald; for France, Monsieurs Poincaré and Bonnet; and for Italy, Signors Grandi and Mussolini.

The room in which the peace conferences took place is now the main dining room of the hotel, and sitting there at a corner table one warm May afternoon, toying with a light luncheon of *Viande des Grisons*, *Les Goujons de Sole à la Persillade*, a green salad mixed at my table with a dressing of my own specifications, and a small bottle of local white wine, one could not imagine a more splendid setting for such a momentous occasion. Through the great windows, indistinct in the heat haze on the far side of the lake, I could see the mountains of the Haute Savoie and the town of Evian-les-Bains nestling at their feet, toward which the occasional steamer would set out, hooting plaintively as though in protest at its heavy load of businessmen and trippers; while all round me, seated at pretty gold and pale blue chairs round little round tables, fellow lunchers ate their way through *Entrecôte Bercy*, *La Piccata Yorkshire*, or *Poulet en Aspic* beneath the elaborately painted ceiling on which were depicted a host of well- (or, depending on which way you look at it, not so well-) covered nymphs, plucking at harps, crowning each other with flowers, and irresponsibly disporting themselves with an air of languid content that must surely, one felt, have transmitted itself to the grim statesmen struggling away beneath to bring continuing peace to the world. Although, on the other hand, if my experience is anything to go by, it is not only that room that produces in hotel guests such a feeling of well-being. For 125 years the Beau Rivage, with its great corridors, its uncluttered entrance hall, its plain but comfortable gardens, has succeeded in maintaining an atmosphere of old-fashioned gracious living that has largely disappeared from the face of the earth; and sitting on the terrace one morning sipping at a Campari and soda in the sun and contemplating the prospect of lunch, I experienced a feeling of total contentment, quite unsullied by the slightest twinge of guilt.

The story of the Beau Rivage begins in the middle of the last century with the opening of the Simplon Railway, which threatened

to end the profitable lake traffic between Switzerland and France. In 1853 a group of eleven influential Lausanne citizens—landowners, bankers, lawyers and the like—presented to the Commune of Lausanne and the Canton of Vaud a plan to transform the little port of Ouchy into a great resort to compete with Vevey and Montreux further along the Swiss Riviera. Up to then, Ouchy's main claim to fame was that it had attracted and inspired Byron who, after a visit to Shelley at nearby Chillon, had written *The Prisoner of Chillon* one stormy night at the Auberge de l'Ancre, now the Hotel d'Angleterre. The ambitious proposal was accepted, the eleven men formed the Société Immobilière d'Ouchy, capitalized at a million dollars, built a beautiful square and pier by the lake, purchased a large tract of land covered with vineyards from the Alliette family and there, at the cost of 1,400,000 francs (about $700,000 then), built the Beau Rivage. The hotel opened on the evening of March 24, 1861, to the accompaniment of brass bands, a *bal champêtre* in the square and a huge banquet for big-wigs in the hotel itself.

From the beginning the hotel was a huge success, so much so that European aristocrats and American millionaires were prepared to wait for weeks to get a reservation in one of the 150 rooms, enjoy its impeccable service and stroll in its fine salons. Particularly popular was the bath house, with its forty cabins from which one could swim in the lake, and the two small enclosed pools, one for men and one for women, divided by wooden bars through which one guest was able to have an excellent view of "elegant nymphs in high-necked bathing costumes of thick serge with white soutaches."

Soon it became fashionable for English and American tourists to spend the summer in St. Moritz and then come down to Ouchy for a few weeks in the autumn before returning home. During the Franco-Prussian War of 1870 several followers of Napoleon III spent time there in exile and three years later Adolphe Thiers, the great French statesman, lived there.

Toward the end of the century great schemes of modernization took place. Gas and candlelight were replaced by electricity, for which the hotel itself produced the power, and many rooms were improved. When there seemed a danger that the hotel would either have to be closed or else the whole bang shoot would have to be moved down to Cannes to avoid the cool weather, the entire problem was solved by the introduction of central heating. Elevators were installed and, an even more newfangled idea, private bathrooms! It was at about this time that the fame of two great doctors, César Roux the surgeon, and Combe, the specialist in stomach complaints, began to attract a whole new clientele to Lausanne. Soon the hotel was full once more to bursting.

Two views. *Above:* The hotel from the Lac du Léman. *Below:* Sacha Guitry's favorite view of France and the Haute-Savoie.

1908

And so it was that in 1906 the Palace building was opened at a cost of nearly 4 million francs—2.5 million more than the original. At the same time, the Société persuaded all those who owned property around the hotel not to put up any new buildings within fifty meters of the quai. This move not only ensured that Ouchy would remain as beautiful as the society had promised it would be but also that the hotel should continue to be surrounded on all sides with a beautiful garden of lawns, shaded walks, flower beds and even, in one corner, a little cemetery for the dogs of old and favored clients.

Toward the end of the First World War the Beau Rivage experienced, as did so many other big European hotels, the sudden arrival of aristocratic Russian refugees, many of whom, through force of circumstance, had had to leave their homeland without a penny to their names. As a result, unpaid bills piled up year after year, causing some concern to the board of directors. But, in the words of an official company report, one cannot be inhuman . . . and besides, what with the discovery of the delights of Ouchy by the rich Dutch, and the choice of the Beau Rivage in 1923 for the Lausanne Peace Conference, business was beginning to boom for Mr. Egli the manager. For the English Royal Family it was almost a Swiss home away from home. Edward VII came when he was Prince of Wales, and George V; the Duke and Duchess of Kent in 1939; and in later years that inveterate royal hotel guest, the Duke of Windsor, came to Lausanne for health reasons. Walter Schnyder tells how His Royal Highness was so delighted with a private dinner party Schnyder gave for him and the Duchess in a private dining room in the cellar of the hotel that he asked if Schnyder would be good enough to arrange a repeat performance for them plus a few friends a few days later.

From what one can make out from the hotel's *Livre d'Or*, which contains the signatures of its more illustrious guests, the entrance hall during the thirties must have been a positive Victoria Station of regal and ex-regal personages—the Prince of Wales rubbing shoulders with Alfonso XIII and Queen Eugénie of Spain, Queen Amelia of Portugal smiling graciously at the Grand Duchess of Luxembourg or the Infanta of Spain. The forties and fifties also produced a fair sprinkling of Big Names—from King Michael of Rumania and his mother Helen, and Queen Geraldine of Albania, to Norma Shearer Arrangé, Richard Strauss, and Sacha Guitry (who honeymooned at the hotel with every one of his four wives, and wrote in the visitors' book, *"Rien n'est plus beau que ce qu'on voit de ma fenêtre en ce moment —on voit la France."*)

They have all been to the Beau Rivage at one time or another—the Monacos, the Windsors, the Thailands, the Luxembourgs, Hirohito, Edinburgh—all the stars. . . . Christina Onassis came there for the reading of her father's will and had to be smuggled out through the kitchens to avoid the pack of *paparazzi* who follow her and people like her into even the most exclusive buildings in the world. Manager Walter Schnyder doesn't care for that sort of publicity; just as he

OPPOSITE *Top left:* A detail from the balcony. *Bottom left:* The corridor leading to the Palace building. *Top right:* The first-floor balcony overlooking the entrance hall. *Bottom right:* A detail from the ceiling of the dining room. OVERLEAF The dining room, in its time the setting for four international peace conferences.

doesn't care for young men with very long hair, be they the sons of ever so powerful men; nor for luggage in the front hall; nor for an entirely American clientele, since he feels that, unlike the French, they do not set the staff a high enough standard; nor for all the streamlined methods adopted by the larger hotel chains: "Working at the Hilton," he remarked, "felt like being a front-line soldier without a gun."

Schnyder, as might be expected in one of the greatest hotel managers in the world, was taught his job by men who did not believe in settling for second best: men like the great Santorelli, under whom he worked as a waiter at the Savoy in 1930. (The day he was made a station headwaiter happened to be August 12, the opening day of the grouse-hunting season, and Schnyder had never really learned how to cope with a grouse. So at lunchtime that day he took himself off to the Trocadero Restaurant and ordered a grouse, just to see how it should be served. It cost him an entire week's wages to discover that all you do is put it on a plate, and that evening not one of his clients asked him for one anyway.) After the Savoy he moved to Shepheard's in Cairo as assistant manager and later reception manager, and in 1938 he was appointed manager of the Semiramis in Cairo, where one day a young man marched into the hotel in full flying outfit, goggles and all, having just flown himself down from England in his own airplane, and asked for an Irish Whisky. Schnyder, having never heard of Irish Whisky, thought it was a stunt and laughed it off. Whereupon the young man sent his man upstairs to fetch one of a dozen bottles from his suitcase, explaining that he never traveled without some. The young man's name was Jameson.

During the war Schnyder went to America and fought in the US Army in some top secret intelligence outfit. On his discharge he went to work first at the Waldorf-Astoria and then at the Carlton House. In 1954 he was asked by Conrad Hilton to be responsible for getting his very first European hotel, the Castellana Hilton in Madrid, off the ground, and it was with some degree of nervousness that Swiss hoteliers, not to mention the big-wigs of Ouchy, learned of his appointment in 1957 as the Beau Rivage's sixth manager in a hundred years. Some people had heard it said he wore light gray suits. I mean to say . . . !

Schnyder believes in tradition in hotel-keeping and is proud that the Beau Rivage has a history second to none. Yet at the same time he is desperately keen to ensure that his hotel keeps up to date. When I last saw him, he was talking excitedly of the swimming pool he was planning, with a view over the lake. He was equally keen to show me the hotel laundry and to explain how, by doing the work themselves, a linen sheet could last twice as long as it would if laundered by an outside firm. For the same reason he keeps on his own electricians and plumbers, two furniture-polishers and two upholsterers. Not *just* because it is cheaper that way, but equally because by keep-

ing a close eye on it himself, he can be sure of offering his guests those small personal touches—like linen napkins, and favorite flowers in the room and even, for anxious parents, a consumer's guide to the local girls' finishing schools—for which people who still appreciate such things continue to come to this great hotel.

Left: The first-floor balcony overlooking the lake, said to have been the one Noël Coward used as the setting for the first act of *Private Lives*. *Above:* Another detail from the dining room ceiling.

Hotel
BEVERLY
WILSHIRE
The
Beverly
Wilshire

BEVERLY WILSHIRE
LOS ANGELES, U.S.A.

OPPOSITE The original brick and stucco entrance on Wilshire Boulevard.

IT WAS ELEVEN o'clock at night. I had been dining in El Padrino, the Beverly Wilshire's conspicuously equine Grill Room, with a woman who has known the hotel intimately for over twenty years, and has, one would have imagined, seen them all come and go—the rich, the famous, the beautiful, the eccentric. Indeed we had been privileged to see one or two in action earlier that evening. There were about twenty of them and you could tell they were somebodies by the inordinate amount of fuss they and the El Padrino staff had made between them over the seating arrangements, as well as by the fact that they were wearing evening dress. I had not managed to recognize one of them; the problem was, neither had my companion—a state of affairs that was seriously impairing her enjoyment of the fish she had ordered, not to say her eyesight as she peered across the low-lit room in a vain attempt to place at least one member of the party. Clues were plentiful but unhelpful. "See that man in a blue frilly shirt and no tie?" she said. "Now the point is, he's part of the establishment but he's trying to show he's not by not wearing a tie. See, he's wearing a blue shirt. That means he's been doing something on TV. Blue shirts show up better than white on TV."

At that moment, who should walk in but Bebe Klein, the well-known Hollywood publicity agent. "There's Bebe Klein," said my friend. "Thank heaven for that. Will you excuse me for a moment?" And she leapt to her feet and beetled off through the tables in the direction of this obviously unimpeachable source of information. Seconds later she was back. "They *have* been on TV!" she announced triumphantly.

Anyway, back to the scene later that evening as we stood with one of the assistant managers of the hotel beneath an Edinburgh street lamp in El Camino Real, the elegant granite-paved drive that divides the old Wilshire Wing and the newer Beverly Wing, waiting for her car to be brought up from the garage.

Suddenly an expensive-looking vehicle drew up beside us and out stepped an attractive blonde lady who gave the assistant manager a big hallo before heading for the front doors of the Beverly Wing.

"Who was that?" my friend hissed at the assistant manager.

He told her. She turned to me, her eyes alight with excitement. "Did you hear that?" she said. "Worth eighty-five million at least. Wouldn't you say?" she added, turning back to the assistant manager.

"At least," he said.

"She gave a party here recently," she said. "How much . . .?"

"About a hundred thousand," said the assistant manager.

"Only three hundred people," she said.

"The flowers alone cost thirty-five thousand," said the assistant manager.

"That's just the flowers," she said.

After that Mel Ferrer strolled past, and Jack Lord from *Hawaii Five-O*, and what with Barbara Hutton and Abe Lastfogel (what do you mean, who's Abe Lastfogel?) ensconsed in their respective suites upstairs in the Wilshire Wing, and Warren Beatty popping in and out of his penthouse apartment on the roof, and Tatum O'Neal wandering about aimlessly, and Mick Jagger expected any moment, I was beginning to wonder if people who are not rich or famous ever get much of a look-in at the Beverly Wilshire.

And then the most wonderful thing happened. As my friend was driving away, the assistant manager turned to me and said, "I don't believe we've met before. You're Mr. Matthew, aren't you? Room 875, isn't it?"

If no one else had uttered a single word to me during my entire stay, that one remark alone would have been sufficient to place the Beverly Wilshire high on my personal list of favorite hotels in America. I suppose that, on the face of it, there was no reason I should have been surprised that in an hotel of over 500 rooms, so many of which were occupied with stars and presidents of big corporations, an assistant manager should have known who I was. On the other hand, I was not unfamiliar with that awful feeling of anonymity that overwhelms one in so many big American hotels, and frankly Beverly Hills, of all places, seemed the least likely location for a haven of gracious living that is almost European in its friendliness and hospitality.

But I had not, by that stage in the proceedings, met Hernando Courtright. When I did meet him, all was, as they say, revealed.

Not that I had any complaints about my accommodation. Far from it. As a professional traveler, I have more than once found myself alone in a splendid room that would look better with two people in it. But never have I been confronted with quite so much space and grandeur and luxury as I was in the Principes de Bourbon Honeymoon Suite in the Beverly Wilshire Hotel. Any complaints I might have had were strictly of my own and not the hotel's making.

The point is that the Beverly Wilshire is such an extraordinary mixture of the grand and the intimate, the old and the new, the bizarre and the traditional, the European and American, that for a while you really do not know whether you are on your head or your heels. And then you meet Mr. Courtright, and you begin to understand. Because Mr. Courtright *is* the Beverly Wilshire, or at least he has been for the last fifteen years or so.

Had he been around when that looming mass of brick and stucco first went up on Wilshire Boulevard in 1928, it might have got off the ground thirty years or more earlier than it did. The basic problem was that it was a staid old lady in bloomers in a town of busty blondes in bathing suits. And anyway, at that time Mr. Courtright was busy working his way up the ladder in the Bank of America in San Francisco.

It was in 1936 that the bank found, to its dismay, that it had somehow inherited the more or less moribund Beverly Hills Hotel, and Vice-President Courtright was sent down to try and bring it back to life. The following year, with the help of such friends as James

ABOVE Hernando Courtwright, *El Padrino* of the city of Los Angeles. OPPOSITE The loggia of the Grand Ballroom in the Beverly Wing. The marble and the craftsmen were specially imported from Italy.

Stewart and Irene Dunne, he bought the place, retired from the bank and spent the next fifteen years turning it into one of the greatest hotels on the West Coast.

In 1956 he sold out and went off to try and sort out Century City, but the lure of the hotel business was too strong. In 1961 he bought the Beverly Wilshire, and before long another old lady was on the road to recovery.

His single greatest triumph in the years that followed was undoubtedly the twelve-story Beverly Wing, which was opened in 1972.

For years the Beverly Wilshire had been an island without a harbor in a sea of fast-moving traffic. Courtright's solution was to turn the hotel round the other way and make the entrance at the back, between the old part of the hotel and the proposed new wing. It was a simple enough idea, yet it took seven years of battling with local authorities, city planners and bankers before his plan was given the go-ahead. During that time, the architect appointed to design the new wing died, and so in the end it was Courtright and his late wife Marcelle who undertook the daunting task.

OPPOSITE El Camino Real, and the entrance to the Beverly Wing. ABOVE The hotel pool was modeled on Sophia Loren's.

The idea of a canopy of mission arches to tie the two wings together over El Camino Real was Mr. Courtright's, as were the two-story townhouse suites with their interior staircases, the bay windows like curved Paris balconies, the Winter Garden and the Ballroom. Mrs. Courtright decided to follow California history by designing every floor in a different authentic style—Spanish, Mexican, modern Californian, Italian, French and ultra-modern. The seventh and eighth floors consist of townhouse suites named after such eminent Courtright friends and old guests as Christian Dior, Dolores del Rio, Maurice Chevalier and Vasarely, and suites named after all the different champagnes—Moët et Chandon, Dom Perignon, Krug, Lanson and so on.

No expense was spared, and Mrs. Courtright literally scoured the world for the finest fabrics, the most beautiful materials, the best craftsmen. For instance, having settled for only the best white Carrara marble, she then bought over a group of Italian stone-cutters to ensure that every inch of it would be shown off to its very best advantage in the Ballroom, on the floors, in the bathrooms and outside facing the Camino Real. She traveled to a remote Mexican village

Clockwise, from upper left-hand corner: The bow-fronted windows of the Beverly Wing were modeled on Parisian balconies; Spanish tiles around the swimming pool; Dior is only one of Courtwright's friends to have a suite named after them: the Christian Dior townhouse suite.

to find craftsmen who would make the particular tables she had in mind.

On the Spanish floor, the headboards on the beds are upholstered in calf leather, painted in antique gold and decorated by hand in an authentic and extremely rare Majorcan floral design. The furniture consists of hand-carved sixteenth-century reproductions, the lamps are made out of hand-painted ceramic vases from Talavera and the curtains and bedspreads are hand-loomed in pale gold mohair. In each of the rooms there is a different embroidered tapestry representing each of the provinces of Spain.

The astonishing Honeymoon Suite, in which I stayed, was named after the Prince and Princess of Bourbon who were the first couple to grace it. It was inspired by the Hindu God of Love and his earthly mate, who together symbolize eternal devotion, and the two main themes of the suite are the Exotic East and Matrimonial Joy—which tends to be rather confusing if you happen to be there on your own.

The Grand Ballroom, which seats just one thousand for dinner or dancing, is entirely Louis XV in style with its crystal chandeliers, its Trianon—white *boisserie* and its marble statues. Directly above the ballroom is a fifty-foot baroque swimming pool, which was modeled on Sophia Loren's. Surrounded by Mediterranean cabanas with gay hand-painted Spanish murals, Spanish tiles and hand-wrought iron grill-work, orange and lemon trees to provide a little shade and a tinkling waterfall to lull away one's cares, one can quite easily imagine oneself to be lazing in the courtyard of some Spanish grandee's private palace.

And yet it would be wrong to suppose that the success of the Beverly Wilshire lies solely in its outward appearance. The genius of Hernando Courtright lies equally in his unceasing and almost obsessive efforts to make a guest feel at home.

For a start the guest will receive a letter thanking him for his reservation. When he arrives, he will be gratified to discover that they are not only expecting him at the front desk but actually know who he is. An assistant manager will take him up to his room—just as they do in European hotels. Once in his room he will very likely find fruit and champagne and flowers. If he is a magazine editor he may well discover the latest copy of his publication on the coffee table and, if a drinks manufacturer, then a bottle or two of his patent medicine in the pantry. OG's (old guests) like Arthur Rubinstein will find that the Steinway is not only there in the room when he arrives but in his very favorite spot, while a successful race horse owner will have messages delivered to him by a page-boy dressed as a jockey and wearing his colors.

As well as being a perfectionist, Hernando Courtright is something of an extrovert. Not for nothing was he elected third Padrino (Godfather) of Los Angeles by the city fathers in succession to Harry Chandler and actor Leo Carillo.

Nowhere does his flair for showmanship express itself better than in the big balls for which the Beverly Wilshire is justly renowned. For one Vienna Opera Ball, fifty violinists were brought over specially to play Viennese Waltzes, and the cabaret consisted of a real ballet. Guests at a Navy Ball were piped aboard over a gang plank, while at an Indian Ball, people hardly had time to recover from the discovery of a single goldfish in every water glass, before they were confronted by the arrival of an elephant in full ceremonial outfit.

The Beverly Wilshire has over the years become a home away from home for the biggest stars—of television and cinema, of finance and industry, of politics and of society. But the biggest star of them all in that city of stars is the one whose home they all come to stay in. As my dinner companion remarked, "If people don't see Mr. Courtright when they come here, it's like going to Universal Studios and not seeing Rock Hudson."

OPPOSITE One can easily imagine that one is lazing in the courtyard of some Spanish grandee's palace. ABOVE An old Edinburgh street lamp in El Camino Real.

LE BRISTOL
PARIS, FRANCE

THE LAST PARTY Josephine Baker ever went to was given in her honor at the Bristol Hotel. It was attended by, among others, Princess Grace of Monaco, Alain Delon, Mireille Darc, Jeanne Moreau and Jean-Claude Brialy. She wore a long white dress and looked as stunning and young as ever. Two days later she was dead. They buried her in the same white dress and they say she looked younger than ever.

As a last place to cut loose in your life, the Bristol Hotel in the Faubourg St. Honoré might be equaled, but hardly bettered. It is one of the great institutions of Paris (at the time of the party its fiftieth-anniversary celebrations were in full swing) and, what is more, it continues to be owned and run by the same family who conceived, built and launched the hotel back in 1925.

The story of the Jammet family was related with great wit and charm in June, 1975, by an old family friend, Monsieur Jean-Louis Horbette, director-general of Sud-Radio, on the occasion of the conferring on Pierre Jammet, the hotel's present director-general, of the Legion d'Honneur.

He had read somewhere, he told the assembled company, that Pierre Jammet had been born fifty years previously in the drawer of a Louis XVI commode that was being moved from one room to another in the Bristol shortly before the hotel was opened. To a family whose connections with the hotel business go back nearly a hundred years such an early introduction into the business would probably seem perfectly reasonable; hotel men are born in the drawers of commodes in the same way that actors are born in trunks.

Pierre's brother Philippe was an exception. He was born in a wine bin, which explains why today Pierre is to be found almost anywhere above ground in the hotel and Philippe almost anywhere below—in the Bristol's wine cellars, cosseting the hotel's hundred thousand or so bottles, some of which date back to 1865. These were acquired by the Jammet brothers' grandfather in 1880 when he was *chef de cuisine* at the Café de Paris before becoming in 1890 the owner of the famous Boeuf à la Mode. It was in that restaurant that Hippolyte Jammet, Pierre and Philippe's father, was born a few years later. In 1900 the family moved to Dublin, where Grandfather Jammet and his brother opened a French restaurant and where, but for the outbreak of war in 1914, they might very well have stayed. After the war Hippolyte bought a little hotel in the Avenue de l'Opéra called the Edouard VII, and with the money he made from the sale of this property he was able in 1923 to buy the land in the rue Faubourg St. Honoré. Two years later, Hippolyte was able to offer Paris a hotel worthy of the *quartier* in which it had been born.

From the word go the Bristol's closeness on the one hand to some of the very best shops in Paris, and on the other to the Elysée Palace and the American and British embassies attracted a select and distinguished clientele.

The name itself contributed a certain amount to the hotel's early

OPPOSITE Detail from the ceiling in the dining room.

success. Frederick Augustus Hervey, 4th Earl of Bristol and Bishop of Cloyne and Derry, was a famous traveler at the end of the eighteenth century, and any hotel known to have met up to his very demanding standards became known afterwards as Lord Bristol Hotels—the eighteenth-century equivalent of four stars in the Guide Michelin.

In 1930 Hippolyte built a fine new extension of eight floors at a cost of twelve million francs. ("Just think," Monsieur Jammet exclaimed when he reached this particular part of the story, "the whole of the Plaza Athenée only cost fifteen million!")

This new wing included some of the hotel's finest suites. The one on the top floor, for instance, is an enormous affair with four bedrooms on two levels and two salons, all decorated in fine Directoire and Empire style.

In 1940 it attracted a rather different type of clientele than usual, in the form of German army officers who arrived to take up residence only to find, flying defiantly from the flagstaff, the flag of the United States of America. Hippolyte, never one to miss a trick, had persuaded the American ambassador, William C. Bullitt, to move in there with his staff, and the Germans were forced to find alternative accommodation. When America came into the war and the ambassador had to

leave Paris, the Luftwaffe tried to move in where the army had failed. But they too failed, after numerous and forcible complaints from members of the diplomatic corps already in residence at the hotel.

But long before the war had even started, Hippolyte had been training his son Pierre to take his place when the time came. And so at the age of seventeen, Pierre entered the hotel business for the second time, working at the ovens in the Bristol kitchens. Later he went to work in the kitchens of the Hotel Laperouse and later still at the Lucas-Carton. After wartime service in the navy, Pierre went to London as a *commis* waiter and barman and to Germany as receptionist. Then he worked in the Ritz in Madrid and later the Atlantic in Hamburg, where he became manager.

Of all these different aspects of hotellery to which he was introduced so intensively in those early years, Pierre is perhaps most interested in the kitchen. Always a gourmet, he launched in 1972 a regular weekly lunchtime gastronomic *atelier* in the hotel restaurant, to which Parisians and foreign visitors could come and sample some of his chef's latest *"recherches et créations culinaires."*

On the other hand, it is not merely for the cooking that people like President Sadat, the Shah of Iran, and President Harry Truman choose the Bristol over any other hotel. Nor is it merely for the pleasure

LE BRISTOL
PARIS
Le siége de WC est changé au départ de chaque client.
Celui qui est dans cette enveloppe protectrice a été traité dans nos ateliers de telle façon qu'il peut être considéré comme neuf.
(BREVETE S.G.D.G.)
Ne pas jeter l'enveloppe dans la cuvette.
The toilet seat is changed after each departure. This one, in its protecting envelope, has been treated in our cleaning workroom so that it can now be considered as new.
(PATENDED)
To avoid obstruction of pipes please do not throw this bag into the toilet.

of taking tea beneath the 1798 Gobelin tapestry—a gift from Napoleon to his mother—or the weight off their feet under the Drouhais portrait of Marie Antoinette which the Queen presented to her chaplain in 1781, or a cocktail beside the Pajou bust of Louis XVI, which His Majesty gave to the brother of the Marquise de Pompadour, that five Chancellors of West Germany (Adenauer, Erhardt, Kiesinger, Brandt and Schmidt) have checked into the seventh-floor apartment. The Bristol is now recognized as *the* home (after the Hotel de Marigny in the Avenue Matignon which was recently donated to the Republic by the Rothschild family as the Blair House of Paris, where the President's personal guests stay) of all the top-ranking diplomats and senior government ministers when they are in Paris on official business.

And yet, beneath its grandness, its great marble foyer, its tapestries and fine furniture, its air of seriousness and sobriety, the Bristol remains what it always was: a family-run hotel. And as long as it remains in the hands of the kind, gentle, generous and at all times wildly enthusiastic Jammet family, it will stand unique among the great hotels of Paris.

PRECEDING PAGES *From left to right:* The main lobby; Marie Antoinette by Drouhais in the corner of the lounge; the dining room, scene of the hotel's weekly gastronomic *ateliers*.
OPPOSITE *Above:* A double bedroom. *Bottom left:* Louis XVI by Pajou, in the lounge. *Bottom right:* Standard procedure throughout. *Right:* The Jammet brothers—Philippe, Pierre, and André.

CLARIDGES
MODELS

CLARIDGE'S
LONDON, ENGLAND

HERE'S AN INTERESTING statistic for your book," Michael Bentley, the assistant general manager of Claridge's, said to me one evening. "1975 showed a rise in the occupancy of courier rooms of 113. I don't know quite what that signifies, do you?" Apart from signifying that Claridge's must be one of the last hotels left in the world that still have courier rooms at all, I cannot imagine. Oil sheiks, I am told, tend to travel with a paid lackey or two; so it might be that more oil sheiks stayed at Claridge's in 1975 than in 1974. On the other hand, on that very night, the Earl and Countess of Derby were also paying one of their frequent visits to the hotel, accompanied by three servants—a valet, a lady's maid and a chauffeur—and since I am assured that the Derbys are far from alone in being thus attended, the answer might simply be that Claridge's welcomed more aristocratic guests like the Derbys in 1975 than it did the previous year. It is a very grand hotel, and it does look after very grand people—from the Japanese lady who likes to bathe every morning in twelve pints of milk to the Countess Fitzwilliam who once left some trifle in her room—a diary or a diamond necklace or something. When they called her country home to inform her of her loss, the telephone was answered by the butler who announced that her ladyship would be unable to speak with anyone since she was at that moment shooting on the lawn.

A lesser assistant manager of a lesser hotel might have been tempted to wonder, shooting *what* on the lawn? The staff of Claridge's, however, have a long tradition of dealing with titled ladies, and gentlemen, with lawns spacious enough to allow a little rough shooting on a summer's afternoon. In fact the original Claridge was a butler who had seen many long years of service in some noble household before saving up enough money to buy a small hotel in Brook Street, Mayfair, next door to an establishment consisting of a couple of town houses run by an ex-chef named Jacques Mivart as a small lodging house for English families up from the country.

By 1855, Claridge had made enough money to buy Mivart's hotel. Long experience of butling had taught him exactly how to cater for rich and titled landowners, who had come up to town with their families and servants for a spot of card-playing or blood-letting, in such a way that they hardly noticed they had left home at all.

Before long, Claridge's became *the* place to put up in town, and when in 1860 Queen Victoria had tea there with the Empress Eugénie, its future was assured once and for all.

So too was its clientele. When Baedeker's Guide referred to it shortly after that as "the first hotel in London," it was referring not to its antiquity, nor to its prices, nor to its excellence of cuisine or services, but to the elevated status of the large majority of its guests. And when the hotel was bought in 1895 by the Savoy Company and entirely rebuilt, the new proprietors anxiously pointed out to their esteemed guests that "the spirit of modernism in the nine-story building would not in the least interfere with their comfort and privacy."

OPPOSITE The Brook Street entrance.

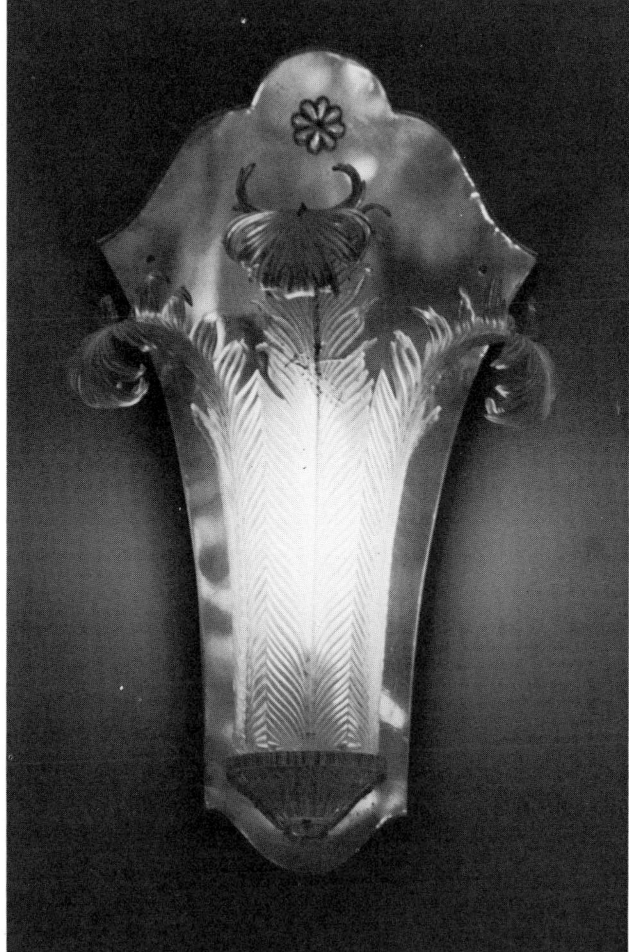

The present hotel, shown above from the corner of Brook Street and Davies Street, is a fine example of red-brick Victorian architecture. Elsewhere on this page are details of the décor, much of which dates from the period between the two world wars.

Top left: It has been known for five heads of state to be dining in the ballroom at the same time. *Top right:* At lunch in the Causerie, smorgasbord is served free of charge with the first drink. *Left:* Part of a suite.

Nor, I am happy to report, does it appear to do so to any great extent today. One can only conclude that precisely the same degree of genuine concern for the comfort and privacy of Claridge's guests is felt by Sir Hugh Wontner and his board of directors as was felt by his predecessors eighty years ago. The atmosphere is still very much that of a large private house, where the servants outnumber the guests by two, and in the winter months, three to one, and one's every wish is known and granted almost before one knows it oneself. Within moments of arriving in one's room, a valet is knocking at the door asking if there is anything he can do, such as unpacking one's suitcases or pressing one's trousers.

Some guests, unfamiliar with this way of life and faced with a telephone without a dial, have been known to complain after several days of a complete lack of room service, not realizing that only seconds away on every floor lurk no fewer than six waiters, six chambermaids, two valets, a house porter and three bathroom cleaners, ready at the ring of the appropriate bell to come springing along the corridor to minister to your slightest need. Even a simple whisky and soda arrives on a trolley covered with a white linen tablecloth, together with crisps, black and green olives, and hot salted almonds.

Over a century ago, the original Claridge's guests taught the staff of the hotel a simple, basic principle of life: that true luxury can result only from personal service. They have never forgotten it, nor, as long as the same sort of guests continue to come to the hotel, will they do so.

There is no bar at Claridge's—the explanation being not so much that a bar would lower the tone of the place as that guests feel so much more comfortable when they have their drinks brought to them by a liveried footman. Up to only a few years ago, the footmen wore powdered wigs in the evenings; today they have to make do with only velvet breeches and white stockings—and even those are not quite what they used to be, since no one seems to be making cotton stockings any more, and they are having to resort more and more to nylon, one pair of which are too cold and two too warm.

In the dining room, however, guests still occupy tables that are barely within hailing distance of each other, on chairs that are wide enough to accommodate three people easily, surrounded by Basil Ionides' 1926 glass panels and tended solicitously by François and his minions who treat them as if they were royalty—which, of course, they often are.

Every time I go to Claridge's I see ex-King Constantine of Greece, earnestly discussing some obviously important project—to regain his lost throne, I like to think, but probably in fact only to come up with a not too undignified way of keeping his head above water. Times may be hard for us all, but old habits die equally hard and he seems to fit into the place so naturally that it is almost impossible to imagine the poor chap ever taking his custom to any other establishment.

A shortage of crowned heads there may be nowadays, but men of power and influence are as thick on the ground as ever. It has been known for four or five heads of state to be dining in the restaurant at the same time, acknowledging each other's presence with only the slightest inclination of the head, and, most important of all, ignored by other diners. For privacy is what Claridge's is about; this is why they come here—the Dukes of Marlborough and Bedford, the Derbys and the Fitzwilliams, the Bulgaris, the Pinellis, the Agnellis and the Pignatellis, the kings and the millionaires, Churchill in his time and Douglas-Home. Stavros Niarchos for years maintained an apartment on the top floor, carefully replacing the hotel furniture with his own, their pictures with Van Goghs and Renoirs, and their not inconsiderable latique vases with his own priceless pieces of Fabergé.

These people know that once through that front door they are *chez eux*, protected from the predatory press and the curious eye of the populace by a press office that, someone once remarked, must be the only one in the world whose job is to keep the hotel *out* of the papers, and a small entrance hall that leads nowhere and sharply discourages the casual passer-by from walking in. In many ways it is more like a club than a hotel. Of course, things are not what they

Above, left: the entrance hall. *Right:* W. S. Gilbert's piano in the Royal Suite.

were, even at Claridge's. Today's state visitors—Sadat, Kissinger, Kosygin—while acknowledging the hotel's supremacy in most matters relating to their comfort and well-being, still insist on making their own elaborate arrangements when it comes to the matter of actually staying alive. As a result, occasions do arise when for several days on end Mr. Lund-Hansen, the general manager, and his staff must bow to authorities superior even to themselves.

Time was when Claridge's became, for a few months of every year, one of the hubs around which revolved that series of bizarre social events known as the London Season. Its four ballrooms were forever being transformed at vast expense into South Sea Island lagoons, African jungle clearings or staterooms on ocean liners, to amuse the whims of countless debutantes and their friends who must wish now they'd settled for the money instead. Claridge's did, and although it must all have seemed rather a bore at the time, I thought I could spot more than a tinge of regret in the voice of the reception manager, Mr. Burrows, when he recalled the occasion in 1959 when a famous banker arranged for several crates of mangoes, a fruit unheard of in England in those days, to be flown from somewhere outlandish just to make the flavor for the ice cream. They cannot even rely any more on a burst of extra bookings for the Henley Royal Regatta.

On the other hand, anyone wishing to find a bed at Claridge's during Derby and Ascot weeks would be advised to book well in advance.

Tuesday, Wednesday and Thursday are still, as they have been for a century or more, the day when the aristocrats come up from the country to see their *corsetières* or gunsmiths or Harley Street specialists, and meet each other for a jaw and a whisky and soda in the sitting room at Claridge's and dream of their youth as the Hungarian orchestra scrapes and tinkles its way through *The Pirates of Penzance* and "I'll See You Again."

Heaven knows what the combined ages of the four musicians must be by now. One night I was sitting with a friend listening to them playing the waltz from Noël Coward's *Bitter Sweet*. When they had finished, they packed up their instruments, and as they were leaving the pianist came across to us. "You know," he said, "I played in the original production of that show. Mavelous days they were." He turned to go, paused and added "Of course that was on tour, not in London." *Bitter Sweet* was first produced in 1929, so that gives you some idea. A year or two ago, they nearly lost Albert, the cellist—the one with the permanent smile—when he was mugged in an ill-lit alleyway beside the hotel. Today, on that very spot, hangs a splendid lamp, erected by the hotel, and known ever after as Albert's Memorial.

I am assured that if ever you ask the Claridge's orchestra for a request, they never forget it; and whenever they see you enter the room after that, they will stop what they are playing and strike up your favorite tune. Guests like that—just as they like knowing that they can always be sure of having the same room they had the last time they were there, with the same valet and the same chambermaid, both of whom know exactly how they like their evening clothes laid out on the bed, and the precise temperature of the bath water. No matter how difficult a guest may be, or demanding, or grand, or eccentric, Claridge's, you may be sure, is more than equal to the occasion. Legend has it that one evening an elderly titled lady marched out of the lift on her way to an important dinner, dressed only in her jewelery. She had simply forgotton to put any clothes on: the sort of mistake anyone might make, and one that was instantly rectified by Mr. Van Thuyne, then the hotel's administrator. He at once stepped forward, covered the lady with his own coat and accompanied her back into the lift as though nothing had happened.

Above, right: The bathroom of the Royal Suite. Its sunken bath has received the naked shapes of almost every king and queen in the world.

And then there was the distinctly touchy matter of the two royal suites. Now, there is in fact only one royal suite at Claridge's; it contains a sunken pink marble bath and has been occupied in its time by all the usual sorts of people who stay in royal suites. Then one day two kings, both quite senior as kings go, turned up in London, each expecting, not unnaturally, that he would be given the royal suite. The obvious solution seemed to be to offer it to the older of the two. Kings, however, do not always understand such principles, and the younger monarch was so insulted by this suggestion that for a while it seemed that some dreadful scandal must ensue. At that point, Mr. Van Thuyne ordered workmen to pull down half the ceiling in the royal suite, demonstrated the unfortunate damage to the ambassadors of both countries in question who reported to their respective monarchs that, as luck would have it, Claridge's had two smaller royal suites which they had of course placed at Their Majesties' disposition.

Ah well. It is a source of constant reassurance to know that, however difficult life may become in the next few years, we always have Claridge's to look after us and make us feel that really everything is all right. On Sundays the restaurant is packed with the rich, the titled and the powerful of Mayfair whose own servants have the day off. Obviously they cannot be expected to cook Sunday lunch for themselves, and so, as one member of Claridge's reception staff put it to me, "It's either us or boiled eggs."

THE CONNAUGHT
LONDON, ENGLAND

An English couple who have been staying at the Connaught for years wrote recently to Mr. Zago, the hotel's general manager, to explain that they would be arriving from abroad on a certain day, but unfortunately they might not be getting in until rather late in the evening. Would he, they wondered, be very kind and arrange for them to have something to eat? They realized the restaurant and the grill might be closed by that time and they might be feeling rather peckish. As it turned out, their flight was delayed and they did not finally arrive at the hotel until after midnight, tired, cold and hungry. They went straight up to their room—the one they always have—where they found waiting for them some piping hot consommé in a thermos and a plate of cold meats with bread and butter. It was exactly what they wanted under the circumstances, and after eating it they retired to bed, warm and happy to be home again.

I am quite certain there are many other hotels, in London and all over the world, that could have given these late arrivals something much more elaborate than soup and cold meat—a steak perhaps, sole in a white wine sauce, piccata of veal, if not an entire three-course dinner—even if they had arrived at four in the morning.

But think of it this way: if you were going to stay with friends in the country and your journey took far longer than you had expected so that you didn't get there till long after dinner, your hosts would be unlikely to greet you with a slap-up dinner with wine and all the trimmings. It would be inconvenient for them to have to prepare it and embarrassing for you to have to eat it. You would far prefer to perch a cup of hot soup and some sandwiches on your knee, while you sat with your hosts in front of the fire. And in a well-run house, that is what you would probably get. No one would be embarrassed, you would feel comfortable and well-fed, and everyone would be able to retire happily for the night.

For over forty years now the Connaught has been run exactly like a good private house, and it is as a private house that its regular guests treat it. For them, the Connaught is their London home, and the staff their old family retainers. Whenever they come there they look forward to sleeping in the same room they have slept in for years, to seeing the same faces and being cossetted by the same servants who have been looking after them for as long as they can remember. Some guests and members of the staff have known each other so well and for so long that it is not unusual to overhear a valet ticking off his elderly charge in no uncertain manner—"You jolly well put your coat on, sir. There's a nasty nip out and you don't want to go catching your death of cold!"

Elsewhere in this collection I have compared certain hotels with private houses, either from the point of view of the intimacy of the atmosphere, or the personal attention of the staff, or the constant presence of one's host or hostess, or the homeliness of the food. On the whole, the comparison applies more to small country hotels than to famous city hotels, for the obvious reason that whereas small

OPPOSITE The bar.

country hotels very often were once people's private homes, the majority of big city hotels were not—or, if they were, they have long since been changed out of all recognition. Claridge's, it is true, has always been run as though it were a country house; but a country house of such grandness that one might have been nearer the mark to describe it as a stately home. In the case of only two city hotels in this book is the comparison with a large, comfortable private house really apt, and they are the Lancaster in Paris and the Connaught in London. Both hotels have a sort of small-scale grandeur that was characteristic of large private town houses of the turn of the century.

Both have the luck to be establishments of human dimensions in which both staff and guests stand a reasonable chance not only of getting to know each other, but actually becoming fond of each other. And, most important of all, both hotels were the creations of men for whom the words "friend" and "guest" were interchangeable, whose idea of the perfect hotel was a place where a guest felt as much at home as if he *were* at home. In the case of the Lancaster, that man was Emil Wolf; in the case of the Connaught, Rudolph Richard.

So strongly is the Connaught associated with the name of Richard that to many people it may come as something of a surprise to learn that the hotel even existed before his arrival in 1935. But in fact the story began as long ago as 1803, when Alexander Grillon, who up to that time had been *chef de cuisine* to Lord Crewe, opened a hotel in Albermarle Street. Some years later, an offshoot to Grillon's Hotel was opened in a pair of Georgian houses at 14–16 Charles Street, Grosvenor Square, the property of the immensely wealthy Duke of

Westminster. Toward the end of the 1880's the Duke decided the time had come to have the entire area rebuilt. The street was completely altered and eventually became what is known today as Carlos Place. A man by the name of Auguste Scorrier owned the hotel at the time, and the moment rumors of the planned alterations reached his ears he put in an offer to the Grosvenor Estate (the Westminsters' family name is Grosvenor) to rebuild his own premises himself. At first he was merely offered an extension to his existing lease, but when in 1892 he applied again, permission was granted on condition that he did not have a bar in the hotel. (The solicitors who were advising him on the loan required for the job, and who finally bought his lease, were also acting for a firm of brewers and distillers.)

Demolition of the old building began in the spring of 1894, and in 1896 the new Coburg Hotel (originally named after Prince Albert of Saxe-Coburg, Consort of Queen Victoria) was opened.

To judge by a brochure issued during those early days around the turn of the century, the Coburg wasted no time in establishing for itself a style that could very well be applied to its successor today.

"The cuisine and the cellar will alike be *sans reproche*, and the Coburg Hotel will be found in every possible detail to justify its association with a part of London which has been for generations, and is likely always to be, instinctively identified with all that is aristocratic, refined and luxurious in metropolitan society."

The Coburg continued under its original name until the outbreak of World War I, by which time public feeling was running high against anything even faintly Teutonic. So much so that Prince Louis of

ENQUIRIES

PRECEDING PAGES *Left to right:* The Carlos Street entrance, the elevator, and an upstairs corridor. THIS PAGE The staircase and one of the suites.

Battenberg, at the time First Sea Lord (in other words, the senior serving officer in the Royal Navy), was forced to resign his position and change his family name to something that fell a little more easily upon sensitive English ears. And owners of dachshunds gave their pets an airing only under the cover of darkness to protect them from the anti-German toe caps of passers-by.

Eventually the Coburg was renamed the Connaught, and a happier choice would be hard to imagine. Not only was the Duke of Connaught the King's brother-in-law, but it also avoided the enormous expense that would have been involved in changing the hotel's ubiquitous monogram.

In the years following the Armistice, the large bulk of the Connaught's business came from the rich land-owning families who kept permanent suites in the hotel. Every table in the dining room belonged to some particular family, who often indicated the fact with a forbidding array of bottles of pills and medicine. In fact, such a proprietorial attitude did regular guests take toward the hotel that the mere presence of a casual guest was greeted with shock and dismay. The dining room closed firmly every evening at nine, and the consumption of wine and spirits was pitifully small.

It was with an understandable sense of gloom and foreboding that Rudolph Richard began his first day as general manager of the Connaught in 1935 at the early age of thirty-seven.

His career had been a distinguished one. Born in Switzerland in 1898, he had learned the art of hotellery in various establishments abroad before coming to the Carlton in London, where the names of Ritz and Escoffier were still fresh in people's memories. From there he moved to the tiny Stafford in St. James's and in 1931, at the invitation of the Marquess of Bute, went to Gibraltar to open the Rock Hotel. Once that was on its feet, he returned to London to take up his appointment at the Connaught, a position to which he was to devote the remaining thirty-eight years of his life.

From the very beginning Richard was determined to run his hotel like a very good private house, with marvelous food, a great wine list and the very highest standard of personal service. On the other hand he did not wish to upset the old families already in residence; so in the years immediately preceding the war such changes as were made were discreet to the point of imperceptibility. He began to build up what had been a more or less non-existent wine cellar and to make small improvements to the menu. Just as he was beginning to attract some attention the war broke out, the old families retreated to the safety of the country, and he was faced with the need to create a whole new clientele. The problem was, as it turned out, solved for him: partly by General de Gaulle, who chose the Connaught as his London headquarters, and partly by the staff of the American embassy just up the road in Grosvenor Square. The happy result was that the Connaught emerged into the warmth and sunshine of peacetime London with a reputation as a highly civilized hotel with a good restaurant and wine list.

By 1952 the *Good Food Guide* was describing the Connaught Restaurant in fairly glowing terms—"Exceptionally good international cooking in the atmosphere of a comfortable Edwardian hotel." As Gregory Houston-Bowden points out in his excellent book on English gastronomy, the Connaught's specialities at that time included *Crêpes de Volaille Connaught, Sole Carlos* and *Oeufs Pochés en Surprise*; while the wine list was boasting such notable numbers as a Château Pavie 1924 for £2.25, a magnum of Château La Mission Haut Brion 1945 for £3.00 and a Beaujolais 1949 for a laughable 85 pence.

In 1955 Mr. Simmons, then under-manager of the restaurant, proposed the idea of a grill room with its own entrance. His idea was taken up and in May of that year the tiniest, most charming and most intimate grill room in London was opened, with Mr. Simmons as its manager.

The next major landmark in the Connaught's steady progress toward excellence came in 1965 with the appointment of Mr. Daniel Dunas as *chef des cuisines*. His credentials were impressive: chef to the United States embassies in Paris and Cairo; *commis* chef to the Duke of Marlborough at Blenheim Palace; pastry chef to the Governor-General of Canada in Government House in Ottawa; then Blenheim again as chef, an experience that proved invaluable when he moved to a hotel renowned for its great English food. The regular daily luncheon dishes are, with one exception, as English as you can imagine: steak, kidney and mushroom pie on Mondays, braised gammon California or Irish stew on Tuesdays, roast sirloin of beef with Yorkshire pudding on Wednesdays, boiled silverside on Thursdays, ox tail on Fridays, steak, kidney and mushroom pudding on Saturdays, and chicken pie on Sundays.

At the same time, Richard knew the necessity for leavening this strongly English flavor with the delicacy of classic French cooking. In Dunas he had a man who not only had an extensive repertoire of

standard dishes at his fingertips, but was perfectly capable of coming up with one or two of his own masterpieces—for example, *Truite de Rivière Soufflée au Riesling*, which is boiled river trout, stuffed with mousseline of sole and truffles, then cooked in Riesling and served with cream and Riesling sauce. He was also a first-class teacher, and in 1972 one of his sous-chefs won the coveted Pierre Taittinger Award.

In 1975 Dunas was lured back to Government House in Ottawa, amid a certain amount of understandable dismay from Connaught regulars.

However, any fears as to the standard of the Connaught's kitchen were proved groundless by the appointment of Michel Bourdin. At the time of writing (and I have no reason to suppose that, by the time you read these words, anything will have altered one jot) the Connaught restaurant is considered by many who know about these things to be the best in London—a distinction which must presumably, since they share exactly the same kitchen, apply to the Grill as well.

But of course, as any amateur gourmet will aver, good grub alone doth not a great restaurant make. Nor, for that matter, a sensational wine list. Although, I must say, when Mr. Zago told me that he sometimes had the impression the hotel was floating on wine, I took it to be a joke until his secretary showed me the bag full of corks that were the result of just one day's consumption in the restaurant and the grill. I would not like to guess the number, but the bag was very large and every cork bore a distinguished name.

When you order a table for dinner at the Connaught—whether you arrive at six thirty or ten thirty, and stay for half an hour or four hours—that is your table. Only on the rare occasions when guests dine very early and then leave for the theater, will they reset the table and allow someone else to use it. A woman recently complained to Mr. Zago because she was not able to drink her after-dinner coffee in the lounge. The manager explained politely that coffee was always taken at the table. "Why?" persisted the woman. "Because," said Mr. Zago, "if we tell a guest that coffee is served in the lounge he will take that to mean that we need his table."

Obviously, the increase in daily revenue, were he to start letting a table two or three times in an evening, would be considerable. On the other hand, he would no longer have one of the best restaurants in London.

On June 13, 1973, Rudolph Richard died. Within three months, Mr. Gustave, the man who for thirty-five years had managed the reception side of the business and without whom the Connaught would not be the *hotel* it is today, was also dead. How nervous Paolo Zago must have been at the thought of following Mr. Richard and Mr. Gustave at the Connaught, when he was summoned from the Berkeley to become general manager.

Wisely he decided to do as Mr. Richard himself had done in 1935

—which was not very much. For the first six months or so he merely looked and listened and learned, until he felt he was in a position to understand the sort of hotel it had been for the last forty years.

PRECEDING PAGE The grill.

"Have you noticed, for example," he said to me, "the way the flowers are done here? I had always been used to very formal arrangements and it took six months before I realized that here they are arranged in a nice, natural way, just as you might expect to find them in someone's home."

In any larger establishment, such arrangements would almost certainly be out of place. But then everything that is special about the Connaught springs, as Mr. Zago soon appreciated, from the essential smallness of the place. Even at its busiest the 140 guests can expect to be looked after by 280 staff, and often the proportion is three staff to every guest. Of course, when you come right down to it, no hotel, not even the Connaught, can be exactly like your own home—unless you happen to live in a house where people walk in and out at all hours, and where parcels and newspapers and luggage and messages are forever being delivered or removed, and people sit behind a desk

ABOVE *Left and right:* Two views of the small sitting room.

adding up figures and answering the telephone. But all that goes on only in the hall and along the corridors that lead to the dining rooms. Climb the wide oak staircase between the massive gleaming banisters and you are in a very different world indeed—of sitting rooms warmed by open fires, of bedrooms furnished with good solid furniture which has been there since the hotel first opened, of silent, deep-carpeted, meandering corridors hung with English pictures, of glass-fronted cabinets filled with English porcelain, of tranquillity and seclusion, where close friends can be staying only a door away from each other without even realizing it, and bankers, politicians and film stars can come and go without anyone giving them a second glance.

And yet, despite the inevitable comings and goings in the front hall, the occasional clutch of businessmen hunched around a table, the ringing of telephones, there are certain moments in the day when the atmosphere in the lounges quite matches that of the corridors above. Tea-time is one such moment. The last time I was there, with the curtains drawn against the winter rain, the little tables with their pink linen cloths already laid and the sound of the cake trolley making its way along the corridor, I might very easily have been, if not a guest in someone's house, then at least the member of a very small, very exclusive London club. Only one of the other seven tables was occupied—by an elderly gentleman reading *Country Life*. We both took tea—Darjeeling for me, Earl Grey for him. The choice between the egg, the tomato and the cucumber sandwiches was impossible, so I solved the matter by having one of each. I passed on the thin bread and butter and jam, preferring to reserve my appetite for the black cherry tart and a slice of the Connaught fruit cake. I did not notice what my companion ate, though he seemed to be doing full justice to the cake trolley. Naturally, we did not speak to each other; one does not like to disturb a fellow while he is having his tea and reading *Country Life*. Still we nodded briefly at each other as I got up to go—as though agreeing that if by chance we were to bump into each other again, we might even say "Good afternoon."

The larger lounge was also empty that afternoon. I paused for a moment in front of one of the writing tables (dip pens still, I was glad to notice) to examine more closely the picture that hung above it. It was of a young man, descending a huge staircase, at the top of which stood an older man, his father presumably, pointing an angry finger in the direction of the front door. Below, a number of servants peered anxiously out through the half-open door that led below stairs as the boy, his head hung with shame, slowly descended the stairs, condemned never to darken the doors of the ancestral home again.

Had he run up terrible gambling debts? Been sent down from Oxford? Misbehaved with one of the maids? Whatever the cause, his father's action was one with which the majority of people who stay at the Connaught would, I feel sure, thoroughly approve.

THE DORCHESTER
LONDON, ENGLAND

FOR SOME REASON I have always thought of the Dorchester as a rather American hotel. Perhaps it is because of Elizabeth Taylor's association with the place, or because so many visiting American actors seem to hold interviews there. Perhaps it has something to do with the curious flat, sweeping, 1930's–style façade that appeared in so many American film musicals of that period. Or perhaps it is that whenever I drop into the bar for one of Roy's famous dry martini cocktails, my fellow drinkers seem to be nearly all Americans. And yet, the Dorchester is very much an English hotel. Mr. Bruce, the head concierge, has known three generations of one English family that has been coming to the hotel since it opened in 1931. Drop in there at lunchtime on a weekday and you will find any number of smartly dressed Englishmen, sipping gins and tonics, either with their wives and children or with business colleagues, before moving into the nearby grill for lunch.

The blue-mirrored ballroom is the traditional venue for those most English of institutions—the literary lunches which are given from time to time by Foyles, the famous booksellers, to celebrate the publication of particularly important books. I remember one in particular, given in honor of Noël Coward, whose biography, *A Talent to Amuse*, by my old friend Sheridan Morley (son of Robert) had recently been published. The list of guests at the top table was, I suppose, as distinguished as any that have gathered for such an event before or since: Mr. and Mrs. Richard Attenborough, Lady Diana Cooper, Dame Gladys Cooper, Sir Michael Redgrave, Dame Sibyl Thorndike, Mr. and Mrs. Robert Morley, Lord David Cecil, Sir John Gielgud, Sir Michael and Lady Balcon, Sir Alan Herbert, Miss Cicely Courtneidge, Mr. Harold Pinter, and Mr. (now Sir) Charles Chaplin. Sadly, Coward himself was prevented by illness from attending, and it was left to Chaplin to make the speech instead. Afterwards he posed for a sentimental photograph with all the waiters.

Equally glittering, though in rather a more obvious way, were the state banquets given in the sixties by King Hussein of Jordan, President Ayub Khan of Pakistan and King Feisal of Saudi Arabia. All three, having been guests of the Queen, ended their state visits in the Dorchester where they threw the banquets by way of thanking Her Majesty for her hospitality.

On each occasion, Oliver Ford, interior designer and design consultant to the Dorchester, was commissioned by the heads of state to decorate the ballroom in a manner befitting the occasion. For the first banquet, given by King Hussein, Ford transformed the room over-night into a garden in the middle of which, surrounded by banks of flowers and tropical plants, was a sixty-five-foot pool filled with water lilies and goldfish. The walls of the room were draped with green and white silk, in front of which stood great pyramids of white carnations, and the Jordanian coat of arms behind the royal table was flanked by the flags of both countries.

OPPOSITE A detail from the doors to one of the reception rooms.

It was in the Dorchester, too, that Princess (now Queen) Elizabeth was dining with friends on July 9, 1947, when her engagement to Prince Philip was announced from the Palace, and on November 19, Prince Philip held his stag party at the Dorchester the night before the wedding. Eleven men, including his best man—his cousin the Marquess of Milford Haven—and his uncle, Earl Mountbatten of Burma, sat down to a dinner of sole, pheasant, fruit salad, ice cream, coffee and champagne, after which the Prince marched into the kitchen to thank the chef personally for a memorable evening.

If I seem to be harping on the more glamorous aspects of the Dorchester's career, this is only because it has always been a rather glamorous hotel.

It was built on the site of the old Dorchester House, the home of Captain Robert Stayner Holford, a man of taste and wealth, who over the years had amassed an astonishing private art collection including works by Titian, Velasquez and Van Dyck. His house became one of London's most famous showplaces, and was renowned for its glittering gatherings.

In 1905, Dorchester House was leased to the American ambassador in London, Whitelaw Reid, and became the American embassy. In 1929 it was bought by Sir Robert McAlpine & Sons, the British construction firm, together with Gordon Hotels Ltd.

The hotel opened with a great flourish in 1931, the last in a series of large luxury London hotels that had begun with the Mayfair in 1926. Mr. Charles, who had first made his name at the Ritz before moving on to Claridge's, was brought in at great expense to open the restaurant. He is reputed to be the only waiter in London ever to have ridden in Rotten Row, Hyde Park, every morning—and that was in the days when only people with the longest pedigrees went riding in Rotten Row. It was inevitable that such a man would command a great following, and at the beginning his loyal supporters flocked to the Dorchester Restaurant. An added attraction in those early days were the Dorchester floor shows, featuring the famous Dorchester Girls with their lovely long legs, and great orchestras led by such figures as Jack Jackson and Lew Stone.

But almost at once the hotel was hit, like everything else, by the depression. In the days before flying became commonplace, the majority of those who traveled at all did so by sea; the turnover of guests in large luxury hotels was consequently very much slower, and, in time of hardship, almost nonexistent. By 1936 Gordon Hotels had lost interest in the hotel and that year McAlpines bought them out and took over the running of the hotel themselves. By the late thirties, the Dorchester was again beginning to prosper.

There are still one or two members of the staff left who were there in those early days—Roy in the bar, Mr. Sim in the front hall, Gordon in the lounge, and Mr. Bruce, who was helping to shift furniture around before the hotel even opened its doors. Talking to him, I was interested to hear about the role played by the Dorchester in the Second World War. Built as it was in reinforced concrete, it was

PRECEDING PAGE The famous Oliver Messel Suite, designed in 1953. THIS PAGE *Clockwise from upper left-hand corner:* The Spanish-style grill room; the hand-painted walls of the elevator; the entrance hall and lounge at tea time; the bedroom of the Oliver Messel Suite; a pair of hand-painted doors in the same suite; and part of the Terrace Restaurant.

The
Dorchester
Bar
Ground
Floor

believed, no doubt with some justification, to be the hotel in London where one would be safest from enemy bombs. As a result, the Dorchester became not only General Eisenhower's headquarters while he was in London, but also the London home of such prominent wartime leaders and cabinet ministers as Lord Halifax, Duncan Sandys, Duff Cooper, Lord Portal and Oliver Lyttleton.

The war over, the Dorchester became a permanent residence for powerful men of a different sort. Lord Camrose, the newspaper proprietor; Lord Rank, the man responsible more than any other for the success of the British film industry in the forties, fifties and early sixties; and Sir John Ellerman, the fabulously wealthy recluse shipping magnet; and for a couple of maiden ladies too, one of whom has been ensconsed there since the hotel opened. I have no idea what the number of her room is, nor how it is decorated, but I'll warrant it is a great deal more charming and elegant than it was when she first took up residence in it over forty years ago.

In those days the corridors were so plain and lacking in decoration that a visitor, newly arrived from America, might have had good reason to wonder if he had ever stepped off the liner at Southampton at all. The bedrooms, comfortable though they unquestionably were and as well-appointed as any in Europe, were decorated in an essentially straightforward style, with few pretty grace notes to break up the monotony of the color.

As for the public rooms, the colors throughout were so pale and neutral that, no matter what a female guest decided to wear, there was never the slightest danger of a nasty clash.

Today the Dorchester is one of the brightest, prettiest, most colorful hotels in the world.

The transformation began in 1953 with the opening of the famous Oliver Messel Suite in a new wing that jutted out at the back of the hotel. On the floor immediately above, Messel (Lord Snowdon's uncle, incidentally, for those who like to be up in these matters) created a penthouse suite in which elegant people could swan about at elegant gatherings in a vaguely sylvan setting.

So successful was the Messel Suite and so much was it in demand that in 1956 a ninth floor was added on to the hotel comprising four roof garden suites, each of which was designed by a different interior decorator.

It was shortly after this that Oliver Ford, a highly successful interior designer, who had recently extended his sphere of activities to the Bahamas, was commissioned to do two designing jobs in Nassau. One was the East Hill Club and the other was a private home, the owner of which one day quite casually asked Ford if he would be interested in decorating one of the corridors in the Dorchester Hotel, which he owned.

Ford's first impression of the corridors of the Dorchester was of a succession of "endless, impersonal tubes." His prime aim, therefore, was to introduce a feeling of intimacy, and this he did by breaking

Above: The hotel was built on the site of the old Dorchester House—for a while the American embassy in

the long tubes up with pretty fanlights, columns and moldings, little console tables with flowers and plants on them, wall-lights reminiscent of old London street lamps, and chairs grouped in such a way that one has the impression as one walks along of moving from one charming little area to another. This effect is further heightened by the different patterning in the carpets that he had made specially for the purpose. On every floor the basic color is different—beige, blue, rust and so on—which not only adds variety, but also gives guests who return to the same floor a feeling of continuity and a sense of coming back home.

In 1961, Ford was appointed design consultant to the hotel and since then, apart from the Messel suites, the Spanish-style grill, and some of the original Jacobean-style suites, he has been responsible for the redecoration of every single part of the hotel—from the marble floor of the front hall, to the circular Gold Room with its draped and painted ceiling; from the honey-beige and green suite the Burtons always have, to the hand-painted walls of the lifts; from the Orchid Suite with its charming mural of the English countryside, into which Ford painted his own country house in Oxfordshire, to the little green boxes of hotel matches.

Few people, on seeing the Dorchester from the outside for the first time, would think of calling it a pretty hotel. For those with a passion for Art Deco, it has a certain architectural interest, some may say charm. But it is essentially a rather severe, slightly cold-looking place, a city hotel built for a city of hotels. It is that much more of a triumph, therefore, that Oliver Ford has succeeded in making one feel, almost the moment one steps through the front door, as though one were outdoors in the English countryside. Whatever the color he uses (and he has a strong preference for country colors) one always has the impression of being surrounded with light, and air, and leaves, and sunshine.

London. *Right:* The rural colors of Hyde Park are reflected in much of the hotel's decoration.

GEORGE V
PARIS, FRANCE

If you pick up a book of hotel matches in the George V you will find inside the cover the words *"Le George V. Le plus Parisien des Hotels."* You will also find the same thing on the breakfast menu in your room, on the mini-bar price list, and on the little card that tells you which number to ring for medical service and how much it will cost you to have a urine test or an inter-muscular injection.

For a long time I pondered on this claim. Since it might reasonably be attributed as much to the Ritz or the Bristol or the Plaza-Athenée or the little Hotel Neron in Montparnasse, I took it to imply some deep philosophical truth which the well-traveled would recognize the moment they walked through the front door and which would be revealed to less sophisticated mortals in time. Occasionally I thought the light had dawned. At dinner the first evening, sitting out in the open courtyard, it suddenly occurred to me how very Parisian was the superstructure of the hotel. Again, at lunch in Les Princes Restaurant with André Sonier, the hotel's director-general, and some of his staff, I found myself involved in one of those pointless intellectual discussions on love and life of which the Parisians are so inordinately fond. During the course of our discussion Monsieur Sonier propounded the theory that the happiest man in the world is the cuckold, who can go off and have a bit of a thing himself without feeling the slightest bit guilty. You know the sort of thing—all very Parisian to be true, yet hardly enough in itself to justify the boast, *"le plus Parisien."*

The location—just off the Champs Elysées, in the Avenue George V—could that be what was meant? Or perhaps the restaurant. Certainly very highly regarded by Paris gourmets. Or the bar, spilling out into the lobby, very much the meeting place of *le moitié* if not *le tout Paris.*

"Tell me," I said to André Sonier finally, "why do you say yours is '*le plus Parisien des hotels*'?"

He shrugged his massive shoulders beneath his pinstriped suit. "I had to think of something to call it," he said.

It is the sort of remark that, coming from anyone else, would smack of gross affectation. But Sonier is a showman, a figure rather larger than life, from whom such off-hand comments fall easily and, in this case at any rate, probably truthfully.

In 1970 Sonier, aged sixty years, was snatched from the jaws of retirement by Sir Charles Forte, who had two years previously bought the George V, the Plaza-Athenée and the Tremoille, and who persuaded him to come to Paris and put the George V back on its feet. They had met in Cannes, where Sir Charles had his yacht, and Sonier, after thirty years at the Carlton, had just launched the Cannes Marina. Though poles apart physically (Sir Charles is small and dapper, André Sonier is huge and shambling), they share a high degree of professionalism and discovered in each other some admirable qualities that could be used to each other's advantage.

The hotel had been built in 1929, and its fame during all those

Above and left: "Le plus Parisien des hotels"; one of the suites. OPPOSITE *Top left:* Part of the main staircase. *Top right:* The Louis XIII room, with its Renaissance fireplace from a château near Orleans. *Bottom left:* Napoleon by Houdon. *Bottom right:* The previous owner of the hotel was a passionate collector of bits and pieces.

"The Hotel George V is also a museum." That tapestry above the registration desk (*top left*) is a Gobelin.

years had been due to the efforts of one man—François Dupré—who had owned the hotel from 1931 to 1968. By that time, sadly, it was offering too little luxury for too much money. As a result, the occupancy figures were falling, the restaurant was virtually empty, the profits were non-existent. After careful deliberation, Sonier did a number of things. He held prices, renovated bedrooms and created a great new restaurant called Les Princes, sacked tired old staff and brought in keen young men of his own. One way and another he began to breathe life into the old place again.

He also turned the George V into a living museum. One of the first things he did upon arriving was to go through the inventory. François Dupré had been a great collector of fine things: tapestries, carpets, paintings, clocks. Sonier determined that the sort of clientele he was going to attract would appreciate being surrounded by such things. And so, when the guest signs in now, he does so beneath a great Gobelin tapestry; on his way to the restaurant he may stop and admire a Houdon bust of Napoleon; in the Louis XIII room he can sit in front of a great Renaissance fireplace from a château near Orleans; and on the way to the bar he can check his watch from a splendidly ornate eighteenth-century Regency clock. Also in the inventory Sonier found mention of a painting by Renoir. Unfortunately, of the painting itself there was no sign, and it wasn't until several weeks later that somebody decided to unwrap an uninteresting-looking parcel at the bottom of the safe. The Renoir *Vase de Roses* had been put there for safe-keeping over ten years before by François Dupré. It now hangs in a Louis XV gilt frame in the Renoir Suite. One cannot help feeling that the hotel's number-two slogan, "The Hotel George V is also a museum," stands up to scrutiny a great deal better than the other one.

Moreover, there is always an exhibition of one good painter or another (it might be Utrillo, or Renoir, or Dufy) either in the Findlay Gallery or in Les Princes Restaurant.

But Monsieur Sonier's concept of gracious living does not begin and end with valuable paintings and antiques. A tremendous amount of thought and planning has gone into the refurnishing of many of the hotel's suites and bedrooms, and Sonier has even persuaded various embassies like the Mexican and the Irish to help him with schemes for decorating certain rooms in national styles. There is a Fontainebleau Suite containing Empire furniture; a Hyde Park Suite in which the fireplace is guarded by a pair of fine china King Charles Spaniels; and a Penthouse with walls covered in an exotic oriental tissue.

In the old days all the big Hollywood stars traditionally stayed at the George V, while the princes and princesses went to the Plaza-Athenée. But of course with the decline of Hollywood, fewer and fewer big names in the entertainment business were to be found in the hotel register. Again, it was Sonier, who had met and known many American and British stars while he was at the Carlton, who brought back a little of the old-time glamor to the George V. Pierre Trudeau, Oliver Reed, Michael York, Peter Ustinov, the Osmonds, Danny Kaye, Roger Moore, Yul Brynner, Burt Lancaster, Jeanne Moreau, Jean Seberg, Gina Lollobrigida, and many others have been to the hotel in recent years either to stay or to attend some social event dreamed up by Sonier. Art Buchwald is one of his oldest friends and always stays at the hotel; so does Harold Robbins; Georges Simenon used the hotel as a setting for *Maigret Voyage*.

There always seems to be something going on at the George V, even when nothing is. People are forever coming and going—beautiful women, interesting-looking men, exotic princesses in yasmaks, and strange musicians in goodness knows what.

It may not be the most Parisian of hotels but, thanks to André Sonier, it is certainly the most lively hotel in Paris.

LE GRAND HOTEL
ROME, ITALY

ABOUT AN HOUR'S drive outside Rome, perched on a hillside in Tivoli, are the ruins of the villa to which the Emperor Hadrian was wont to retire whenever the pressures of life in Ancient Rome became overwhelming. It must have been an enormous place in those days; almost an ancient Roman version of Versailles. Today white rose bushes grow on the spot where the Emperor and his friends stretched out on couches to eat and drink; swifts and swallows swoop and twitter about the walls of the great rooms; and through halls that once were rife with gossip and political intrigue creeps nothing more sinister than the occasional breeze, cooling the shimmering heat of a summer's afternoon and making you feel glad to have escaped, if only for an hour or so, from the noise and traffic and swarming crowds along the Via Veneto.

Nothing increases one's appreciation of a great city more than the knowledge that one can, whenever one so wishes, escape from it into a refuge of peace and calm and beauty.

Mind you, for those without the time or the inclination to journey quite so far, there is one famous sanctuary that is much closer to hand—within walking distance of the center of Rome. I refer, of course, to Le Grand Hotel in the Via Vittoria Emanuele Orlando, only a step away from the Via Veneto.

Once inside that sumptuous lounge, with its huge, intricately patterned carpet, its gleaming floorboards, its glittering chandeliers and its potted palms, one has the feeling, as surely as at Hadrian's villa, of having stepped back into another age, when life for the rich was slow and luxury was taken for granted. Le Grand Hotel is and always has been *the* place for Roman patrician gatherings, especially weddings, and if you arrive when one of those is in full flow you begin to realize that in style and elegance and downright grandness, no nation can touch the Italians.

The women all seem to have stepped straight out of the pages of Italian *Vogue*; without exception they are stunning in those stiff, off-white, wild silk frocks that English and American women never seem quite to be able to carry off. The men would stand out a mile anywhere else in the world in their dark suits and shirts that have somehow achieved a new level of whiteness; here they pass virtually unnoticed.

One has the impression, though, that no matter how naturally they may appear to fit into the sumptuous surroundings, people like this are merely passing through—up from their villas on the coast or in the Tuscan hills. For the upper-class Romans, the Grand is the place to meet their friends for a meal in Le Maschere Restaurant or a drink in Le Rallye Bar, but one feels they rarely stay there.

Who then does?

Essentially, the same sort of people who stay at hotels like Claridge's in London and the Bristol in Paris: well-to-do out-of-towners, distinguished foreign visitors, people who care passionately about being looked after hand and foot by a devoted army of servants

OPPOSITE The Ritz Banqueting Hall.

who are capable of interpreting every slightest wish before it has been expressed or even thought of, and who are prepared to pay handsomely for the privilege.

It goes without saying that the Grand is endowed with the most beautiful public rooms and bedrooms you are likely to find in any hotel anywhere in the world. Even more magnificent than the lounge is the Ritz Banqueting Hall, with its curved painted ceiling, its mirrored walls and its great chandeliers. Le Maschere Restaurant, opened in October, 1969, is arguably the prettiest and most romantic eating place in the world. The bedrooms are all in impeccable taste and Le Rallye Restaurant is one of the most successful in Rome. Between 1963 and 1970, CIGA, the owners of Le Grand (and of the Gritti and Danieli in Venice and many other great Italian hotels) spent approximately 3,000 million lire (over 4½ million dollars) modernizing and redecorating. And yet no matter how much they had spent and how beautifully they had done it up, it would all have been a complete waste of time and money had they not also continued to offer their clients the one thing that in the end separates the great hotels from the rest—personal service.

I doubt if there is a single hotel in the world that does not claim to provide visitors with personal service. However, there is a difference between plain comfort, which means that if you pick up a telephone or ring a bell and ask for something it will automatically be provided, and real luxury, which is when things are done for you *without* your having to ask.

Such close personal concern for all your needs takes many forms at Le Grand Hotel. For instance, if you spill coffee on your jacket at breakfast, as happened to one guest, the head waiter, without waiting to be asked, will take the jacket away and have it dry-cleaned and returned to your back before the meal is over. The second time you walk into Le Rallye Bar, the barman will remember not only your name but also the way you had your drink the previous night.

Mind you, personal service of this sort is not achieved without a great deal of care and effort on the part of the staff. They don't just happen to remember your name by chance. There is not some mysterious spirit whispering in their ears that you like your whisky with soda and no ice. Nor is it necessarily because of the force of your personality that they remember that when you were there two years previously you had to speak sharply to someone about the air-conditioning in your room. The fact of the matter is that everyone who stays at Le Grand Hotel automatically becomes part of the hotel's permanent records. The name is entered on a card: a blue one if you are an old guest, a red one for travel agents, yellow for VIP's, hotel managers or journalists, and a green one for people who have ever had cause to complain about something. The moment you make a reservation, your name is looked up in the files. The least you can expect as an old or favored guest is a bowl of fruit and some flowers with a welcoming note from the manager. Should you ever have had

Above: The front entrance of the hotel, with the ruins of the Fontanove del Mose, built in 1584 by Pope Sixtus V. *Right:* Concierge Renzo Chiaranda can arrange for you to have an audience with the Pope.

cause to utter the least criticism, be it only to remark that you have never understood how people can live with yellow bedcovers, then you can be sure that your sense of taste will never again have to withstand such a body-blow. The reception manager will make sure either that you are put into another room, or else that the bedcovers are changed for those of another hue.

But these are mere run-of-the-mill stuff compared with the demands that are made by some guests. The card of one New Yorker records that when he says he likes new sheets every day (which is normal practice in CIGA hotels anyway), he means newly *bought* sheets every day. Another tells that the wife of a Californian likes to speak Italian to the staff; a third that a particular client requires a personal maid to wash and iron his laundry. Whether they go in for flattery on the scale of one German hotel which has cards marked with remarks like "Remember to enquire after dog's health", I do not know, but it is a fact that the concierge, Renzo Chiaranda, if he likes you and cares to put his mind to it, can arrange for you to have a private audience with the Pope without *too* much difficulty. . . .

Why is it, though, that certain hotels are able and prepared to cater to guests' every whim while others, equally adept though they may be in all the normal departments of hotel-keeping, are not?

In the end, I suppose, it comes down to two things. One, tradition; two, class of manager. In both of these the Grand in Rome is as well-endowed as any hotel in the world.

First, tradition.

In the *New York Times* on Monday, January 17, 1910, an advertisement appeared for Le Grand Hotel which announced, to the surprise of many who were not up in these matters, that it was "Under the same Proprietorship and Direction as the Savoy Hotel, Claridge's Hotel and the Berkeley Hotel, London."

In fact, the story goes back to the inauguration party for the Savoy in London in 1889, when the Marchese di Rudini happened to remark to Madame Ritz that Rome could do with such a hotel. Soon afterwards her husband César, at that time managing director of the Savoy, paid his first visit to Rome and instantly fell in love with the city. "Rome," he wrote later, "is the most beautiful city I have ever known."

The upshot was that five years later, on January 11, 1894, Ritz and Escoffier opened Le Grand Hotel for the Savoy Company. César himself was in charge of all the planning and construction. The inauguration celebrations were as elaborate and impressive as anything that Rome has ever witnessed.

A day or so later, 150 of Rome's leading citizens sat down to a banquet during the course of which the mayor of Rome, Prince Colonna, proposed a toast to "the new César returned to conquer Rome."

Other Ritzian innovations included baths in every room, and dining in the hotel restaurant for non-residents. So powerful was his

Clockwise, from upper left-hand corner: Le Maschere Restaurant; the lounge; the main staircase; Le Rallye, one of *the* meeting places in Rome; the walls of Le Maschere are decorated with scenes from the old Commedia dell'Arte.

Le Rallye
BAR
GRILL

influence in such matters that when Ritz announced, shortly after opening, that it was high time the city had a winter social season, his proposal was instantly taken up. From the end of December to the end of April the following year, Rome was alive with balls, and galas, and banquets, all of which were of course held at the Grand.

The second season was even more brilliant, and numbered among the hotels guests were various German and Montenegrin princes, the German Kaiser, and Emile Zola (who had a curious habit of retiring to his room at the first hint of a thunderstorm and disappearing beneath the sheets until it had abated). During the several months that he stayed at the hotel, his wife took a course of Italian lessons from an extremely good-looking young tutor, at the end of which, they say, she was unable to speak a single word of the language.

But the ability to attract a wealthy, gifted and heavily titled clientele was only one of Ritz's talents. More significant in the long run was the gift he shared with Escoffier of simplifying everything—from the food they served in the restaurant to the decoration of the bedrooms. Of course, the simplest meal eighty years ago seems like the most exotic banquet compared with the average meal one eats today in even the grandest restaurants. Yet the tradition established by Ritz and Escoffier of simpler dishes and plainer sauces continues today in all the hotels with which they once had any connections.

Le Maschere Restaurant in the Grand, for example, with its charming atmosphere of a Venetian *festa* and its walls decorated with scenes from the old Commedia dell'Arte, is devoted primarily to the great Italian staple dish—pasta. Having searched for and found the

most accomplished *sfoglina* (pasta cutter) in Italy, the hotel was then in a position to offer thirty-eight of the most distinctive regional varieties of pasta, one of the most exotic of which is the *Pansoti al Latte di Noci*, which consists of triangles of pasta, stuffed with a wild herb called *borage*, and served in a sauce of fresh crushed walnuts, garlic and olive oil.

In Le Rallye Room, too, simplicity is the order of the day. Its two outstanding dishes are *Bresaolo*, an air-cured beef from the Italian Tyrol, which is here cut into very thin slices and arranged on a plate with grapefruit segments and a pungent variety of lettuce called *rughetta*; and *Spaghetti Balduini*, an invention of the maître d'hôtel of the same name, the actual ingredients of which are, alas, a closely guarded secret.

Le Grand Hotel's tradition of simple luxury could be said to extend further back into the past than the late nineteenth century, for in the days of Ancient Rome, where today their patrician successors swan about in the main entrance hall, there was a warm water swimming pool that was part of the Baths of Diocletian.

But tradition is only one of the blessings that go to make up the really great hotel. The other is, as I said earlier, a great manager, and the Grand has that too in the form of Dr. Nico Passante, a man of enormous charm and elegance. Dr. Passante has that cool, somewhat withdrawn air of one who would think he had failed terribly if he ever gave you the slightest hint of the amount of sheer hard work that goes into the smooth running of that hotel.

I remember once asking a friend who had just come back from Le Grand Hotel what in particular she remembered about the place—outstanding examples of service, complicated problems overcome, delicate matters handled in a particular way, that sort of thing. She thought for a while and then said, "Do you know something? Everything seemed to run so smoothly, especially with everyone speaking perfect English, that I really didn't notice anything in particular at all."

Dr. Passante would be very pleased.

Above left: The sitting room of the Royal Suite. *Above right:* The bedroom of the Royal Suite.

GRITTI PALACE
VENICE, ITALY

I KNEW THE passage almost by heart already. It was not a very distinguished piece of writing, but it *was* by Somerset Maugham and it *was* about the place we were heading for along the Grand Canal in the shiny brown motorboat on that overcast, dozy Venetian afternoon. "At the Gritti," he wrote, "you are not merely a number as you are in those vast caravanseries that are now being built all over the world. You are a friend who is being welcomed as you step out of your motor boat. . . ."

Unfortunately, as it happened, we had arrived on the day of a national strike of hotel staff. Not only was there no one on the wobbly floating landing stage to welcome us as friends, but we had to totter in through the elegant front door, our knees buckling badly beneath the weight of fourteen suitcases. It was not a very propitious start to a stay in one of the world's greatest hotels. On the other hand, even if we had been forced to swim all the way from the parking lot, carrying our luggage in our teeth, I do not believe we should have climbed out of the stinking water feeling anything other than delight and childish excitement at being back in Venice once more. But to be in Venice *and* to be staying in a fifteenth-century Doge's Palace, surrounded by palaces, with the church of Santa Maria della Salute facing you on the other side of the water and beyond, San Giorgio and the infinitely mysterious waters of the lagoon—this surely is more than any twentieth-century traveler deserves.

I doubt if there is another hotel anywhere that can compete with the Gritti for the sheer loveliness of its setting. That alone places it among the greatest hotels in the world, staff or no staff.

The thing that gives the Gritti such an enormously unfair advantage over almost every other hotel, in addition to its unique location, is that it was not originally built as a hotel. As a result, nothing is uniform, inevitable, artificial or forced. The public rooms lead off one another in a haphazard sort of way; the corridors ramble; the bedrooms are of all shapes and sizes; the furniture and ornaments look as though they have been collected, one at a time, by someone who knows and cares about beautiful things, and not by a highly paid interior decorator. The hotel's *direttore*, Natale Rusconi, likens it to the nearby garden of Toscanini's daughter, the beauty of which has grown out of years of care and affection; it has not been created overnight by professional know-how.

Robert Morley, writing about the Gritti, described how in the course of one of his visits he sent a valuable-looking bedside lamp crashing to the floor. "If I can afford to pay for it I will," he told the desk, but they dismissed the suggestion with a chuckle.

And yet the extraordinary thing is that this little palazzo, the home of Andrea Gritti, 1455–1538, the sixty-seventh Doge of Venice, became a hotel only twenty-six years ago.

True, for a while it had acted as the annex to the Grand Hotel next door; but it was not until 1947 that it was taken over as a separate establishment by CIGA (*Compagnia Italiana del Grandi*

OPPOSITE Evening on the Grand Canal, from the hotel terrace.

Alberghi) who at once set about remodeling it and turning it into the finest jewel in their glittering chain. The man largely responsible for the metamorphosis was a formidable gentleman by the name of Raffaele Masprone. His closest collaborator in those early days was the dark-haired lady who is still the hotel's head housekeeper, Signora Cosima Giandomenici, who took the job under the misapprehension that she would be working in a private house. In a way she was.

She remembers the place as looking quite terrible when she first walked into it. It seemed an impossible task, and she believes it was only the personality and enormous drive of Masprone that created the initial team spirit on which the success of the hotel was built.

In June, 1948, the Gritti opened its doors for the first time. For a year, nothing much happened. Business was satisfactory but far from spectacular. And then, suddenly, after about a year, the place exploded into life. One guest whose name did more to transform the Gritti into one of the most famous hotels in the world was Ernest Hemingway; and the fact that he stayed there in Suite 115–116 on the corner of the first floor (now known as the Hemingway Suite) on several occasions and wrote *Across the River and Into the Trees* there has continued to be a powerful if understated selling point for the hotel ever since.

Clearly he made a profound effect on Signora Giandomenici, who still, after all this time, goes quite dreamy whenever she talks about him. Apart from his soft eyes, she particularly remembers how he used to write, looking out through the window at the buildings on the other side of the Grand Canal. At ten every morning he would ring for caviar and champagne. Then he would move on to more champagne and after that whisky. But for most of the day he would keep his spirits up on Valpolicella, an ample supply of which was kept permanently in the bath. Northing much, it seems, distrubed the great man—not even the constantly argumentative *gondolieri* at the landing stage beneath his window, to whom he would from time to time send a bottle of wine. She has fond memories too of Mary Hemingway, who would more often than not slide down the banisters in preference to taking the stairs.

The Gritti has always had a special attraction for writers. Long before it was ever thought of as a hotel, John Ruskin wrote part of *The Stones of Venice* in an upstairs room; Dickens came there, so did George Sand; and more recent literary guests have included Sinclair Lewis, John Dos Passos, Ben Hecht, Cornelia Otis Skinner, C. P. Snow, Peter Ustinov, Sir Winston Churchill, Noël Coward, Georges Simenon and Somerset Maugham, whom Signora Giandomenici remembers sitting in Suite 112–114 surrounded by red carnations and a strong scent of Schiaperelli "Shocking," doing *piccolo punto* (petit point) while his secretary read to him.

"There are few things more pleasant," he wrote, "than to sit on the terrace of the Gritti when the sun, about to set, bathes in lovely color the Salute which almost faces you."

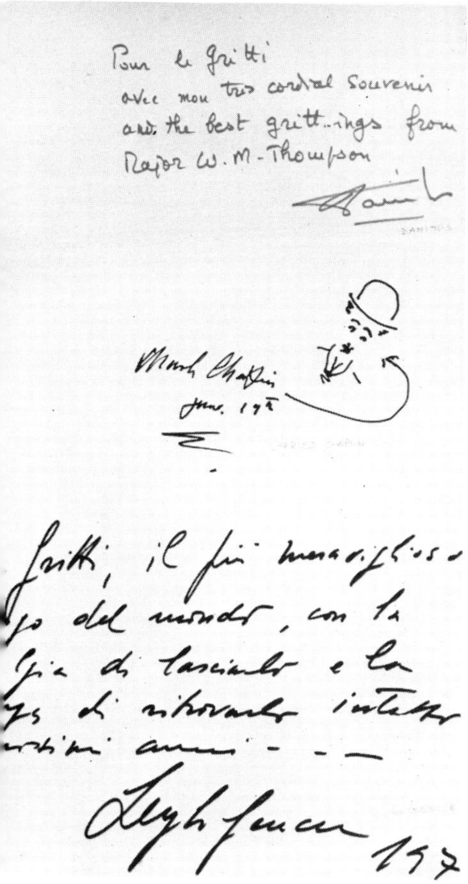

If I attempt to explain why writers in particular should have found the Gritti such a sympathetic setting in which to practise their art, I do so only because I believe that it reveals certain aspects of the hotel's character and quality that anyone blessed with the smallest amount of sensitivity would understand and appreciate.

The point is this: the two worst problems the writer faces are, first, persuading himself to sit down at the desk in front of the blank sheet of paper; and second, having done so (no mean feat in itself, I may say), forcing himself to remain there and not be distracted by thoughts of more amusing activities. The temptations are doubly strong when the weather is fine and the sun is shining. From this one might suppose that Venice, where the sun shines a good deal in the summer months, is not the ideal place to try and write. However, I can only tell you that as I sat writing one brilliant morning in one of the corner suites overlooking the Piazza Santa Maria del Giglio, with the windows open on two sides, I could not have been more composed. The sounds of life in the streets below—dogs barking, women screeching, pigeons flapping, boats swishing and whining their way past along the Grand Canal, and organists practising in the church—poured in through my open windows in such profusion and with such vividness that I was perfectly content to remain at my desk, in the cool comfort of that spacious room. And if at any time I felt the need to rest my eyes from the paper, no matter where I looked through the windows I could be certain of enjoying some visual delight or other—a roof, a tower, a dome, or just the pigeons wheeling against the blue sky.

Clearly the Gritti is not alone among the great houses and palaces of Venice in offering writers these very attractive facilities. Robert Browning lived and wrote at the Palazzo Rezzonico; D'Annunzio made love to Duse and wrote *Notturno* in a Venetian palace; Byron once threw himself into the canal from the balcony of the Palazzo Moncerigo. Nor, to pursue my earlier point about people of taste and sensibility, is it only writers who have found peace and inspiration at the Gritti. "Not only the best in Venice—but the best in the world," wrote Moss Hart and Kitty Carlisle Hart in the hotel's *Livre d'Or*. "I will come back," Mrs Stravinsky inscribed rather threateningly. Lord Aberconway wrote that he was "leaving once again his favorite hotel in his favorite city". When Toscanini stayed there he used to sleep with a little black devil doll between his sheets; Nkrumah preferred a pistol.

In the VIP book the signatures of Isaac Stern, Poulenc, Sviatoslav Richter and Nathan Milstein rub characters with those of the Queen Mother of Bulgaria, Cole Porter, Clark Gable and Dean Acheson. De Gaulle, Harry Truman and Alexei Kosygin all stayed at the Gritti; so too did the Windsors. Signora Giandomenici remembers her as being a very strong woman and him as being very kind, sometimes offering her a cup of tea in their suite.

ABOVE Three leaves from the Gritti's *Livre d'Or*.

One evening Dr. Rusconi, the hotel's director, was entertaining

some friends to drinks on the terrace. The façade of the hotel glowed red in the warm rays of the setting sun; boats of all shapes and sizes chugged past on the Grand Canal; gondoliers leaned on their poles, easing their craft effortlessly through the choppy water; San Giorgio shone white across the lagoon; waiters moved noiselessly among the tables. We were talking about the extent to which the Gritti owed its success to the fact that it was not an hotel to begin with. "What is more," agreed Dr. Rusconi, "it still doesn't want to be."

One of the problems of writing about a hotel like the Gritti is that one tends to be overwhelmed by the beauty of the surroundings, the elegance and the history of the building, the romantic literary associations, the nostalgia, and all the fame that has preceded it. One runs the risk of assuming that somehow all that luxury and grace and elegance and comfort just, well, happens: silently, effortlessly, in a self-perpetuating sort of way, like those clocks which once you have wound them sit on the mantlepiece spinning backwards and forwards, apparently forever.

All of which is precisely as it should be. One of the marks of a great hotel is that one should be aware only of the hands keeping perfect time, and never of workings of the motor. Thus, when a guest orders *fegato alla Veneziana*, he will never know that at that very moment the chef is having trouble with his vegetable cook, one of the ovens, and the quality of the liver. And when Signor Lis, the chief concierge who has been with the hotel from the beginning, knowing a particular guest is unable to buy a ticket to a certain operatic event, hands him two tickets, the guest may never discover how it was done. Things like that happen at places like the Gritti.

The reason they do is, of course, that somebody somewhere—Signor Lis, the chef, Dr. Rusconi, a waiter, Signora Giandomenici, a chambermaid—cares sufficiently about the hotel and its guests that he or she has gone to a great deal of trouble to make sure they do; and, what is more, never to let on just how much.

On July 1 every year, Madam Valentina Schlee, the designer, takes the 8.35 train from Paris. When she arrives at Venice that evening, she knows that she will be met by someone from the Gritti. It is marked on her card—*"arriva sempre de mattina treno Paris."* On arriving at the hotel she will be greeted by Dr. Rusconi and accompanied to the same room she has had every year since 1951. In that room she will find the same familiar furniture, lamps, china, books, paintings, even the same breakfast napkins. And when she goes down to the restaurant for dinner she will find that her table has been pulled out of line and placed at the slight angle that always gives her a perfect view of everyone in the restaurant.

As Maugham put it: "When you sit down to dinner at the very same table you sat at the year before and the year before that, and when you see that your bottle of Soave is in the ice pail waiting for you, as it has been year after year, you cannot but help feel very comfortable and very much at home."

OPPOSITE *Top and bottom:* Gritti Palace from across the Grand Canal; Signora Giandomenici in the Hemingway Suite. ABOVE Santa Maria del Giglio.

IMPERIAL
VIENNA, AUSTRIA

I SOMETIMES WONDER, as I am being shown up to my hotel room by the assistant manager and we make small talk along the carpeted corridor, what thoughts pass through the minds of important state visitors—kings and queens, presidents and sheiks, prime ministers and foreign secretaries and the like—during the first minutes after their arrival. Are they impressed by their royal suities, or disappointed? How many of them feel that the accommodation they are being offered is rather a step up, and for how many is the grandest suite of rooms not quite up to the sort of thing they are used to at home? Does the President of France look up at yet another ornately decorated ceiling and run his eyes over yet another vast canopied double bed and long for a single room at the back with a TV? And what about someone like the peripatetic U.S. Secretary of State? Does he ever have time to distinguish one room from another anyway?

They say the Queen's private rooms in Buckingham Palace are surprisingly modest; even so, I cannot imagine there are many hotels with royal suites that can actually impress her by their grandness . . . except, possibly, the Imperial in Vienna.

The Imperial Suite occupies most of the front of the hotel's first floor, and is arguably one of the most aptly named in Europe. It comprises four vast baroque double rooms, decorated in pink with elaborate white moldings, leading one into the other through arched doorways that are not quite big enough to accommodate a double-decker London bus. Everything in these rooms has been designed to remind their occupants that the curiously provincial town they are staying in was once, and not so long ago at that, a great capital city; and that Austria, before it was reduced to a neutral state of seven million people, was once the center of a mighty empire of fifty millions that stretched right across Hungary, Czechoslovakia and Northern Italy.

Today the crowds of sightseers swarm through the gardens of the Schönbrunn Palace and clamber to the top of the Gloriette high on its hill for one of the best views of the city to be found anywhere. How many of them, one wonders, realize that on that same spot, but even more elevated, was to have stood the original palace—a kind of super Versailles—from the highest point of which the Empress Maria Theresa, the mother of Europe, might have viewed her empire stretching away in the distance toward Prague and Budapest?

To understand Vienna today, you must understand what she once was. Age has withered her as it withers a great courtesan who has lived with kings and princes, and influenced mighty decisions. Her heart still beats, but only lightly. At times it seems almost to have stopped. The people, who know of her great fame only by repute, come to stare and wonder that such a frail frame could once have supported such mighty trappings—vast buildings like the Hofburg, great palaces like the Belvedere, Fischer von Erlach's amazing Nationalbibliothek—and then pass on, shaking their heads.

OPPOSITE Night in the Karnterring.

But nowhere is one more forcibly reminded of the grandeur that

The Imperial Suite. *Top left:* A corner with the portrait of Maria Theresa's mother. *Top right:* One of the three bedrooms. *Right:* The corridor outside.

was Vienna than in the Imperial Suite of the Imperial Hotel. It requires little imagination to believe that at any moment the double doors at the end of the room might open and the aged figure of the Emperor Franz Joseph, in his white uniform, his head bowed beneath the weight of those great moustaches, might totter in.

Just to descend the great staircase, past the two famous Winterhalter portraits of Franz Joseph and Elizabeth, between massive marble walls surmounted by columns, balustrades, statues, chandeliers and yet another portrait of the Emperor, is enough to endow a modern guest with unwonted delusions of grandeur.

Curiously enough, of all the people, grand and humble, who have been associated with the Imperial throughout its hundred-year history, the only one who never enjoyed the satisfaction of strolling down that splendid staircase was the one responsible for putting up the building in the first place—the autocratic Duke of Württemberg. A Prussian by birth, he decided in 1867 to commission the famous Italian architect Zanotti to build him a large town house on the Ring—on the site where the old city ramparts used to stand. No sooner

had the house been completed than the city council put through a plan to build a side street between the house and its gardens. The overbearing Duke, never a popular man at the best of times, announced that he would never set foot inside the house, and left the city forever.

The house remained empty for several years until its was bought in 1873 by the city fathers, who were anxious to find first-class accommodation for visitors to the Vienna International Exhibition. At huge cost, they turned it into a hotel of such splendor that the Emperor Franz Joseph himself declared that it should be named the Imperial and Royal Court Hotel.

Little is known of the history of the hotel during the years that followed, beyond the fact that it was the meeting place for the aristocracy who came to Vienna from every corner of the empire for the winter season of balls and entertainments, and that Wagner lived there for two months in 1875 with his family while he was putting the final touches to *Tannhaüser* and *Lohengrin*. The end of the First World War saw the final disintegration of the Austro-Hungarian monarchy, and the hotel, moving with the times, began to open its doors to a wider circle of guests that now included businessmen, bankers and artists.

And then, in 1938, Hitler came to Vienna.

Mr. Heinke, now the hotel's reception manager, still retains a vivid memory of standing on the far side of the Ringstrasse, looking up at the small, rather comic figure on the hotel balcony as he waved and smiled at the silent crowds beneath. "I doubt," he told me, "if I had any idea that this man was going to destroy the whole of Europe, condemn me to years of soldiering, and take away both my older brothers."

(A tiny footnote to this event: Goering took one of the large state rooms at the front of the hotel where he could be more easily seen; Hitler slept in a small room at the back of the building.)

By the time the war finally came to an end much of Vienna was in ruins. The Imperial was badly damaged. Many of its highly prized possessions had been destroyed or stolen. And to add insult to injury, almost immediately after hostilities ceased the hotel was taken over by the Russians, who maintained it as their headquarters until, under the terms of the 1955 Austrian State Treaty, the city was returned to its own people and the occupying forces finally withdrew. "All the time the Russians were here," Mr. Heinke told me, "you crossed the road when you passed the Imperial. No one dared go anywhere near the main entrance."

The first, and indeed only manager of the Imperial Hotel after that time was Mr. Karl-Peter Littig—a remarkable Munich man who had been responsible for, among other things, helping to make the Vier Jahreszeiten in Hamburg the great hotel it is today.

The task of clearing away the mess, redecorating and refurnishing, and building up a new clientele, would, if mastered, have been a major triumph on its own. But to have restored the Imperial within a space of only a few years to its former position as one of the best hotels in Europe is an achievement of which few men would be capable. Robert Morley stayed there shortly after it reopened while filming *The Journey* with Yul Brynner and Deborah Kerr, and to this day he counts it among the greatest hotels he has known. He marveled that an establishment which had been occupied for ten years by Russian soldiers—who had stabled their horses in the ballroom and roasted whole oxen on the marble staircase—should have managed to get everything back into place and be open for business within a year.

I do not know whether any of the distinguished world figures who have stayed there since the war ever wondered at the amount of energy, imagination, attention to detail and sheer single-mindedness, not to mention money, that Mr. Littig and his colleagues must have devoted to the re-creation of that hotel. That they came there at all is perhaps a compliment in itself. The kings of Sweden, Denmark, Belgium, Norway, Nepal and Saudi Arabia have all occupied the Imperial Suite, as have the queens of Holland and England. The

OPPOSITE *Top left:* A lamp in the Imperial Suite. *Top right:* the Imperial arms above the Grand Staircase. *Bottom left:* An old plan of the city, discovered in an attic after the war and assembled in a first-floor corridor. *Bottom right:* The bar.

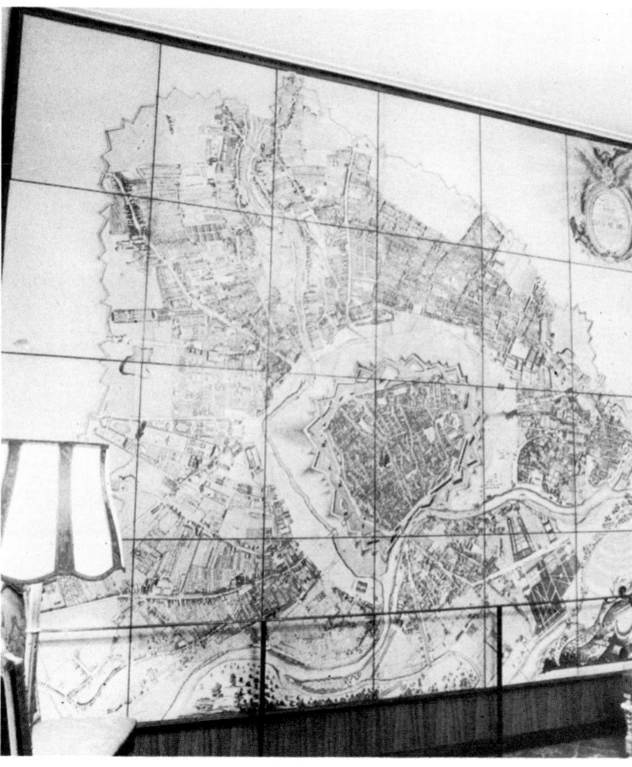

pages of the book are littered with the signature of presidents, prime ministers, and other assorted high government officials: Rusk and Gromyko, Kissinger and Sadat, Pompidou and Couve de Murville. Krushchev stayed there for his famous meeting with Kennedy in July, 1961. (The President, for reasons of protocol, stayed at the American embassy.) Certainly, no one I have ever come across who has stayed there is anything other than wildly complimentary about the endless pains to which the staff always go to make life as easy for their guests as is humanly possible.

During his stay, Mr. Morley was joined by his wife and children, who were fascinated by the gas balloons that were sold in the Prater next to the Great Wheel (of *The Third Man* fame). They would carry them back to the hotel and up to their room, where they would invariably forget to hold on to them, and the balloons would float up to the ceiling where they would remain until a man arrived with a ladder to take them down. "As long as the children stayed with me," Morley wrote later, "it seemed as if in our sitting room there was always a porter perched on a step ladder."

Although not a great balloon-collector myself, I am happy to report that the friendly willingness of the staff that was so much appreciated in the early days of the hotel's rebirth are still very much in evidence today. During my most recent visit I cannot remember a single floor waiter, room maid or employee of any sort who did not greet me with a cheerful "Grüss Gott" or "Gute Tag" as we passed.

But then the Imperial, although outwardly grand and rather forbidding, is really a warm, welcoming place, staffed by simple people who are there to make you happy not nervous, who believe in doing things properly but are proud of the fact that you can eat a jolly good meal in the Coffee House for only forty-five schillings. Vienna has lost a great deal over the past fifty years: its empire, its monarchy, its power in the world, its influence and some of its greatest brains. Yet throughout it all, the Viennese have never lost their talent for hospitality. They enjoy nothing more than sitting for an hour or so over coffee and Sachertorte, reading the newspapers or gossiping with their friends—unless it is encouraging visitors to their city to do exactly the same thing. And of all the brilliant ideas Mr. Littig has incorporated into the Imperial over the years, none has been more brilliant and successful than the new Coffee House, whose muted colors, comfortable green leaf-patterned chairs and banquettes, charming table-service designs, simply delicious food, and separate entrance from the Ringstrasse, have combined to make it one of the most popular meeting places in town. Always there is someone in there, be it the distinguished ex-head of the Vienna police force, who has popped in for his morning coffee and a look at the newspapers, or a group of top bankers lunching; or in the afternoons the aged countesses and baronesses who still like to totter in to sit there over a single cup of coffee and re-live their memories of the old days.

The Creditanstalt Bankverein, the company that owns the

107

Imperial, also owns the Bristol Hotel, and Mr. Littig divides his time between the two. Yet traditionally it is at the Imperial that guests of the government are received while they are in Vienna. It is also traditional that when such guests arrive, they are accompanied up the great marble staircase and along the wide carpeted corridor to the Imperial Suite. As it happened, our arrival coincided with that of the Minister of Defence of Hungary. The doorman was naturally anxious that we should unload our hired car and drive it away to the garage as quickly as possible. On the other hand, it is not every day that one is offered the chance to walk into a hotel along a red carpet between armed sentries, and, to the doorman's intense irritation, we took our time over it. No sooner were we in the bright warmth of the main lobby, than from the murky grey of the street outside came the sound of wailing sirens and roaring motorcycles; and a moment later, in a flurry of flashing headlights and frenzied activity, a long dark limousine with a small flapping pendant on its hood squealed to a halt outside the front door. Doors flew open, orders were shouted, heavily booted feet stamped and into the lobby swept a procession of uniformed officers—the Austrians in grey, the Hungarians in Russian-style brown—in the midst of whom trotted a small figure, also in uniform, his eyes staring straight ahead from behind his dark glasses, a long, unlighted cigarette jammed between his lips. Without pausing for a second the group marched silently across the lobby, turned sharp left and disappeared into the elevators which had been kept open in readiness by a number of unsmiling plain clothes security men with constantly shifting eyes and bulges under their armpits, and suddenly they had gone. The tension vanished, normal life returned to the lobby, the limousine drew silently away, and people began talking again.

We asked later why they had not been accompanied to their rooms via the marble staircase in the traditional way. "Ah well, you see," the man explained, "the trouble was they booked their state visit rather late in the day, and unfortunately we had already let the Imperial Suite to one of the senior executives of the Minnesota Mining Corporation who is here for a meeting. Under the circumstances, we could hardly ask him to move out, so we had to put the defence minister and his staff on the third floor at the back. . . ."

If the minister or his staff felt in any way insulted or hard done by, they certainly never showed it. I saw them coming and going on several occasions and they seemed, as far as one can judge, to be thoroughly happy to be there. And so indeed they should have been.

ABOVE *Top:* Shoes are returned in the morning polished, and with shoe trees in them. *Bottom:* The Coffee House.

ÖSTERREICHISCHER HOF
SALZBURG, AUSTRIA

OPPOSITE The manager has a weakness for potted palms.

SET INTO THE floor of the lobby of the Österreichischer Hof in Salzburg is a series of charming mosaic designs. In the very center of the most prominent of these, bang in front of the main desk, can be seen the letters CS. These are the initials of Carl Schwartz, the man who built the hotel between 1863 and 1866. Not a great deal seems to be known about this Baron who deepened the river Salzach, had a street named after him, and gave Salzburg its grandest hotel. One thing is quite clear, however: when it came to picking locations, he was second to none.

Just as he went to great pains to ensure that every guest should be reminded of him every time they walked through the lobby, so he determined that every time they looked out of the window and across the river they would bless him for having had the wit and foresight to choose as the site for his hotel a spot with what is arguably as good a view of the whole of old Salzburg as you will find anywhere.

I remember particularly one cold bright November morning, standing on the little balcony outside my second-floor room. The sun was just warm on my face as I looked across at the multi-colored façades of the ancient houses stretching along the side of the river away to my left, so pretty one could scarcely believe they were not part of some giant stage set. Behind them rose the domes, towers, minarets and steeples that crown what must be one of the richest collections of ecclesiastical architecture to be found anywhere in Europe: the Cathedral with its fat, comfortable-looking central green dome, the severe Gothic steeple of the Franciscan Church, the somber mass of Fischer Von Erlach's University Church; the baroque onion dome of St. Peter's; St. Blasius, St. Ursula and the Convent of Nonnberg.

And again, towering high above it all on its wooden hill, the fortress of Hohensalzburg—one of the largest and best preserved in Europe, began in 1077 by Archbishop Gebhard and home of the Archbishops of Salzburg for 500 years. The wooded skyline dips briefly above the rooftops, then rises again to become the mass of the Mönschberg against whose sheer rock face the old city comes to an abrupt halt and on top of which is perched the funny old Winkler Café.

This was the panorama that I looked out on that cold morning. Any sounds of traffic were deadened by the rush of the river, the cry of seagulls and the clang of innumerable church bells calling the faithful to mass. The city fathers of Salzburg use, as their selling motto, the phrase "a city that keeps its looks." And the most cursory examination of a plan of the city made in the late eighteenth century shows that the view today from a room in the Österreichischer Hof differs very little from the one the keeper of the Lederer Gate would have had from his cottage, which stood on the same spot two centuries ago.

Oddly enough, it was as the result of a period of decline in Salzburg's history that the city succeeded in keeping its looks while others

lost so much of theirs. For many centuries, largely because it was ruled by a series of archbishops who loved beauty and encouraged the building and creation of beautiful things, Salzburg was an important center for cultural and religious life. However, at the beginning of the nineteenth century Salzburg was secularized and very soon became nothing more than a small provincial town. And so it was that, at a time when in Vienna the Emperor Franz Joseph was expressing imperial grandeur by pulling down old houses to make way for the Ringstrasse, Salzburg was allowed to doze quietly, undisturbed and untouched.

It was at the height of this quiet period that Baron Schwartz began work on the Österreichischer Hof. When completed in 1866, it was about half the size it is today, with sixty-six rooms, a dining room with a verandah and a nice garden through which guests could stroll and admire the view. Illustrations of the period tell us that at that time the hotel went under two names, both of which were displayed on the outside of the building. Patrons glancing above the main entrance of the Schwartzstrasse saw that they had arrived at the Österreichischer Hof, while those in the garden or sailing by on the river would have seen on the roof above the dining room the

THIS PAGE *Top left:* The recently restored mosiac in front of the main desk. *Top right:* When it came to picking locations, Baron Salzach was second to none. *Left:* A raspberry souflé in the Subterranean Keller. OVERLEAF The view of old Salzburg is as good as you will find anywhere.

rather more sophisticated sign "Hotel d'Autriche." The Baron, being a builder rather than an hotelier, sold the hotel immediately upon its completion to one Karl Irresberger, and it was he whose name appeared under the announcement in the *Salzburger Zeitung* of June 4, 1886, of the *"Geoffnung des neuen hotel zum Österreischischen Hof im Salzburg."*

From the beginning the hotel enjoyed great success. Early guest lists included distinguished names from all walks of life and all parts of Europe—doctors, lawyers, diplomats, soldiers, princes, aristocrats and artists. Thus, alongside the names of Friedrich Smetana and the painter Pausinger we find those of the rifle-manufacturer Wendl, and, of all people, Buffalo Bill.

However, it was not for another thirty years or more that any serious attempt was made to enlarge the hotel. In 1899 the garden disappeared (followed seven years later by the verandah) to make way for a long low construction which added another forty rooms to the hotel.

Despite a brief crisis during the First World War when there was a strong possibility that the hotel might be requisitioned by the Italians as their new consulate, life at the Österreichischer Hof con-

tinued at a quiet, unhurried and elegant pace. And then, on August 22, 1920, an event took place that was to turn Salzburg from an insignificant provincial town into one of the most important cultural and touristic centers in Europe, and the Österreichischer Hof from a modest, well-run, town hotel into one of the great gathering places for the leaders of European and world society.

That event was the first performance in the Domplatz of Hugo von Hofmannstahl's production of *Jedermann: the life and death of a rich man*. It was the beginning of the Salzburg Festival.

The end of the nineteenth and beginning of the twentieth centuries had seen the flowering in many parts of Europe of small music festivals, but it took the combined talents of Max Reinhardt, Hugo von Hofmannsthal and Richard Strauss to devise a way of bringing them all together in one place and giving them a permanent home. Salzburg was the ideal choice as a setting for an artistic endeavor of the scale they envisaged; and the Österreichischer Hof was the ideal choice of all the top musicians, artists and festival-goers as a place to stay. And it has remained so ever since. The hotel's Golden Book teems with the great names of the musical world: Karl Böhm, Toscanini, Leontyne Price, David Oistrakh, Herbert von Karajan, Bruno Walter, Wilhelm Backhaus, and many others.

So firmly was the Festival established in the cultural calendar and so fond had those associated with it become of the Österreichischer Hof that the moment Austria regained her independence in 1955, after fifteen years of war and occupation, a large proportion of the old guests wasted no time in returning to the hotel. Once again Salzburg was full of music, of beauty, and of life.

In 1960 the Irresberger family sold the Österreichischer Hof to Countess Johanna Blanckenstein and her husband, Joseph. Under their ownership, and the direction of Herr Robert Prinz, another 23 rooms have been added, bringing the total number to 130, and a great deal of money has been spent on every aspect of the hotel: on the rooms, which have been decorated in a variety of styles ranging from modern brass and glass to antique wood; on the subterranean Keller, where one evening I succeeded in consuming a positively indecent quantity of goulash with dumplings, eggs and sausages, followed by a gigantic soufflé made with fresh raspberries; on the Mozartkugel Coffee Shop; on the Salzachgrill, and on the main dining room with its adjoining wood-paneled Zirbelzimmer; on the fine Persian carpets, good curtains and elegant chandeliers that are to be found in every bedroom; on the mosaics, which have recently been cleaned and replaced at enormous expense; and on that most charming of all the hotel's many charming features—the grand staircase, down which elegant festival-goers in their long evening dresses and black ties descend on warm summer nights through a magnificent garden of climbing plants and potted palms, on their way out to one of the best performances of *The Magic Flute* they may ever see in their lives.

THE PIERRE
NEW YORK, U.S.A.

ONE DAY NOT SO very long ago, a guest of the Pierre Hotel decided to take an excursion on the Circle Line, the three-hour guided boat trip that circles the whole of Manhattan Island. As anyone who has ever been on the trip will aver, this is one of the highlights of a visit to New York. Not only does it afford passengers marvelous close-up views of the Statue of Liberty and Brooklyn Bridge, but it also provides a better picture of how Manhattan is laid out and where everything is than any city bus tour. Hardly a single famous landmark or building of note fails to look its very best—the Empire State Building, the Chrysler Building, the United Nations, the World Trade Center Buildings—and the day this particular visitor took the Circle Line not one went unobserved or unremarked by the guide.

And then suddenly he heard the guide say, "And that tall building over there, ladies and gentlemen, with the fine copper roof, is the famous Pierre Hotel, probably the best hotel in New York City."

The hotel guest, while absolutely approving of the guide's opinion of the Pierre, was nevertheless surprised, first that he should have included it among New York's leading landmarks, and even more so that he, a guide on a Circle Line boat, should have been so definite in his opinion of the hotel's quality.

Whether the Pierre really is New York's best hotel is obviously arguable. What is beyond question, however, is that such success as the hotel has enjoyed since it was first opened on October 1, 1930 (a year and one day after the New York Stock Exchange crashed) is due in very large part to its situation (on the corner of Fifth Avenue and 61st Street bang opposite Central Park) and to its elegant and unique structure, which reminds one less of a New York hotel building than of a French château that some giant hand has taken by the roof and stretched upwards for forty-two floors. But then not for nothing is it called the Pierre.

The history of the hotel starts nearly a century ago in Ajaccio, Corsica—birthplace of Napoleon, incidentally—when the wife of a restaurateur by the name of Casalesco gave birth to a son whom they christened, rather unimaginatively, Charles Pierre. As soon as he was able, Charles began working in his father's restaurant. But then at the age of eighteen he left Corsica to seek his fame and fortune in Monte Carlo. Apparently he abandoned his surname at the same time he abandoned his homeland, for it was as Charles Pierre that he was taken on as a page boy at the Hotel Anglais in 1897.

At the Anglais he came into contact with a luxurious way of life he had never dreamed of in his father's kitchen in Ajaccio. This was the Golden Age of the French Riviera, when the hotels were riddled with kings and princes and grand dukes, all apparently hell-bent on disposing of huge sums of money in as short and extravagant a way as possible—largely in the casino. It seems that Charles was particularly impressed by the old Shah of Persia, who would be conveyed to and from the casino every night in a carriage drawn by a pair of fiery Arab horses.

OPPOSITE The Pierre, like an attenuated château, from Central Park.

Pierre also served on the Duke and Duchess of Mouche, whose title, which had been given them by Napoleon III, had evidently gone to their heads: they resolutely refused to appear in any of the hotel's public rooms unless accompanied by the ex-Empress Eugénie.

Later Pierre moved to Paris, where he set to and learned everything there was to know about the restaurant business. Then he went to London where he was taken up by Louis Sherry, the restaurateur, and given a place in the Sherry organization.

It was with Sherry's that he came in 1904 to New York, where he planned meals for, among others, John Jacob Astor, Mrs Stuyvesant Fish, assorted Vanderbilts and Elbridge Gerry.

He stayed for twelve years and might have stayed longer had he not fallen out with Mr. Sherry over the latter's refusal to allow women to smoke in his restaurant. After working for a while at the old Ritz-Carlton at Madison and 46th, Pierre opened his own restaurant at 11 East 45th Street and later another at 230 Park Avenue. He acquired a reputation not only for his food but also for his willingness to escort debutantes home after dinner, if there seemed no other way of getting them there; and with the arrival of Prohibition such problems were not infrequent in New York. Deb parties turned into gin

An upstairs world, high above the noise and bustle of New York City.

parties and before long everyone and everything began to get slightly out of control.

In 1928 came the opportunity Pierre had been waiting for—the chance to own a great hotel. Elbridge T. Gerry, one of his oldest clients, had died, leaving a huge family house at Fifth and 61st to a son who wanted nothing of it. Backed by a group of financiers who had always admired and respected his talents—among them Otto Hahn, Walter Chrysler, Gerry's son Robert, Peter Frelinghuysen and Le Roy Baldwin—Pierre was able to lease the property.

In February, 1929, the firm of Schultz and Weaver produced a design for the building based on a French château and shortly afterwards construction work began. Pierre set himself the very highest standards, based on those he had learned over so many years in Paris, London and Monte Carlo. He even persuaded Escoffier himself to come over and advise him on the kitchen. Things went badly for the Pierre in the thirties, as they did for almost everyone, but picked up again in the war years. This was really the peak of the Pierre's career, with the 42nd Floor Restaurant in full swing and all the big bands of the day booked to play for the swellest functions in town. Those were really the great days of the Pierre. After the war the hotel was

sold to Paul Getty and then later to Robert Dowling who had owned the Carlyle. On his death the hotel was bought by the Trust House Forte group in London which numbers the Plaza-Athenée and the George V among its foreign hotels.

Privacy and discretion are the keynotes of the Pierre today. Many of the original 700 rooms have been sold off over the years as private apartments and now, with only 196 rooms to manage, life is a good deal easier and the standards a good deal higher than many another huge 900-room New York hotel.

Even if the manager, Henri Manassero, did not have the sort of clientele who go there in search of peace and anonymity, the residents certainly would not put up with scruffy décor and sloppy service. The result is the most beautifully run and elegantly decorated hotel. Apart from the few public rooms—in particular the Grand Ballroom—there really isn't much that is spectacular about the Pierre. It has little to offer in the way of grand entrance halls or overwhelming dining rooms, like the Plaza or the Waldorf.

The atmosphere is much more reminiscent of a small Paris or London hotel—rather good carpets, French period furniture, a marble staircase or two, the occasional unexpected nook and cranny containing just a couple of chairs, muted pastel colors and few casual visitors. My bedroom I remember as being small and cream and exceedingly comfortable, with impeccable room service and lots of towels in the bathroom.

ABOVE *Left:* Curry in the Cafe Pierre. *Right:* The East Side from the 34th floor.

Why I should have expected anything exciting to happen at the Pierre while I was there, I cannot imagine. Perhaps simply because I find New York a very exciting place to be in, and when I am there exciting things do seem to be taking place at every moment of the day and night. And because the Pierre is so quiet and restrained, one feels in some odd way completely cut off from the rest of the city—wrapped up safely in a soft, cream cocoon, protected from the rough and tumble of everyday life in Manhattan. Of course, things do go on at the Pierre. Shortly before I was there, they had had an Edwardian banquet at which my old friend Simon Williams—James Bellamy in the TV series *Upstairs, Downstairs*—had been guest of honor, and the very day I arrived there was a dress show going on in the ballroom. Yet it all took place so quietly and discreetly and privately that one did not even like to peep in through the half-open door. Indeed, people who stay at the Pierre rarely look at one another, or seem interested in anything other than hurrying in, taking their key from the concierge and scurrying away into the lift to be whisked silently away from the noisy downstairs world of New York City to the safe, rarified upstairs world of bedrooms and sitting rooms and silent, empty corridors high above Central Park.

THE PLAZA
NEW YORK, U.S.A.

On an appallingly hot August afternoon in 1974, with temperatures in the nineties and humidity up around the 100 per cent mark, some friends and I strolled up the steps of the Plaza, made our way across the lobby, past the elevators with their palatial doors, turned sharp left then right into the famous Palm Court in search of nothing more sensational than a nice cup of tea, or just conceivably, a banana sundae. The maître d'hotel, however (or maître de Palm Court, as I suppose he should be called), viewed us with an unsympathetic, not to say supercilious eye. He was most frightfully sorry but unfortunately we were not wearing jackets. . . . And from this entrenched position nothing was going to shift him—not the fact that we were dying of thirst, nor that we had come all the way from London specifically to have tea at the Plaza, nor that we had once met the Sonnabends (who at that time owned the hotel), a fact that happened to be true.

If perhaps we cared to don jackets kept specially by the hotel for such occasions. . . .? Unhappily, though, my male friend was built along lines that do not readily accommodate such casual wear; besides, Rumpelmeyers was only next door, and if the Plaza did not wish to have us, that, as far as we were concerned, was their loss. So we went to Rumpelmeyers and had iced coffees and sensational milk shakes, and very happy they seemed to be to see us.

Despite my sour-grapes attitude towards the Plaza, however, I have had ever since a sneaking regard for its pompous, random and, some would argue, ineffective attempts to maintain a certain standard of dress (and, by implication, behavior) in its public rooms. There is no good reason to suppose that the Plaza is likely to succeed in stemming the modern tide of informality any more than any other first-class hotel. On the other hand, I admire it for trying.

A few months later, in deepest mid-winter, I stayed at the Plaza for the first time. Since that time I have heard all sorts of reports from other guests of peeling wallpaper, hole-ridden floors and appalling room service. One man I know made the mistake of telling his waiter that the trolley he had just trundled into his room couldn't possibly be his, as he had ordered it under an hour before. The waiter, for whom the antiquated domestic arrangements were probably as much a source of irritation as they are to the guests, was not amused; my friend very nearly had his order wheeled straight out again.

Well, that's as may be. All I can tell you is that the suite I had facing Grand Army Plaza was splendid and luxurious, that my breakfast seemed to arrive more or less when I wanted it, and that one way and another I couldn't have been happier with my lot. Another friend was almost shocked at my expressions of pleasure and satisfaction. "Ah well yes, of course the Plaza was marvelous—once upon a time. But have you seen it lately? I mean, it's falling to bits. It's too big. It's finished. Sad, but there it is."

Perhaps he too had had a bad experience with room service. I don't know. Certainly it is true that for a hotel of that size, in that

PRECEDING PAGE The Grand Army Plaza entrance. ABOVE *Left:* The 59th Street entrance. *Center:* A corner of the hotel roof makes a striking contrast to the glass of a modern skyscraper. *Right:* The most famous guest of all.

situation, employing that many staff, maintaining the first-class service and the air of opulence for which it is known all over the world, is not an easy task. However, Western International Hotels, who took over the Plaza in 1974, have just spent ten million dollars on an enormous program of refurbishing, including cleaning the whole of the outside of the building, redecorating the Persian Room and the Oak Room, and generally putting the old lady back into mint condition. Almost certainly they will need to continue their policy of welcoming groups, sales conferences and other necessary commercial enterprises if they wish to survive. This will continue to be a source of enormous regret to the old hands who remember the Plaza in the good old days, and of smug satisfaction to those smaller establishments who, so far at any rate, have not needed to resort to such drastic means.

How many of them, though, can boast a history half as eventful and glittering as the Plaza's?

A hundred years ago the land on which the Plaza now stands was New York's most fashionable skating rink, where the doyenne of New York society, Mrs. William Astor, and her friends amused themselves of a brisk winter's afternoon. The area was fast becoming the

OVERLEAF The Oak Room, now a dining room, was once a bar for men only; the State Apartments, then and now, have hardly changed.

most fashionable part of the city. St. Patrick's Cathedral had been consecrated in 1879, and in 1883 the property on which the skating rink was situated was sold to two builders, John Phyfe and James Campbell, who had a dream of building on it one of the finest hotels in the country. They ran out of money but the work was completed by their insurance company, and in 1890 the first Plaza, a dignified building of eight stories and 400 rooms, opened its doors to the public. It was a great success, and would have continued to be so had not a German immigrant named Ben Beinecke, who had made a lot of money out of meat, and Harry S. Black, who was president of the huge Fuller Construction Company, taken it into their heads to build a hotel which would, by its size and opulence, be a sort of living monument to the new era of wealth.

Meanwhile, down in Palm Beach, a young man named Fred Sterry was managing the Poinciana and the Breakers. He happened to meet Harry Black, who told the hotelier, not very seriously, that New York was really the place for him. "Build me my kind of hotel," Sterry was said to have replied, "and I will come"; and the subject was dropped.

Back in New York, Beinecke and Black in company with various associates were attempting to raise sixty million dollars to finance their dream hotel—a task they were not finding as easy as they had expected. It was John "Bet-a-Million" Gates, a speculator, gambler and promoter who had made a fortune out of barbed wire, who finally put a stop to many months of discussion and speculation. "Get Fred Sterry to manage the hotel and you can count on me for all you need." So Fred Sterry was appointed supervisor and first manager of the new Plaza Hotel.

From the very beginning no expense was spared. There had been talk of keeping the original building and adding on, but now that money was no object they could afford to demolish the old hotel and start again from scratch. As architect they appointed Henry Hardenbergh, who designed the Waldorf-Astoria, the Manhattan, the Raleigh in Washington, the old Martinique in New York, and the Copley-Plaza in Boston. Hardenbergh called in E. F. Pooley to help plan the interior of the hotel.

From Belfast they ordered linen; from Switzerland, hand-embroidered organdie curtains; from France they brought glass, tapestries, Savonnerie rugs and Louis XVI furniture. Instead of being papered, the walls were paneled and painted and decorated with plaster moldings. The Louis XVI candelabra and candlesticks alone cost over 300,000 dollars. 1,650 crystal chandeliers were bought for overhead illumination; ten elevators were installed and five great staircases lined with marble. Masses of materials were shipped from Europe to give the impression inside of a French château, and for the baronial Oak Lounge they used the same British oak that was used for the tomb of Edward the Confessor in Westminster Abbey.

It was small wonder, therefore, that when the hotel finally opened on October 1, 1907, the crowds that gathered came to stare as much at the building as at the wealthy and famous who were lucky enough to be able to stay in it.

At 9 a.m. the first guest climbed out of his limousine. He was Alfred Gwynne Vanderbilt, whose father, Cornelius Vanderbilt, was reputed to be the richest man in America and lived in the huge mansion just across the street. (Eight years later he was to lose his life tragically on the Lusitania.) Other guests included John Wanamaker, Oliver Harriman, Benjamin Duke of the Virginia tobacco family, and—escorted of course by Lillian Russell—Diamond Jim Brady. Others who attended various opening-day functions included Mark Twain, Billie Burke, Charles Dillingham, David Belasco, Oscar Hammerstein and Maxine Elliott.

The Plaza established on that October day in 1907 a reputation for style, elegance, and class that, despite its many ups and downs over the years, it has maintained ever since. For nearly seventy years it has been a refuge for recluses, a stage for show-offs, a haven for eccentrics, and a source of more good stories than any other hotel in New York.

And yet no matter how extravagant the antics or how outrageous

the behavior, the Plaza management has always managed to retain its composure . . . whether it was at the sight of Mrs. Patrick Campbell lighting a cigarette in the Palm Court one afternoon in 1907; or at the King of Morocco and his retinue demanding that Saks Fifth Avenue be opened up specially for them on Sunday morning; or at Enrico Caruso losing his temper with the whirring of the electric clock in his room and ripping it out of the wall, thereby putting the 224 other electric clocks in the hotel out of commission. (In the last instance, the management sent the great singer a magnum of champagne and a note of abject apology.)

One of the hotel's earliest tenants, the millionaire Percival Kuhne, had a marble fountain, said to have been Marie Antoinette's favorite, shipped over from Versailles and installed in the sitting room of his suite.

Scott Fitzgerald lived at the Plaza whenever he could afford it, and characters in his books were forever behaving badly somewhere in the hotel, as anyone who read *The Great Gatsby* will remember. Hemingway once wrote to Fitzgerald from Key West suggesting he he come down to cover a Cuban revolution, and added, "If you really feel blue enough, get yourself heavily insured and I'll see you can get killed. I'll write a fine obituary and we can take your liver out and give it to the Princeton Museum, your heart to the Plaza Hotel."

S. R. Guggenheim, the metals multi-millionaire and art collector, and his wife occupied a series of rooms that took up almost half the first floor of the hotel, and included two of the beautiful Louis XIV rooms that go to make up the State Suite. Their marble fireplaces, paneled walls and chandeliers served as admirable settings for his collection of Matisses, Seurats, Chagalls, Klees, Bonnards and Légers. Frank Lloyd Wright also lived at the hotel while supervising the building of the Guggenheim Museum just up the road, and declared himself particularly fond of the domed ceiling of the Palm Court.

One of the most extraordinary figures to be associated with the Plaza in the early days was Frederick Townsend Martin, a bachelor from a wealthy family, who became the friend of Skid Row derelicts, and whose hobbies included slumming and collecting family crests from stationery. He knew all the right society people as well as the leading members of the theatrical profession, who in those days were considered very much out of bounds; and it was a mark of his compelling personality that he succeeded in introducing the stuffy Edwardians to the bright stars of the theater.

He did this in the Plaza, of all places. For years he acted as unpaid social secretary for the hotel and an invitation to one of his parties was considered a mark of immediate social acceptance. One of his greatest triumphs was a private theatrical performance of *Mrs. Van Vechtend's Divorce Dance*, starring Mrs. George Jay Gould, in the hotel. The matinée idol Kyrle Bellew, star of *The Thief*, was booked to play the male lead opposite Mrs. Gould. It was *the* social event of January, 1908, and six hundred of the most glittering members of New York

660

6th
FLOOR

The
Terrace

society and the stage sat expectantly as George Gould Jr. pulled back the curtains to reveal a complete Louis XV boudoir, including a dressing table Marie Antoinette had once used at Versailles. Mrs. Gould herself came on wearing her personal jewelery.

The Plaza has been peopled over the years with so many eccentrics that one could almost believe it offered them a special rate. Perhaps the most eccentric guest of all was a wealthy gentleman from Philadelphia who suffered from an exaggerated fear of germs. In addition to his own room, he rented the rooms to the right and left of him, across the corridor, above and below him, and slept in each one in rotation according to an elaborate personal theory about how long it takes for germs to die. Every morning fifty white towels were delivered by the chambermaid. He always wore white gloves and never shook hands. He demanded that letters and cables be read to him over the telephone. His meals were brought to his door covered with a white cloth by a gloved waiter who would ring the bell and leave before the door was opened. He would order whole hams and roast joints of beef so that he could be sure of being able to cut a totally uncontaminated morsel from the very center. On the other hand, he tipped well and for all his bizarre ways was a good deal less trouble than many of the hotel's far less eccentric guests.

Another of the Plaza's distinguished guests from 1940 to 1952 was the Hungarian playwright Ferenc Molnar who, on the Wildean principle that an address inspires confidence, lived in a room at the hotel and ate his meals at a delicatessen on 6th Avenue. It was with understandable astonishment that he discovered that for eight years he had been living under the same roof as the Belgian playwright Maurice Maeterlinck, who wrote *The Blue Bird.* But so insistent had they both been to the hotel staff upon their need for complete solitude that no one had ever thought of introducing them.

In 1943 an event occurred that for the Plaza and its guests was only slightly less earthshaking than the Japanese attack on Pearl Harbor. The Plaza was sold to Conrad Hilton. It could mean only one thing: the hotel was going commercial. It was to the guests' astonishment and Hilton's everlasting credit that it never did. On the contrary, he carefully pursued the tradition of elegance for which the Plaza had been renowned for the previous thirty-six years. He made the Oak Bar into one of the hotel's most famous and most profitable rooms. He commissioned the artist Everitt Shinn to do a series of murals for the room, including the celebrated one of the wintry nights in 1908 showing the old Vanderbilt mansion on the other side of the Grand Army Plaza where the Ford Building now stands. He also hired as promotion and PR director Prince Serge Obolensky who had been married first to one of the Romanovs and later to the daughter of John Jacob Astor. It was his idea to ask various well-known interior decorators, including Cecil Beaton, Christian Dior, and Elsie de Wolfe (then Lady Mendl), to design a number of "Celebrity Suites." The Lady Mendl Suite was a great success with everyone who occupied it,

PRECEDING PAGES *Top Left:* The Palm Court at tea time. *Bottom left:* The Edwardian Room. *Top center:* The elevators in the 59th Street lobby. *Top right:* The Fifth Avenue lobby, originally a summer dining room. *Bottom right:* A corridor off the Palm Court.

MANHATTAN GAZETTE DECEMBER 1, 1973

HERALD, PARIS, SATURDAY, OCTOBER 5, 1907.

THE PLAZA

NEW YORK

NOW OPEN

THE WORLD'S MOST LUXURIOUS HOTEL

LOCATED IN THE CENTRE OF NEW YORK'S FASHIONABLE SECTION AT 5th AVENUE AND 59th STREET FACING CENTRAL PARK

Single Rooms $2.50 to $4 per day. Single Rooms with Baths $4 to $6. Double Rooms with Bath, $6, $8 and $10. Parlor, Bedroom and Bath, $12, $15, $18 and $20. Parlor, two Bedrooms and two Baths, $16, $18, $20 and $25.

FRED STERRY . . . . **Managing Director.**

until Marlene Dietrich booked in, took one look at the bright scarlet-and-gold clock that Elsie Mendl had installed as her pride and joy, announced, "Too much gingerbread," and had the clock banished from the suite.

In 1953 Hilton sold the Plaza to Boston industrialist A. M. Sonnabend, and it was in the hands of the Sonnabend family that the hotel remained until 1974, when it was bought by Western International Hotels.

Whatever the future may hold for this great hotel, one thing is indisputable: the Plaza will live on, in fact as well as in legend, as an example of what a great hotel was once all about. For nearly seventy years now people have been impressed the first time they have walked into that extraordinary Palm Court, and every time they returned they have relived that first moment, and been young again. For them, time has stood still. That is what the Plaza is all about.

PLAZA-ATHENEE
PARIS, FRANCE

OPPOSITE The front of the hotel in the Avenue Montaigne. The Relais Plaza is on the corner at the far end.

ONE OF THE great joys of being a foreign visitor in a city like Rome or Paris or New York is being able to eat in the choicest restaurants, jiggle up and down in the trendiest night clubs, and swan about at the most glittering first nights without having to worry about who is eating, jiggling, or swanning about beside you.

Take the Relais Plaza, for example—the grill room of the Plaza-Athenée Hotel in Paris. The *on dit* in smart circles is that this is where *le tout Paris* has its lunch—where at 1 p.m. on almost any day of the week you can spot Monsieur Givenchy or Monsieur Saint Laurent rubbing elegant shoulders with the Baroness Guy de Rothschild or the wife of the prime minister; where top Paris models flash immaculate mouthfuls of teeth at up-and-coming film directors; and where famous hairdressers blow kisses at notorious actresses. All of which is very nice for people who happen to be part of the setup or for those who aren't but would dearly like to be. For the foreign visitor, on the other hand, who doesn't know who anyone is anyway, and just wants a good lunch, the Relais is simply a restaurant in which the food is either good or not good, the service efficient or hopeless, the clientele either attractive and amusing or totally unworthy of attention.

The same applies to any hotel. All that a guest usually cares about is that he should be comfortable and well fed and looked after. The fact that this famous film star or that well-known politician has stayed in the same hotel becomes, for all except the most hardened snobs, entirely irrelevant if the bed has a lump in it, or the room service is insufferably slow.

None of which, I can confidently report, is the case at the Plaza-Athenée, which currently enjoys the reputation of being not only one of the most fashionable of Paris hotels, but equally one of the best run.

The revolutionary general manager, Paul Bougenaux, would claim that the present success of the Plaza is due to the system of worker participation which he introduced in 1969 when, as head concierge, he led the demonstrations against the new Forte management. It may also have something to do with the six million or so dollars that Forte has spent over the last five years on the redecoration and refurnishing of the entire hotel (not to mention the rebuilding of one entire floor and the construction of a new one). Then again, it may just be the Plaza's turn to wear the crown of fashionableness. Who knows—perhaps this is only a passing phase and, in a year or so, the hotel's glories will have faded? Whatever the case may be, few of the hotel's guests seem to care; and considering the high standards Monsieur Bougenaux sets for himself and his staff, there is no reason they should.

Mind you, it wasn't such a bad hotel before he took over—or indeed before either he or Sir Charles Forte had ever been heard of. The original Hotel Athenée was founded in 1867 in what was then the most fashionable area of Paris, near the newly built Opéra. Throughout the seventies, eighties and nineties it was one of *the*

Clockwise, from upper left-hand corner: The courtyard; the long gallery of the entrance hall, where tea is served to the accompaniment of a tinkling piano; the Régence-Plaza restaurant; the bust of Molière; a double bedroom.

smart places for eating and drinking, and for spending a night or two (thus proving that, in the hotel world at least, history does repeat itself). In 1913 it was moved to its present address in the Avenue Montaigne and renamed the Plaza-Athenée. Within months war had broken out and apart from one night when the police swooped on the hotel and arrested a quiet female guest by the name of Mata Hari, life took on a fairly dreary aspect for the Plaza.

However, what the hotel lost during the war in glamor it made up for in the years following the armistice. Nicknamed "The Millionaires' Hotel," it welcomed, among others, Vanderbilts, Fords, and Rockefellers.

During World War Two it was requisitioned, as were so many Paris hotels, by the Germans. After liberation it became for a while the headquarters of the American Air Transport Command.

Normal service was resumed as soon as possible after the end of the war, and the Plaza-Athenée once more took its rightful place among the great Parisian hotels, with a list of distinguished guests that was second to none: people like the Queen of Denmark and her husband Prince Henryk, King Hussein of Jordan, David Rockefeller, Herbert von Karajan, the Goulandris family, Alfred Hitchcock. In one afternoon, I spotted Jennifer Jones, Gary Cooper's daughter, and Pierre Salinger.

But names, as I indicated earlier, are not my forte. The things I remember best about the Plaza-Athenée (apart from the fact that they win my award for the fastest room service in the world) are, firstly, the enchanting view of the central courtyard which, with its hanging greenery and window boxes of geraniums reminded me of the quadrangle of an Oxford college in high summer; secondly, the long elegant gallery from the far end of which Molière looks askance at the tea and rather good pastries being served to the accompaniment of a tinkling piano; and thirdly, a solitary dinner I had one evening in the main hotel restaurant. Eating alone is never an easy matter; the main problem is making it appear to the rest of the dining room that you

Above: The ornate main entrance in the Avenue Montaigne. *Right:* Monsieur Roland, the restaurant manager, back after a 25-year break at the Tour d'Argent.

are alone by choice, not because you are unable to find anyone who wishes to eat with you. Monsieur Roland, the restaurant manager, who had recently returned to the Plaza-Athenée after a twenty-five-year break at the Tour d'Argent, bent a sympathetic ear as I explained how my dinner companion had at the last minute had to leave for the Greek islands with her husband. "Do not fear," he said; "here you are always among friends."

His claim proved, as the evening progressed, to be far from idle. Rarely have I enjoyed an evening better, or been better looked after. Not a dish was served nor a drink was poured without a detailed, and on occasions deeply philosophical, discussion on the nature of the food or drink in question. Barely had I sunk my fork into the fish mousse (the ideal preface to the *noisette d'agneau*, we had agreed) than the chief sommelier, Monsieur le Bail, was at my side, enquiring idly what wine I had ordered.

On learning it was to be a Corton Pouget 1969, he became very serious and said that in that case I would be well-advised to take a glass of vodka flavored with lemon peel with the fish to ensure that my palate would be entirely clean for the burgundy that was to follow. Much conversation ensued before, during and after the drinking of the vodka—the upshot of which was that if you are eating fish for your first course and you want to be sure that the taste does not linger into the second, then vodka with lemon peel is the antidote you are looking for. The lamb *noisettes*, which were covered with pate de foie gras, also came in for some detailed comment from my waiter Monsieur Matthieu—as did the nature of *bourgogne rouge*, and Corton Pouget 1969 in particular, from Monsieur le Bail. I learned later that I was perfectly correct in my theory that it is wiser just to taste one cheese from the board rather than a selection, but it was Monsieur le Bail's suggestion of a *vielle prune de Souillac* with the coffee (served by a Turkish gent in a fez and full robes) that really got the conversation flowing, not to mention the drink. It all began when I mentioned a fondness for Armagnac. Had I had the slightest inkling that Monsieur le Bail came from that neck of the woods I might have been a little less forceful in my ex-cathedra statements on the drink. "If you say to a *mousquetaire*," he announced, "that such-and-such is a good Armagnac, then all I can tell you is that there is no such thing as a bad Armagnac."

Within moments the table was covered with enough bottles of the stuff to make Dionysos quiver like a jelly in a hurricane.

I don't remember a great deal about the rest of the evening. I do know that, for all the undoubted comforts the Plaza-Athenée bedrooms have to offer, I slept very badly indeed. Which may of course account for the fact that at lunch in the Relais the following day I was somewhat less than fascinated by the news that the man at the next table was a big cheese in political circles or that Monsieur Balenciaga had just come in. . . .

LE RICHEMOND
GENEVA, SWITZERLAND

THERE ARE A number of hotels in the world that are rated very highly by the most demanding of travelers and are to be found year after year among the top ten of lists compiled by the most respected of connoisseurs, but which a transient guest may spend a night in and never think about again. And if afterwards you were to express great interest in the fact that he had stayed there, and explain that such and such a professional hotel critic had for years been calling it one of the best hotels in the world, he would very possibly be absolutely amazed.

One such hotel is Le Richemond in Geneva. My room with its little balcony, on which I was able to sit and enjoy breakfast in the early morning sun and look across the lake, was perfectly adequate without being in any way memorable. Even Room 529, one of the hotel's most outstanding, and reputed to have been in its time the favorite of Sophia Loren, is nothing out of the ordinary: comfortable yes, and in impeccable taste certainly, with its beiges and browns and rusts; but hardly memorable. The so-called Spanish Room—Room 329—with its fine red headboard, red beams and red and gold writing desk, is equally very pleasant. So too are the corridors—dark, red and discreet, with their touches of Swiss rusticity—an antique dresser here, a sacred wooden statue there. I was suitably impressed by the conference rooms, in particular the Louis XVI room where the Aga Khan, who has a villa on the lake not far away, is fond of entertaining his friends. I had also admired the eighteenth-century sedan chair halfway up the main staircase, which is now used as a display case for jewelery. But surely, I kept telling myself, there had to be more to Le Richemond than this, something very special that could attract such distinguished names as Pablo Casals, Anthony Eden, Marc Chagall, and Colette? My neighbor at dinner in Le Gontilhomme Grill the night I stayed was unmistakeably John Kenneth Galbraith, and people like that are very particular about where they stay.

(The meal, incidentally, was delicious. We had *brochette de scampi* and *mignon d'agneau au poivre vert* with a bottle of local wine; Professor Galbraith had some sort of plain fish, with which he seemed thoroughly satisfied.)

Wherein therefore lies the secret to Le Richemond's great reputation if not in its bedrooms, its public rooms, its restaurant or its decor? Surely it must be possible to find some clue at least in its illustrious past. For in 1975 Le Richemond was a hundred years old, no less, and during all that time, the hotel has remained in the hands of the family Armleder. That in itself must constitute some claim to fame, however modest.

The name Armleder, which goes back at least to the thirteenth century, is an interesting one. It was applied to a certain tribe—highly feared for its skill in pillage and general persecution of other tribes—whose members wore a leather armlet as some sort of membership badge. In 1337 the armlet was abandoned, but the name survived and spread to Bavaria, Swabia and Alsace. Centuries later, in 1874

OPPOSITE Balconies overlooking the Lac du Léman.

Clockwise from upper left-hand corner: Room 329, the Spanish Room; Le Gentilhomme Grill-Bar; behind the concierge's desk; one of the upstairs corridors.

HOTEL RICHEMOND
SIMP

One of the old lake steamers in front of the hotel.

to be precise, one A. R. Armleder, a member of the Alstadt-Rottweil branch of the family, settled in Geneva after traveling extensively in England, Ireland and Italy. The following year he took over a humble lodging house known as the Pension Riche-Mont.

Despite its modest beginnings (in those early days it could accommodate no more than twenty-five guests at a time), every effort was made to cater for a guest's every need, no matter how bizarre. For instance, the Genevese painter Francois Diday, who lived on the fifth floor of the hotel, could not bear to be interrupted while he was working; so Monsieur Armleder constructed an elaborate device on rails which carried the artist's meals into his studio. (The observant guest will notice a sculpture by the artist of his own palette and brushes in the entrance of the hotel.)

Business boomed for the Riche-Mont during the seventies and eighties, and by the time the National Exhibition came along in 1896, Monsieur Armleder had shrewdly bought the Hotel Eden next door, joined the two buildings together and thus created the Hotel Richemond.

After the First World War, A.R.'s son Victor continued to improve and expanded the hotel's facilities. In 1920 the hotel was honored to receive the Indian Delegation to the League of Nations—not to say taken aback when the first of the delegates arrived, their noses bedecked with jewels. The guests too were not a little surprised, particularly the evening when they had just sat down to dinner and the door burst open and in rushed a chicken pursued by a huge Indian brandishing an axe. In 1931, to coincide with the Disarmamant Conference, Victor Armleder expanded the hotel even further, and after his and A.R.'s death it was Mrs. Victor who was largely responsible for maintaining the high standards for which the hotel had acquired such a reputation over the years. Today the task is in the hands of Victor's son, Jean, and his wife and son, and it is some measure of the esteem in which he is held by his fellow hoteliers that Le Richemond, the Ritz in Paris, and Hotel de Paris in Monte Carlo are the only three hotels in Europe to have been awarded the high distinction of the *Coupe d'Or de Bon Gout Français*.

It is equally some measure of the esteem in which he is held by distinguished and discerning travelers from all over the world that when they come to Geneva, they come to stay with him. The secret of the Hotel Richemond lies, as it does in so many other great hotels of the world, not so much in outward signs of luxury and opulence as in the inward and, as far as the casual visitor is concerned, largely invisible spirit of the man who owns it.

RITZ-CARLTON
BOSTON, U.S.A

A RECENT ADVERTISEMENT for the Ritz-Carlton Hotel in *The New Yorker* consisted of a thumbnail sketch of a blazing fire beneath an elegantly carved mantlepiece, and beside it the words: "The Ritz is . . . watching birch logs crackle in the fireplace of your suite overlooking Back Bay." Which is very charming except that, as a lady in Wisconsin pointed out in a letter to the hotel's general manager, birch logs do not crackle—not even in the Ritz-Carlton. Ah, well, even advertising copywriters must be allowed a little poetic license from time to time.

On the other hand, it is perfectly true that the suites in the Ritz-Carlton do have fireplaces and they do burn logs in them. Equally beyond dispute is that some of them overlook Back Bay. Others overlook Boston Common, the Public Gardens, the State House and Beacon Hill. In fact the Ritz-Carlton, as is only to be expected with a hotel of that name, is situated in just about the choicest part of town. And the view across the Charles River, especially at night, toward Cambridge and the lights of Harvard, is probably as delightful a view as you'll find in any city on the East Coast of the United States.

Time was when the land upon which the hotel now sits was part of the ocean. It really was a bay, and the water lapped against what is now the Common. But that was long ago. By 1924, when a self-made millionaire named Edward Wyner decided he wanted to build himself a new apartment house, the sea had long since retreated, and it was Back Bay in name only.

No sooner had Mr. Wyner started putting up his building than James Michael Curly, the notorious mayor of Boston, appeared in his office one day with the suggestion that he turn it instead into a hotel. Wyner acceded to the request but determined that in that case his hotel would be the classiest on the whole east coast.

He therefore applied to the Ritz Hotel in Paris for permission to adopt their name. Permission was granted and in May, 1927, the hotel was ready for business.

From the beginning, the hotel has had a reputation for cool elegance, impeccable service, great discretion and an overall atmosphere of understated luxury. At the same time, though, it has never been totally averse to the occasional touch of exuberant eccentricity. Boston being an important city for giving plays their pre-Broadway try-outs, the Ritz-Carlton has played host to all the great producers, actors and writers over the last fifty years. The great showman Flo Ziegfeld was a frequent guest; so too was Tallulah Bankhead. During one of her visits her pet monkey escaped from her room. The staff hunted high and low for the simian refugee until it was finally located swinging from a wire in the elevator shaft.

Music and dancing were a feature of the Ritz-Carlton during the thirties. In 1933 Wyner opened a roof garden where on warm summer nights Bostonians and guests would foxtrot to the great bands of the day—Tommy Dorsey, Benny Goodman, Glenn Miller and many others.

OPPOSITE The hotel from the Public Gardens.

OPPOSITE *Top:* A view from the 16th floor with the Public Gardens in the foreground, Boston Common in the background, with Beacon Hill and the Statehouse. *Bottom:* Birch logs (?) crackling in the fireplace.

ABOVE *Top and bottom:* The restaurant and the main staircase.

Food has been another of the hotel's chief attractions. Before the Second World War Wyner was in the habit of eating from time to time at the Puritan Hotel. The chef there was a man named Charles Banino, and Wyner enjoyed his cooking so much that he engaged him as his assistant chef. Eventually Banino took over the kitchens and, upon the death of Edward Wyner in 1946, the management of the entire hotel. How he was capable of running that *and* the kitchens is hard to imagine. In any event, during his fifteen-year reign the standard of comfort and service and the quality of the food continued to rise. Among his appreciative guests were Winston Churchill, Charles Lindbergh, Richard Rogers, Oscar Hammerstein, Irving Berlin, and more or less all the Kennedys, for whom the Ritz-Carlton was virtually a second home. John Kennedy maintained a suite there while he was a congressman and senator, even though he had an apartment only a few blocks away. Today, members of the Kennedy family are often to be seen around the hotel and Senator Edward Kennedy frequently dines in the restaurant.

John Kennedy was not the only influential figure to keep a permanent suite in the Ritz-Carlton. Soon after the hotel was opened, Mr. and Mrs. Swift of the Swift Meat Packing Company rented the entire 15th floor, which they maintained for many years. Today there are still fourteen permanent guests, including the widow of Captain Edward Logan (after whom Boston's Logan International Airport was named). Legend has it that Howard Hughes lived somewhere in the hotel for a couple of years although no one is prepared to confirm or deny the story; and more recently Henry Kissinger commuted daily between the Ritz-Carlton and Washington while his wife was in the Massachusetts General Hospital undergoing surgery.

In 1964 the hotel was acquired by Cabot, Cabot and Forbes, a firm of real estate developers. The whole of Back Bay held its breath as they waited for the old place to be turned inevitably into a bear garden. But to everyone's astonishment the company held firmly to its promise not to alter in any way the essential character of the hotel. Moreover, such alterations as they did undertake only served to make the place even more comfortable and pleasing to the eye than it had been before. The restaurant was redecorated in dark blue and cream; the suites were made even more attractive and home-like with their open fires and gay, light color schemes; the Ritz Café, too, was given a fresh and simple look, without any nonsense or frippery.

The Ritz-Carlton is a hotel for the sort of people who know what is the best without having to be reminded of it wherever they look. The bar, for example, which in so many hotels rejoices in all manner of fancy names, in the Ritz-Carlton is called simply Le Bar. What else?

RITZ

RITZ
MADRID, SPAIN

KING ALFONSO III of Spain, the grandfather of the present King Juan Carlos, was one of the few men in history literally to have been born a king. His father, King Alfonso II, had died some months previously and thus he succeeded to the throne immediately upon his birth in 1886.

As a young man, with his mother acting as Regent, he embarked on an extensive tour of the world to prepare for taking the heavy weight of kingship upon his own shoulders.

He returned from his travels with his mind full of the great buildings, splendid palaces, elegant parks and charming fountains that he had come across in Italy, in England, in France and in Germany. He also brought home with him as his bride King Edward VII's niece, Victoria Eugénie of Battenberg, and his marriage to Queen Ena, as she was popularly known, heralded not only the beginning of his reign proper, but also the birth of many new ideas for making his capital, Madrid, into a great international city.

Madrid had always been a great city, with wide streets, great plazas and elegant gardens, a wonderful climate and a great art collection, housed in the Prado Museum. And yet, as the king realized, it lacked one important element: a hotel that would rank alongside the greatest in Europe. Way back in the Middle Ages, Spain had been famous for the inns and rest-houses that stood along the Pilgrim Route to Santiago de Compostela; but gradually, over the years, this celebrated Spanish hospitality had been allowed to fall into disrepute.

By the beginning of this century, however, the practice of traveling for travel's sake was becoming more and more common among the rich and the privileged of all nations, and among the delights they had discovered were the cities and coasts and landscapes and blue skies of Spain. As Gabriela Mistral, the Nobel Prize-winning Spanish-American novelist wrote: "Come here during the ugly season of the European winter, from Berlin, Brussels or Paris, or else direct by sea. One leaves behind the indefinable drabness of the industrial world to enter into a kind of aristocratic heaven. From a mentality at once tense and frivolous one suddenly finds oneself in a land of dry brilliance which cleans and awakens the senses."

Which was all very nice, except that unless they could offer wealthy and demanding travelers the kind of accommodation they had found elsewhere in Europe, Spain would run the risk of becoming very much a touristic backwater.

The king therefore called together a group of wealthy Spaniards, outlined his plans, and urged them to join him in making his dream a reality.

His plan was received with great enthusiasm and a site was chosen just above the Paseo del Prado, between the Plaza Canovas and the Plaza de la Lealtad, right next door to the Prado Museum itself. The position alone was enough to guarantee success.

On July 27, 1908, the Ritz Development Company was formed. Two architects were appointed—Charles Mewes, the Frenchman who

OPPOSITE The Plaza Colon. The Prado museum is behind the trees to the right, just out of the picture.

had designed the Ritz Hotels in Paris and London, and Don Luis Landecho of Madrid—and soon the shape of the new hotel began to rise above the elms, cedars and acacias that surround the Prado.

The cost of the venture was enormous: 1.15 million pesetas for the site, 2.6 million for the building itself, a million for furnishings and 17,000 for publicity. One way and another the bill came to over 5.5 million pesetas. Nothing like it had ever been seen in Spain before; but the King himself was one of the original shareholders and confidence ran high.

Four or five bathrooms were provided for every floor—the last word in comfort in those days—not to mention washbasins in all the rooms, an elevator, and a telephone on each floor.

The hotel was opened formally on October 2, 1910, and few hotels have ever got off to a better start. The ABC newspaper reported excitedly: "The inauguration of the Hotel Ritz was an important event since its creation represents the answer to an acute problem. . . ." The problem, apparently, was soon about to be solved:

> Although the inauguration ceremony took place at night, we must first tell our readers of the imposing spectacle which took place in the afternoon. It was then that the King and Queen, accompanied by the Queen Mother and Royal Princes and Princesses, were received by the Prime Minister and the Ministers Merino, Garcia Prieto Calbeton and Burell, the last two accompanied by

Top left and right: A suite on the 5th floor, and the entrance hall. *Bottom:* A detail from the main entrance.

> their wives. . . . A famous orchestra performed the National Anthem upon the arrival of these illustrious guests, and during the royal inspection of the premises various charming musical compositions were played, the well-known conductor, Boldi, having the satisfaction of hearing words of congratulation from these august personages.

But if congratulations were owed to anyone it was surely to those responsible for "the comfort and luxury on display . . . the care and profusion devoted to every detail . . . the magnificent lighting . . . the snowy bed and table linen from the Irish firm of Robinson and Cleaver . . . the Louis Quinze silver service consisting of more than 15,000 pieces, the Limoges porcelain, the hairdressing salon, and the offices of the International Sleeping Car Co. (Wagons Lits) installed in the building for the greater convenience of travelers."

It soon became clear that King Alfonso's gamble had paid off, for from that day forth the elegant salons, terraces and gardens of the Ritz have witnessed an endless procession of distinguished Spanish and foreign guests—kings, prime ministers, ambassadors and general. Practically every member of every ancient Spanish aristocratic family has stayed at the Ritz and continues to do so, as a matter of course, to this day.

The Windsors always used to stay there, as have the Archduke Francis Joseph of Austria (when he was commuting between his estates in Spain and Austria), Prince Louis Napoleon, Baron Eugène de Rothschild, Earl Warren, France's foreign minister Couve de Murville, Prince Hugo of Bourbon Parma and his wife, Princess Irene of Holland, Henry Ford II, King Hussein of Jordan, Prince Rainier and Princess Grace of Monaco, the President of Brazil, Sir Alexander Fleming, the discoverer of penicillin, Senator Edward Kennedy, Konrad Adenauer, Henry Cabot Lodge, the Count of Paris, the Pretender to the French throne, and the Crown Prince of Japan.

The only famous guests who are not welcomed with open arms at the Ritz are the film stars. At the larger Palace Hotel, also owned by the Ritz Company, they can cope with newsreel cameras, crowds of gawking fans, TV cables and the general brouhaha that tends to accompany visits by such people, but the Ritz clients do not care for that sort of thing at all. Some actors have been known to stay there: Myrna Loy, who in private life is a diplomat's wife; James Stewart, who is also a US Air Force General; and Laurence Olivier, who is also a lord. But poor old George Sanders (who, to quote himself, came disguised as a gentleman) never made it past the front desk.

The Ritz in Madrid is, like all Ritzes, old-fashioned, snobbish, grand and patronized exclusively, it would seem, by a breed of men and women, almost extinct now, to whom such attributes are not only admirable but essential to a continued existence on this earth.

It is the sort of place where you will never see a man sitting in the lounge in a topcoat or hunched over a table full of papers with a business colleague, for the simple reason that no one can get further

than two steps into the lounge without someone hurrying forward to remove his coat and relieve him of his attaché case.

The man responsible for maintaining this gracious way of life is the general manager, Alfonso Font, who also manages the Palace.

Señor Font is one of the greatest European hotel managers since the war. He took over the Ritz in 1962 from the famous Doña Carmen Guerendiain, "The Lady of the Ritz," as she was once dubbed, who was, by all accounts, a remarkable woman. On her retirement at the age of sixty-eight she went straight off to manage another hotel in southern Spain.

A less remarkable figure than Alfonso Font might have found the task of succeeding Doña Carmen extremely unnerving. But Font was by that stage a man of enormous experience. After graduating from the hotel school in Lausanne, he immediately reduced himself to the ranks and began working as a *commis* waiter, fetching and carrying dishes and washing up. He worked at the Baur au Lac in Zurich and the Adlon in Berlin where he came in contact with many of the Nazi leaders whom he was to come across again later in Spain. In 1939 he was at the Meurice in Paris where the kings of Norway, Denmark, Rumania and Bulgaria often stayed and where Britain's Prime Minister, Neville Chamberlain, and Leslie Hore-Belisha, the Secretary of State for War, met their French counterparts at a session of the Allied Secret War Council.

At the outbreak of war Alfonso Font returned to Spain which, having just recovered from its own internal struggle, had lapsed into an uneasy neutrality.

In the Ritz Hotel, war was being waged as fiercely as anywhere else in Europe, though in a rather less obvious way. Suddenly the place was filled with the strangest collection of guests—apparently unpatriotic English aristocrats, rich South Americans, and Germans claiming to be sick of Hitler. It was no secret among the staff that few of them were quite what they seemed. Some of the most important secret agents from England, Germany and the United States used the Ritz as the base for their operations. One of the best known routes home to England for RAF pilots shot down over occupied Europe was via Spain, and there is little doubt that many of these secret life-lines were planned and organized from inside the Ritz Hotel.

And during it all, life at the Ritz flowed serenely on very much as it had done before, and very much as it has done ever since.

Above: Alfonso Font, one of the great hotel managers since the war.

RESTAURANT
RITZ

RITZ
PARIS, FRANCE

IT IS STILL with feelings of faint disbelief that I look back on lunch that day at the Ritz as the best I have ever had. Everything was against it from the start. For one thing, I was not the slightest bit hungry. Still, I hadn't anything better to occupy me for the next hour or two, and the garden, viewed through the windows of the cocktail lounge, was looking particularly alluring: warm May sunlight filtering down through the trees onto the pink cloths of the laid tables, the turquoise-blue umbrellas, and the water trickling in a summery sort of way from the fountain at the end. Unfortunately, by the time I had finally concluded, with the help of a couple more *champagnes fraises*, that I might possibly be able to force down a little light something, the sun had disappeared behind some ominously grey clouds, a nasty little wind had got up, and the waiters were beginning to usher some of the older and less intrepid lunchers into the adjoining dining room.

However, so determined was I by now that I was going to lunch, come wind, rain or snow, that I marched firmly out to the garden, plumped myself down at the most sheltered table I could find and began ordering. My choice was singularly uninspired, and certainly not one that was likely to qualify for one of the great lunches of a lifetime—Cavaillon melon, *brochette d'agneau* and a half-bottle of Nuits St. Georges 1967. However, an astonishingly beautiful young woman had by now arrived at the adjoining table, and with her arrived the sun. Between them they succeeded in casting over the entire proceedings a warmth and a light that somehow elevated even my dull choice of food to an altogether higher plane. The melon was the sweetest and softest I have ever had, the pieces of lamb melted inside my mouth like morning dew, the rice—not too little, not too much—was fluffy and of just the right moisture, and the wine ("I couldn't have chosen better myself, Monsieur," murmured the sommelier) not only improved with every mouthful, but also slipped down with such ease that the bottle seemed to be empty almost before I had started it. Some raspberries to follow and a brief discussion with the waiter about the advantages of sprinkling the sugar over them *before* the cream (I had the feeling I might have set him thinking there for a moment), and finally the coffee and a small brandy.

Well, if he thinks *that* was a good lunch, I hear some of you murmuring, heaven knows what he would make of the lunch *I* once had at the Pére Bise or Lasserre or Maxime or wherever. Melon, brochette of lamb and a half-bottle of wine indeed! Why this meal should feature so vividly in my memory I cannot say; perhaps simply because one is so used nowadays to finding something wrong with almost everything, that the day you have nothing to complain about stands out from the rest for that reason alone.

Actually, I think the answer was summed up years ago by the great Ritz regular Marcel Proust, who explained his liking for the hotel in four words: no one jostles you. In my experience, not only does no one jostle you at the Ritz but they apologize just in case they

OPPOSITE The Place Vendôme entrance.

OPPOSITE Perhaps the most famous dining room in the world. OVERLEAF *Clockwise from upper left-hand corner:* The main staircase on the Place Vendôme side. The concierge's desk is on the right; one of the small salons; part of one of the great first-floor suites overlooking the Place Vendôme; just to wake up in the Ritz is the greatest event of all; a staircase on the way to the restaurant; the glittering array of showcases that line the corridor between the rue Cambon side and the Place Vendôme side.

might be *about* to jostle you. For instance, on the afternoon of the day I was leaving, I had left my suitcase packed in my room, aware that the next guest was expected later that day. Unfortunately, the guest arrived earlier than expected, and insisted on being able to use the room. The assistant manager explained that he was very sorry but the room was still occupied. If the gentleman would care to rest temporarily in another room. . . . ? But he was not to be fobbed off so easily. In the end my suitcase was removed to a safe place and the guest was able to take his snooze. Now, it made no difference to me whether my suitcase remained in the room or elsewhere; I had no further use for the room anyway. But for Monsieur Moreau, the assistant manager in question, this was a matter of the greatest concern, as he explained, *sotto voce*, in a corner of the lobby to which he had solicitously drawn me. He hoped I would forgive him . . . this sort of thing never normally happened at the Ritz . . . if I would care to have the use of another room before I left . . . ?

It is experiences like that that lead me to believe that any lunch I might have at the Ritz would probably be something of an event. After all, nearly everything else that happens to one in that hotel is—whether it be drinking in the bar next to Jeanne Moreau; being nodded to by the governor of the Bank of England in the hall after breakfast; walking from the Place Vendôme side of the hotel to the rue Cambon side through the elegant arcade with its showcases full of porcelain, jade and *broderie anglaise*; or just stepping out of a taxi at the Place Vendôme entrance and walking under those three yellow blinds, shaped like shells, with the one word *Ritz* on them, through those ancient gray pillars and into the lobby of what is unquestionably the greatest hotel in the world.

In fact, just to be able to lie in a great brass bed in one of the more modest rooms, surrounded by gilt and glitter and tall wardrobes and great mirrors and small sofas, and to keep telling myself that there I was staying at the Ritz. That was perhaps the greatest event of all.

It was with a feeling of similar awe that I found myself one morning shaking hands with Charles Ritz, now in his eighty-sixth year. He shouted at me, "I'm not the founder of this hotel, you know; that was my father." True. Even so, it is not every day that one has the opportunity to pass the time of day with the son of the man whose name passed into the English language as a word conveying all that is most chic, deluxe, and swell.

(It is amusing though useless to speculate that if the man who had founded that hotel had happened to be called Jones, Irving Berlin might have written a song called "Putting on the Jones," Scott Fitzgerald a story entitled "The Diamond as Big as the Jones," and we might today be referring to a particularly smartly dressed woman as being "pretty Jonesy.")

The name and word Ritz seem to have been part of our language for so long that it is something of a shock to realize that it was only just before the turn of the century, 1898, that César Ritz, a shepherd's

son from Niederwald in Switzerland, first opened with much pomp and circumstance what he referred to as "a little house to which I am very proud to see my name attached."

The story of César Ritz has now been told so often (and so well by Stephen Watts in his book *The Ritz*), that I do not propose to cover the well-trodden ground more than cursorily.

Ritz began his career in 1870 as a waiter at Voisin, then the most fashionable restaurant in Paris, and it was there that he first began hearing the name Escoffier. Almost at once the Franco-Prussian War began, and having survived the terrible Siege of Paris and the ensuing famine (for years afterwards both Ritz and Escoffier would reminisce about the days when Voisin bought two elephants from the Paris zoo and *tronc d'éléphant sauce chasseur* first appeared on the menu), Ritz went to Vienna to work at the Imperial Pavilion.

When he was twenty-three he moved to the Grand Hotel in Nice, where he became restaurant manager. That summer he went to Rigi-Kulm in Switzerland to run the Mountaintop Restaurant. One of his clients there, Colonel Pfyffer, ran the National at Lucerne and it was at that hotel that Ritz really began to make his mark in the hotel world. In the winters he went to the South of France, where he became manager of the Grand Hotel, Monte Carlo, and finally met up with Escoffier. Together they evolved their ideas of what a deluxe hotel should be, and after that there was no stopping César Ritz. He gave up Monte Carlo and Lucerne, took over the Hotel de la Conversation in Baden-Baden, then bought the Hotel de Provence in Cannes (where the Prince of Wales came every year), then another small hotel in Baden, the Minerva, and finally came to the notice of Richard D'Oyly Carte who was in Baden taking the cure. He asked Ritz to come to his recently opened Savoy in London, and there between them Ritz and Escoffier conquered London. It was a group of admirers in the City of London who first suggested that Ritz should consider opening his own hotel in Paris.

At first he was not all that keen; he was not French and had never worked in Paris above the rank of restaurant manager. Above all, he knew that the location of the hotel was of the utmost importance and at that time there didn't seem to be anywhere in Paris that was both suitable and available. At all events, in 1896 a company called the Ritz Hotel Syndicate Ltd. was registered in London under the chairmanship of Henry Higgins, a fashionable and wealthy lawyer.

No one quite knows to this day how the Place Vendôme was chosen as the location for Ritz's hotel. Whatever the real story, the decision of the Credit Mobilier to leave what had once been the town house of the Duc de Lauzun was an opportunity not to be turned down. The problem was money. And then Ritz remembered that some years before a man called Marnier Lapostolle, a wealthy vineyard owner, had come to him with a liqueur he had invented. Ritz had tasted it, thought it rather good and suggested he call it Grand

Photograph: C. Veron

Above: Lunch in the garden.

Marnier. As a result Lapostolle had announced that he would be under a debt of gratitude to Ritz for life. . . .

Lapostolle put up the money without a murmur and an option on Number 15, Place Vendôme was secured.

The house was exactly what he wanted in order to create a small, intimate and exclusive hotel. He planned to leave the elegant mansard façade exactly as it was and somehow to rebuild the interior with all the refinements that a prince might hope to incorporate in his town-house. He also insisted that the existing gardens should remain where they were.

Ritz remained at the Savoy for a further year, and only left after a bizarre battle of wills between himself and one of the head housekeepers, who had for some reason taken against him. In the end Ritz resigned, taking with him Escoffier, Echenard his maître d'hôtel, Agostini the chief cashier, and Henry Elles the restaurant manager, all of whom were to form the nucleus of his team in Paris. The Prince of Wales at once cancelled a party he had arranged at the Savoy saying "Where Ritz goes, I go."

For the next two years Ritz devoted all his energies to the creation of his "little house" in the Place Vendôme. His architect, Charles Mewes, was horrified when Ritz explained he wanted his hotel to be the most modern in Paris—until, that is, he understood that what he really meant was that it should be "hygienic, efficient, and beautiful." "A beauty that would last for ever," said Mewes. "Exactly," said Ritz, and from that moment on they understood one another perfectly.

Ritz's attention to detail was keen and relentless. Months were devoted to the lighting alone (Ritz was a great pioneer in the art of indirect lighting); heavy velvets were rejected in favor of light fabrics that were easy to clean; metal beds were chosen over wooden ones; wherever possible, large built-in wardrobes were installed, and even a special drawer for ladies hair-pieces; the lobby was made small to discourage loiterers; even when a room seemed perfect to Madame Ritz, her husband would find something that was not quite as he would like it. On the afternoon of the day the hotel was due to open its doors for the first time, he had all the tables in the restaurant sent off to the makers to have two centimeters cut off every leg.

But in the end it all paid off, as Ritz knew it would. "I am going to dismiss my chef," Boni de Castellane remarked to him as he was leaving at the end of the evening. "It is foolish to try and compete with you and Escoffier."

With the Ritz successfully launched, César and Escoffier turned their attentions to the Carlton in London in which he and his backers had acquired a controlling interest, and everything he and Mewes had learned from the building of the Ritz they proceeded to apply to the rebuilding of this famous London hotel. The Carlton opened two years after the Ritz and was an immediate success. At once, Ritz began to apply himself to the building of the London Ritz in Piccadilly.

Two years later, while in the midst of preparing the Carlton to be

the center of all London's celebrations for Edward VII's coronation, Ritz collapsed. He lived for another sixteen years, but he was never to be the same man again. His efforts and his enthusiasm had destroyed him, and although he continued to take a keen interest in all his hotels, he was a sinking man. He died in a clinic at Kusnacht, near Lucerne, just a few weeks before the armistice. He was sixty-eight.

In the years immediately following Ritz's death, the continued success of the hotel was due to the combined efforts of three men: Henry Elles, Victor Rey, and Olivier Dabescat.

Olivier was one of the greatest maîtres d'hotel of all time. So great was his fame that the writer Edouard Bourdet made him his central character in a play called *Le Sexe Faible*, under the name of Antoine. One of his closest friends was Marcel Proust, of whose generosity many stories have been told, notably by André Maurois in *The Quest for Proust*:

> At long last the dinner actually took place, in a private room at the Ritz, paneled in cerise brocade and filled with gilded furniture. Considerable surprise was caused by the presence, in this scheme of decoration, of "two furred and padded Lapps," who turned out to be Proust and Mme de Noailles. Risler, engaged at the last moment, played Wagnerian overtures. Dinner done, the tips had to be distributed. Marcel wanted to give Olivier 300 francs, but the guests flung themselves upon him in an effort to modify his generosity. He promptly gave more.

Nothing was too much trouble for Olivier of the Ritz, and he took enormous pride in the fact that while he ordered most of the food to be served he always went shopping for the fruit himself.

Harold Nicolson called Olivier "the Napoleon of Maîtres d'Hôtel." He tells of the time in 1919 when he was in Paris with Lord Curzon, the British Foreign Secretary, for a conference, and they had returned home for a late supper. After they were seated. Olivier said to Lord Curzon, "The last time you had supper you had an omelette. I remember I gave you a kidney omelette but I cannot remember if you liked it or not." Before Curzon could reply, Olivier produced a dish and continued, "So, to be sure, I have prepared you two omelettes, one with kidneys, so that you shall have what you prefer."

Victor Rey, who later became manager of the Ritz was a Swiss who based himself unashamedly on César Ritz. Once, when he was reception manager, the English newspaper magnate Alfred Harmsworth (later Lord Northcliffe) arrived at the hotel and remarked on how pale and unwell Rey was looking. Rey tried to pass it off, but Harmsworth insisted on knowing what was wrong. Rey finally confessed that his wife had been taken to a maternity hospital during the night and he did not know what was happening. Harmsworth immediately announced that he had always wanted to know what it was like to work on the other side of the desk, and he marched round the back of the desk, sent Rey off to the hospital and took over in his place. By the time Rey's relief arrived, Harmsworth had let rooms to a party of Americans and was looking extremely pleased with himself.

Another of the great men of the Ritz who ran the hotel as Ritz himself would have had it run was Claude Auzello, who was manager for twenty-five years and saw the hotel through two of its trickiest times. The first was in the early days following the Wall Street crash, when American and later English custom dropped off badly—a state of affairs that Ritz himself had never envisaged. Economies had to be made, but at the same time Auzello did not want to have to lay off any staff. So instead, he did away with all the suppliers in the neighborhood through whom the hotel bought its meat and vegetables and bread and fruit, and set about doing all the buying himself. For three years he would get up every morning at 5.30 in order to be down at Les Halles as soon as the market opened. In that way he could be sure that the hotel continued to serve its customers only the very best of everything. At the same time he was working until after midnight every night on his managerial tasks. Never at any time during those three years could anyone complain that the standard of the Ritz had dropped. And when bookings eventually began to pick up again Auzello returned, exhausted but satisfied, to his normal duties.

But his most difficult task came during the war when the Luftwaffe took over the whole of the Vendôme side of the hotel, leaving the rue Cambon side as a hotel. Although he had been told that the Germans staying at the Ritz were all very high-ranking personal friends of the Führer, Auzello was taking no chances, and just to make sure there was no damage he made all the German officers shareholders in the hotel.

Another of the great Ritz characters of the past was Maxim Charrier, a man whom many great men and women have leaned on over the years for moral and practical support—people like the Cuban Colonel Caraf who took Max along with him to sugar conferences in Brussels and Berlin; the Maharajah of Kapurthala, whom he used to escort to Italy and who had a special gold medal struck for him; Barbara Hutton and Bernard Baruch; King Ferdinand of Rumania and King Alfonso of Spain; and the old Aga Khan, who once despatched Max to London to deliver a personal letter to George V.

One of the things for which the Ritz is justly famed is its bar. The Ritz has three bars, but the real Ritz Bar is the one just inside the rue Cambon entrance on the left. They say it was due to Frank Meier, head barman here from 1921 until he died in 1947, that the Ritz Bar earned its reputation. He it was throughout those glamorous years between the wars who mixed his sophisticated clients some of the great cocktails of all times: concoctions with names likes Bees' Knees, Whizz Bang, Monkey Gland, Pink Lady, Chatterley, Gin and Sin, Golden Slipper, and Green Hat (in honor of Michael Arlen). Many

Top: A detail from the mantelpiece in one of the suites. *Bottom left:* A commemorative plaque just inside the Place Vendôme entrance.

were named after celebrities of the day: Alfonso XIII, Caruso, Prince of Wales, Seapea (Cole Porter's initials), Nicky's Fizz (for a Russian prince) and Blue Bird, in honor of Sir Malcolm Campbell. One of his most exotic concoctions was the Rainbow (anisette, mint, yellow chartreuse, cherry brandy, kümmel, green chartreuse, and cognac, each poured on top of the other in equal quantities), and his Special was peach brandy, vermouth and gin.

It was his successor, George Scheuer, who was in the bar on liberation day dishing out free champagne to all and sundry when the door burst open and in marched his old friend Ernest Hemingway in war correspondent's uniform and carrying a sten gun, announcing that he had come to liberate the Ritz in person. Hemingway had been introduced to the Ritz Bar by another expatriate drinking man, F. Scott Fitzgerald, and among other famous clients George could boast Winston Churchill, the Aga Khan, various maharajahs, Mayor Jimmy Walker of New York, Andrew Carnegie, Woolworth, Rockefeller, Pierpont Morgan, Rudolph Valentino and Greta Garbo.

The list of names of people with whom the Ritz has been associated over the years is endless. One of the most famous was of course Coco Chanel who lived in an apartment in the hotel on the rue Cambon side for years.

So too are the stories. The Ritz has always attracted the sort of people who create them—the famous, the powerful, the eccentric. For nearly eighty years they have been coming, and they will continue to do so as long as the Ritz continues to provide impeccable service, marvelous food, sensational suites, and all those other leftovers from a bye-gone age that are themselves fast disappearing from the face of the earth.

For me, though, it was all summed up by Monsieur Moreau, who, once the matter of the suitcases had been forgiven and forgotten, shook me by the hand and said, with the utmost sincerity, "Come back home soon." And that was the first time I had every stayed there.

SAVOY

THE SAVOY
LONDON, ENGLAND

When you register as a guest at the Savoy Hotel in London, you do so not with the customary ball-point pen but with a very expensive-looking fountain pen. I daresay it would be less expensive for the hotel to provide a ball-point job, and certainly less trouble for the man whose task it is every morning to make sure the pens are filled with ink and in working order. No doubt a few elderly eyebrows would be raised were such a change ever to be made, but the majority of guests would probably not even notice the difference.

Not that such considerations would ever enter into the Savoy's thinking. As far as they are concerned, there are ways of doing things that are correct and others that are incorrect—and expecting your guests to register with a ball-point pen is incorrect.

The Savoy, like every other great hotel in these hard times, is having its troubles. The cost of maintaining a building of that size, let alone of continuing to offer the sort of service that Savoy guests have over the years come to expect, must be phenomenal. Rumors fly hither and thither that the old place is going to the dogs, giving slightly at the seams, not quite what it used to be. For all I know, the worst fears may, as far as some guests are concerned, be fully realized. Well, that may be so. All I know is that the last time I stayed there, I had in the Grill the best meal I have had in London, or anywhere else, for many months; my room was extremely comfortable; room service was brisk and efficient; and the breakfast arrived—as it does in all the best hotels—on a trolley covered with a white linen table cloth, with the butter on ice in a little dish and the marmalade and jam in little pots, each with its own spoon, the croissants fresh and warm from the pastry chef's oven, the coffee hot, rich and plentiful. I emphasize the excellence of the Savoy breakfast partly because I care a lot about breakfast—in many ways it is my favorite meal; partly too because it typifies the Savoy's insistence upon doing things the correct way—that is to say, the way they have been doing them and, more importantly, teaching others to do them for the best part of a century. I remember the manager of the famous Empress Restaurant in Berkeley Street, Mr. Negri, once saying to me, "The Savoy was and still is the Catering University not only of England but of the whole world. Take the great head waiter, Giordano. Many people will say that Giordano made the restaurant at the Savoy. But I tell you, it was not the great Giordano who made the Savoy; it was the Savoy that made Giordano!"

It also made John Iversen, general manager of the Lancaster in Paris; Peter Stafford, lately of the Mandarin in Hong Kong; Walter Schnyder of the Beau Rivage in Lausanne; the present general manager of the Savoy, Beverly Griffin, and literally hundreds of managers, reception managers, maîtres d'hôtel and chefs all over the world who at one time or another have been through the Savoy system.

When you stay in the Savoy, you are aware at all times of a

OPPOSITE The famous entrance in the Strand, with the statue of Peter of Savoy.

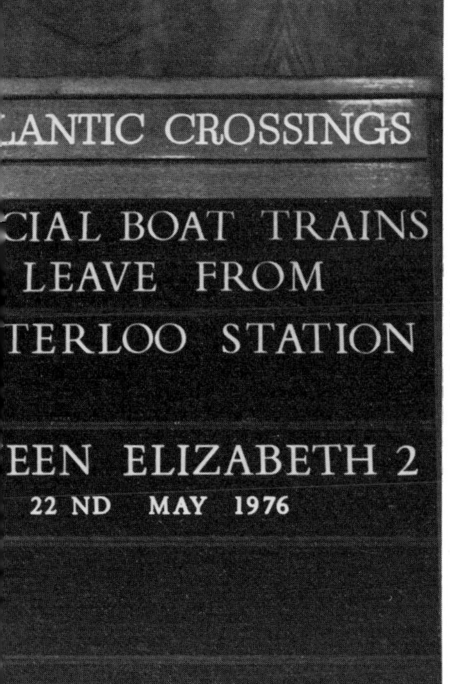

Top: The view from one of the River Suites. *Bottom left:* A hazy view of the main entrance hall on the Strand side. *Bottom right:* Once upon a time, the board would have been full.

general feeling of enormous self-confidence that they are doing things the way they ought to be done. Few hotels in the world wear this air of self-confidence as easily or as naturally as the Savoy; but then few hotels have enjoyed anything like such a distinguished career, and been associated with quite so many great names, and at the same time succeeded in remaining as great today as they were the day they were opened. No other hotel in the world can boast quite an extensive bibliography, which includes a full-length book by Stanley Jackson, a book by Sir Compton Mackenzie, and literally countless magazine and newspaper articles.

Arnold Bennett based his novel *Imperial Palace* on the Savoy, and as for the anecdotes that have been recounted over the years concerning the hotel's more celebrated and extravagant guests, they would surely fill a six-part encyclopaedia. Can it be possible, I ask myself, that any part of the Savoy story will come to you like a fresh breeze from the slopes of Parnassus? It seems unlikely. Still, there is nothing people like more than hearing old stories repeated, and the story of the Savoy, more than that of any other hotel I know, always bears repetition.

It all began in 1246, when Henry III gave Peter, Count of Savoy, uncle to his wife Eleanor of Provence, a piece of land that bordered a rather rough bridle path known as "le Straunde" and sloped down sharply to the river.

On this site Peter began to build a great palace that—thanks to his fondness for bringing over beautiful young women of noble birth from France and marrying them off to eligible young Englishmen—soon earned the reputation of being "the fayrest Mannor in Europe."

The English, however, had never much cared for foreigners, especially when they were as highly favored by the king as Peter had been; and it came as no surprise when in 1264, following the king's defeat at the Battle of Lewes by Simon de Montfort, Peter returned to his native land.

The palace was occupied for a while by Simon de Montfort, who founded the House of Commons, and later by John of Gaunt, Duke of Lancaster, who entertained Chaucer there. Gaunt's son, Henry Bolingbroke, after defeating Richard II and becoming Henry IV, amalgamated the Duchy of Lancaster and the Crown, so that the precincts of the Savoy are to this day a Liberty of the Duchy of Lancaster.

The palace was ransacked by Wat Tyler during the Peasant's Revolt of 1381 and left empty until 1509, when Henry VII rebuilt it as a hospital for poor people. This in turn was finally dissolved by Queen Anne, and by the early nineteenth century the whole area was a collection of tumble-down dwellings and dirty coal sheds.

And then onto the scene stepped Richard D'Oyly Carte, the young impresario who had begun to make a huge name for himself as the producer of the comic operas of W. S. Gilbert and Arthur Sullivan. He had already put on *The Sorcerer, H.M.S. Pinafore* and *The Pirates of*

Penzance when in 1881 he decided the time had come for the operas to have their own permanent home. He found the ideal site in the Strand, among the remains of Peter of Savoy's great palace.

On October 10, 1881, *Patience* transferred from the old Opera Comique to its new home in the Savoy Theatre. Shortly after this D'Oyly Carte went to America, and it was during this trip that he conceived the idea of building a great luxury hotel on the site next door to his theater. In those days hotels were, as far as the upper class of English were concerned, simply places you slept in when you had no other choice. Certainly no responsible person would have dreamed of being seen dining out in a hotel restaurant. In America, however, where hotels of great luxury and magnificence had been built, it was fast becoming acceptable for even the very best people to spend an evening or even a night in surroundings that were every bit as splendid and comfortable as their own homes, and in which they could expect service of the very highest standard.

If the Americans were ready for such radical change in their social habits, argued D'Oyly Carte, might not the English be equally ready—provided that the hotel in question offered the most up-to-date comforts, the finest kitchen and conscientious staff to rival the grandest private homes in the country? Convinced that he was capable of satisfying every one of the most stringent demands he had imposed upon himself, D'Oyly Carte set to work on the steel- and concrete-framed seven-story building that must have seemed to the citizens of London in 1884 nothing less than the eighth wonder of the world.

The installation of six hydraulic elevators, despite the company's assurance that they were "perfectly safe, their movements smooth, pleasant and rapid," was surely a dangerous form of extravagance. And seventy bathrooms! Why, the most luxurious hotel in London at that time, the Victoria, provided four for their five hundred guests; and that, compared with many other modern European hotels, was going a bit too far. And then there was this business of the electric lighting. This without doubt was the most daring and dangerous innovation of all.

On the other hand, one had to admit that this quite extraordinary edifice did possess one or two outstanding, pleasant and useful attractions—like the six thousand-square-foot courtyard into which the carriages and cabs drove from the main entrance in Savoy Hill; and the fact that this was the first building in England to be constructed entirely from non-combustible materials; not to mention Mrs. D'Oyly Carte's notion for providing service on every floor at all hours of the day or night, which gave guests the reassuring feeling that they were, if not in their own homes, then at least in that of a very rich and thoughtful friend.

The restaurant, reached from the Genoese Hall via a double staircase, was also something of a sensation with its mahogany paneling surmounted by a gold and silver frieze. For smaller, more intimate affairs, there were a number of charming private dining rooms named after the Gilbert and Sullivan Operas—Pinafore, Mikado, Iolanthe and so on.

Yes, on the whole, this newfangled Savoy Hotel really did have one or two things to commend it—the one serious drawback being the deep-rooted English reluctance to dine out in a public place. All right with friends who were staying there, of course, but not as a general habit for respectable society. But then D'Oyly Carte, perceptive as ever, made a brilliant move. Realizing that good plain English cooking and pretty decoration stood precious little chance of attracting the sort of clientele he was looking for, he determined to offer his guests the very best French cuisine possible.

In the summer of 1888, only months before the Savoy was due to open, he was in Baden-Baden taking the cure, when whom should he bump into but César Ritz, who, although not yet a world-famous figure, had nevertheless made something of a name for himself at the National in Lucerne and the Grand in Monte-Carlo, and had recently taken over the Minerva in Baden, just next door to Brenner's Stephanie-Hotel. D'Oyly Carte, recognizing in this Swiss peasant's son the qualities that were later to make him the most famous of all European hoteliers, invited him to come and run the Savoy. Ritz was doubtful until he saw what D'Oyly Carte was creating down there beside the river. He at once accepted the Savoy board's invitation to handle the opening of the restaurant, and four months later, on December 21, 1889, he was appointed general manager of the Savoy Hotel.

Ritz brought a lot of people with him when he took up his appointment. He brought Autour as his assistant manager, Agostini as his chief cashier, Echenard as his maître d'hôtel. He even brought the Prince of Wales, perhaps the only man in Europe whose patronage of any establishment was a surefire guarantee of its immediate success. But of all the people Ritz brought with him, none did more to establish the Savoy Restaurant than his chef Escoffier. Among the many famous dishes he invented at the Savoy were *Pêche Melba* for Dame Nellie and *Cuisses de Nymphes a l'Aurore* (frogs' legs served cold in cream and Moselle, and reddened with paprika) for the Prince of Wales. Some spoil sports might be tempted to comment that if he fancied that he would fancy anything. Which of course he did.

Another of Escoffier's famous dishes was *les Suprêmes de Volailles Jeannette*—breasts of cold chicken in jelly surrounded with foie gras—created in memory of the crew of the Arctic exploration ship *Jeannette* who lost their lives in 1881 when the vessel became ice-bound off the coast of Siberia. Escoffier introduced this dish in the restaurant one evening fifteen years later, with the individual portions served somewhat tastelessly on beds of crushed ice.

The right food, the right company—only one thing more was needed to guarantee a perfect evening out, and that was good music; and since Savoy guests had come to expect nothing but the best, only the very best music would do. Everyone loved the waltz and who better

OVERLEAF *Top left:* Kaspar the Cat, the fourteenth guest. *Top right:* One of the Savoy's green-tiled bathrooms. *Bottom:* Noël Coward demanded that his medicine be laid out for him in a certain way, and Marlene Dietrich liked a particularly large bed.

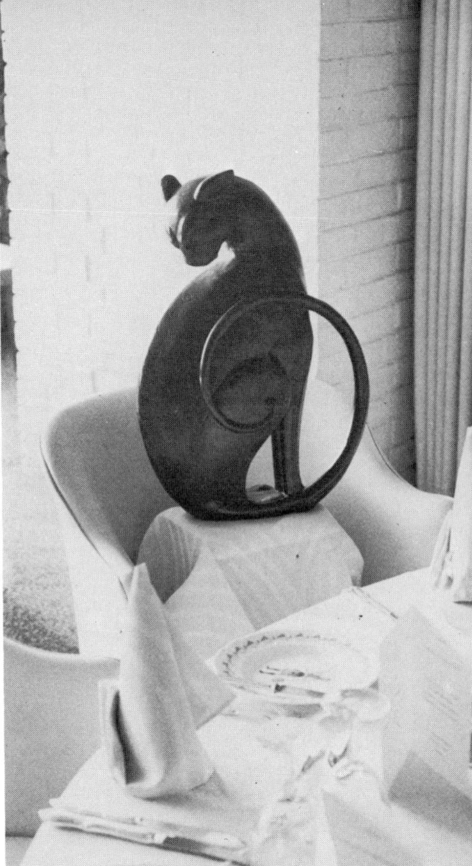

to play waltzes than Johann Strauss himself? The hotel's directors protested with typical English caution: "His fees will be astronomical!" "Yes," riposted Ritz, "but at the same time people will linger longer over their dinner, and just think of all those bottles of wine they will order!"

César Ritz stayed at the Savoy for eight years, after which he and Escoffier went to the Carlton, which was opened in 1897.

At first the Savoy directors were terrified that Ritz and Escoffier would take all their faithful clients with them, but their fears were unfounded. By that time the Savoy was firmly established as an essential part of English social life.

In 1900, at a party to celebrate the opening of Claridge's, D'Oyly Carte met a young man who was managing a small hotel called the Berkeley. His name was George Reeves-Smith, and he struck D'Oyly Carte as being just the sort of chap the Savoy needed to carry on where Ritz had left off. Reeves-Smith joined the board of the Savoy and soon afterwards became its managing director—the post he was to hold with outstanding success for the next forty years. The appointment, as it turned out, had been made just in time, for within months D'Oyly Carte was dead. His son Rupert succeeded him as chairman and with him and Reeves-Smith at the helm, the Savoy sailed forth into the second phase of its long and brilliant history.

The end of the South African War heralded a renaissance in English life. The gloomy Victorian age was past, Edward VII was on the throne, and suddenly all was summer. In keeping with the general air of light-heartedness and optimism that suddenly overcame the nation, the Savoy began to expand and renovate. They pulled down the male-only Grill Room and in its place built the much larger Café Parisien. They also built a new entrance in the Strand, paved it with rubber to deaden the sound of horses' hooves, and constructed a great arch over it on top of which they planted an effigy of Count Peter of Savoy, who to this day keeps a rather forbidding eye on guests arriving at the hotel. They also expanded the restaurant. A million pounds that cost, and, as though to keep pace with this outburst of opulence, a series of wildly extravagant parties began to take place at the Savoy. In 1906 the German industrialist Krupp threw a little do for a few friends during the entire course of which the majolica fountain in the courtyard gushed champagne. In the same year, the champagne magnate George Kessler had the whole courtyard flooded in order that his guests should be able to eat their dinner seated in large gondolas and serenaded by none other than Caruso himself. To celebrate the discovery of the North Pole by Commander Peary, the Pilgrim's Club gave a dinner for which the Winter Garden was transformed into a fantasy of ice and snow and the waiters dressed up in Eskimo furs. The same organization also gave a dinner in honor of a visit by the American Naval Squadron at which all twenty tables were turned into models of famous British and American battleships.

Such outbursts of theatricality came as no surprise to the staff of the Savoy which, for obvious reasons, always has been, and, I'm delighted to say, still is, a wonderfully theatrical hotel. Sir Henry Irving, the theater's first knight, lived there, and Sarah Bernhardt very nearly died there (from an overdose of chloral taken after a performance of Jules Barbier's *Saint Joan* at Her Majesty's Theatre). Puccini entertained Melba there after the opening of *Manon Lescaut* at Covent Garden, Franz Lehar entertained his cast there after the first night of *The Merry Widow*, and the chef entertained Chaliapin there in his own little dining room. Tetrazzini used to stand on a chair and sing "Home Sweet Home" and Oscar Wilde used to sit on a banquette and make witty remarks. Pavlova once danced there in cabaret, and Charles Frohman, the American producer, once got stuck in a lift there for some hours. (When finally released he remarked to his secretary that it was the first holiday he had had in years.)

And what figure could be more theatrical than that of Kaspar, the sleek black wooden cat, who sits on a mantlepiece in front of a large Art Deco mirror in the Pinafore Room, and who, whenever there is a dinner party for thirteen guests anywhere in the hotel, is taken down to become the fourteenth guest at the table! Not only is he given his own chair to sit on, but a napkin is tied under his chin, and a complete place is laid out before him, wine glasses and all. He is not actually served with any food, but as each course is completed the appropriate items of cutlery are removed from in front of him.

During the First World War the Savoy became a great center of American life in England. It was in the Mirror Room that America's entry into the war was celebrated in 1917, and it was in the same room that six years later a bust of Abraham Lincoln was unveiled by the British Foreign Secretary, Lord Curzon, and the room renamed the Abraham Lincoln Room.

But the moment the war was over, the hotel resumed its task of making life as agreeable and amusing as possible for as many people as could afford it.

Dancing had been one of the hotel's most popular features ever since Strauss first raised bow to strings in 1889. By 1910 ragtime was beginning to take over from the waltz, and during the war one-steps, two-steps and foxtrots were what the young men danced in the few brief moments left to them before returning to meet their deaths in the mud of France.

Reeves-Smith was a perfectionist about wine, about food, about decorations, about everything. No detail escaped his eagle eye, and it was he who established so many of the high standards which are still maintained.

To this day, the hotel builds its own beds and makes its own mattresses (with 967 individual springs, I might say!). Its linen and towels are made to exact specifications, as are its silver, its glass, and its china. If you want a velvet suit pressed when you arrive, it will be done on the spot—no mean achievement if you know anything about velvet suits. Similarly, if you want your food cooked in a particular way, Silvino Trompetto M.B.E., *chef des cuisines*, will be only too happy to oblige; indeed, he insists on his waiters writing the diner's name on each order, so that he can always be sure of who is going to eat each dish.

For special guests—that is to say, old friends of the Savoy who have been there for years—there is almost nothing Beverly Griffin, the hotel's general manager, will not do. Once a distinguished guest with a son at Eton entrusted Mr. Griffin with the responsibility of handling the boy's pocket money and giving him more only when he, Griffin, thought he genuinely needed it. On another occasion he was assigned the delicate task of going through the effects of an American impresario who had recently died, and having to decide what he should do with certain compromising odds and ends.

People who stay at the Savoy sometimes have trouble settling for anything less. Still, if the hotel will insist on maintaining a ratio of one guest to every three members of staff, each of whom genuinely believes that guests should be given everything they want when they want it, is it any wonder that anyone who stays there, if only for one night, comes away completely and utterly spoiled? They say that the late Sir Noël Coward was so insistent on having his various bottles of pills and medicine laid out in a particular order on his bedside table that eventually the housekeeper took a Polaroid of the correct lay-out and followed it in minute detail.

Ah yes, I hear you cry with scorn, but of course they are going to run round after the rich, the famous and the titled. And you would be perfectly correct in so crying. The Savoy always has been and still is very proud of its famous clientele, and would be hypocritical if it pretended otherwise. And because the rich, the famous and the titled are frequently a good deal more demanding of a hotel staff than the

Top left: Room service in one of the River Suites. *Top right:* Silvino Trompetto, M.B.E., *Chef des Cuisines.* *Bottom:* Vic, the head barman in the American Bar.

less humble, and because hotels like the Savoy derive enormous satisfaction from solving the most complicated problems for their guests and coping with their most outlandish demands, one is more likely to hear about Marlene Dietrich's fondness for a particularly large bed than about Fred Bloggs's overwhelming urge to consume scrambled eggs and coffee at four o'clock in the morning.

On the other hand, I am neither rich, famous nor titled. Nor am I the hotel's most frequent guest. Yet all I can tell you is that I have never yet walked through the front doors of the Savoy without feeling thoroughly happy, comfortable and at home. Perhaps the explanation is that, being a Londoner, I tend to think of it more as my local than as one of the greatest hotels of all time; or else quite simply that I always associate the Savoy with happy events—weddings of friends, family dinner parties, and lunches with pretty girls in the Grill; or that I have an enormous fondness for the decoration that has been a feature of the place since the 1930's.

Or is it something much more than that? The late Sir Compton Mackenzie, in an attempt to define the greatness of the Savoy, wrote the following:

> From the August day in 1889 when it was first opened, the Savoy has been the mirror of its period; but year in year out it has never for a moment ceased to possess a creative life of its own, and therefore one never hears it said that the Savoy is no longer the leading hotel in Europe. True greatness is almost always approachable and always immune from the contempt which familiarity is supposed to breed. What is the formula that enables a hotel to put a resident or a casual visitor quite so quickly at ease, make them quite so completely at home? The Savoy has the unmistakeable stamp of a well-bred host by whom every guest is made to feel particularly welcome. I have pondered on the secret of this hospitable ease, but if it were really discoverable, it would not be so remarkable. In the end one falls back on the two words: imaginative direction. . . .

Imaginative direction. It is not at all a bad way of describing the vision, the flair, the attention to detail, the love, and, above all, the genuine fondness for people and a genuine desire to make them feel happy and at home. This attitude was expressed first by Richard D'Oyly Carte nearly a hundred years ago, was continued by his son Rupert in partnership with George Reeves-Smith, and is still maintained today by Sir Hugh Wontner and his fellow directors.

Perhaps Beverly Griffin touched on the secret better than anyone when he told me, "You see, the Savoy is not an industry, nor is it a business. It is a family."

I think I am inclined to agree with Compton Mackenzie that some secrets are best left unexplored and unsolved.

HOTEL VIER JAHRESZEITEN
HOTEL VIER JAHRESZEITEN
VIER JAHRESZEITEN
TAXI
TAXI
TAXI

VIER JAHRESZEITEN
HAMBURG, GERMANY

OCCASIONALLY, JUST OCCASIONALLY, you walk into a hotel and you know at once, almost instinctively, long before you have lain on your bed, or eaten in the restaurant, or rung for room service, or even written your name in the hotel register, you know that you have arrived at one of the dozen or so hotels left in Europe that are in a class of their own.

The Four Seasons in Hamburg is one such hotel.

Other hotels may go in for all manner of gimmicks to attract guests and give them the impression they are getting the best value for their money: fancy uniforms for the staff, expensive-*looking* furniture, color TV in all the bedrooms, piped classical music . . . the whole mish-mash.

At the Four Seasons, on the other hand, they prefer to do things the correct way. The reception staff are dressed in black jackets and pin-striped trousers, the waiters in short jackets and long white aprons, while the barman's jacket is a long wine-colored one. Guests dining in the grill can expect their orders to arrive quickly, correctly (that is to say, under silver covers) and to be served in the correct manner—in two helpings. The bedrooms, furnished with good comfortable hotel furniture, are essentially simple and unfussy, with just one or two pictures or old prints to enliven the walls.

To the hotel's two chief concierges, Mr. Jurgen-Porzelt and Mr. Lepke, who have both been there for over thirty years, it is second nature to know the names of all the guests in the hotel and to greet them by name every time they see them. The sort of people who stay in hotels like this expect personal treatment of this nature, and because of it they return time and time again.

In case I have made the staff and management of the Vier Jahreszeiten sound self-satisfied, not to say cold, arrogant and snobbish, let me hasten to reassure you that if such were the case, neither this hotel nor Claridge's in London nor the Ritz in Paris would still be in business. For quality of service and doing things the way they should be done are only the outward and visible signs of a genuine inner desire to make guests feel as much at home as possible during their stay; and I have stayed in few hotels anywhere in the world where I have been more aware of the ceaseless effort made by staff and management alike to ensure my pleasure, comfort and convenience at all times of the day and night.

I can cite no better example than breakfast in the Restaurant Haerlin (a charming room, even at seven o'clock in the morning), served by three waitresses in pretty floral-patterned frocks and a couple of formally-attired waiters: six different types of roll and three types of bread in a wicker basket; pats of butter on ice; honey, jam and marmalade in little pottery jars; coffee that had obviously just that moment been brewed, with its own little cosy to keep it warm; delightful china in a delicate pink and green design; a tiny arrangement of roses and carnations to one side of the table. . . . How many hotels take that sort of trouble over dinner, let alone breakfast?

OPPOSITE The main entrance in the Neue Jungfernstieg.

Another example: how many hotels do you know where every morning they move the telephone from your bedside table to your writing desk and back again at night? Or where the concierge goes to the trouble of telling you, as you deliver your key after changing before dinner, that your companion has just gone into the bar? (He hadn't, as it turned out, but it certainly got the evening off to a good start to think that anyone cared.) Have you ever sat down to eat in a room, and been presented by your waiter with a leather case containing three pairs of men's glasses of different strengths and three of women's? I cannot believe there are many guests these days who care about the precise temperature of their bath water; even so, it says something for a hotel that it should provide a large wooden thermometer in every bathroom for the few who do care.

Superlative service, enormous attention to detail, genuine care and concern for the guests—these, then, are the essential elements that combine to make the Vier Jahreszeiten the great hotel it is. Yet there is one more factor, more fundamental than all those three put together; the driving force behind the whole thing; the reason that a waiter in the restaurant, whom I have never seen in my life before, somehow knows my name; the reason that people like the King of Greece, the Danish Royal Family and the Queen Mother of England, have so much enjoyed staying there; and why the Fürstenbergs, the Fürst-Bismarcks, the Prince van Hanover, the Thyssens and the van Finks continue to come there as their parents and grandparents did before them; and why the opera singer Anna Moffo has stayed there 115 times since 1969 and the Austrian artist Theo Lingen 500 times since 1959; the reason that so many distinguished travelers always rate it among the top ten hotels in the world; and why I knew, the moment I walked in, that I would be including it too. I refer of course to the Haerlin family who have owned the hotel since 1897. It was in that year that Friedrich Haerlin, a native of Württemberg, who, despite a secret ambition to be a farmer, had served his apprenticeship in the hotel business at the Bellevue Palace in Lucerne, raised his finger during the auctioning of a big house on the Neue Jungfernstieg overlooking the little lake known as the Inner Alster and, to his astonishment, found he had bought it.

From the beginning, Friedrich Haerlin was determined that his guests should live in a style to which not only they, but also he, was accustomed—surrounded by good furniture, good pictures and good staff. To ensure that the food they ate should be of the best quality, he bought a farm on the outskirts of the city where he grew his own vegetables, reared his own meat and produced his own eggs. He also cultivated his own flower garden, and to this day all the flowers, all the vegetables, and at least half the meat and eggs used in the hotel still come from the farm.

In time the hotel was taken over by Friedrich's son, Fritz, who with the help of his wife, Agnes, and his two daughters, Anne and Thekla, carried on the tradition of perfection laid down by his father.

PRECEDING PAGES *Clockwise from upper left-hand corner:* Mr. Jurgen-Porzelt and Mr. Lepke; the lounge where drinks are served from a side table; the main staircase; one of the suites; the Condi tea room and pastry shop; the grill room; the hotel seen from across the Inner Alster Lake.

Sadly, Fritz Haerlin died only a week or so before I visited the hotel and I was never able to meet him. His staff spoke of him as an essentially simple, hard-working man, who at the age of seventy-six was still parking his little Volkswagen in the hotel garage every morning and carrying out a full day's work, pausing not even at lunchtime. At the same time, as one of his daughters pointed out to me, one should never underestimate the part Mrs. Haerlin has played in providing all the little touches that, taken together, give the hotel its unique charm. Her work can be seen everywhere—in the ubiquitous flower arrangements, in the Condi tearoom and pastry shop, with its pretty pieces of porcelain and Biedemeyer-style decor where in the afternoons ladies with nothing better to do sit sipping coffee and gossiping cosily with their friends, watching the sun setting across the water and the gulls wheeling above the little boats. . . .

Looking at that scene now it is hard to believe that by the time the Allied bombers had finished with the place in 1945, almost nothing was left standing. How the Four Seasons managed to survive the holocaust is difficult to imagine. "Ah, you see," explained Mr. Lepke—or was it the other one?—"the English pilots were very clever: by that stage they knew they had won the war, and that when they came to Hamburg afterwards they would want somewhere nice to stay; so of course they made sure their bomb aimers always missed the Four Seasons!" A joke perhaps, yet what did the hotel become for the first six years following the war? A club for RAF and Royal Naval officers.

Am I being fanciful when I suggest that a club-like atmosphere pervades the hotel to this day? Perhaps I am a little. Nevertheless, my outstanding memory of the Four Seasons is coming down the stairs that first evening—past huge gleaming pieces of furniture, past mirrors in beautiful mahogany and walnut frames—and hearing below me on the ground floor, increasing in strength as I approached, the slow, ponderous ticking of a grandfather clock. From there I made my way straight to the sitting room and plumped myself down in one of the heavy, upholstered armchairs in front of a log fire blazing cheerfully beneath a massive chimney piece. The barman, in his wine-colored apron, brought me a large whisky and soda, and there I sat for fully an hour, sipping my drink, watching in one corner a family talking in excited but subdued tones, in another a group of businessmen bending each others' ears with propositions and figures, and on a sofa near the fire, Lilli Palmer going over a new script with a friend, and thinking to myself that if ever I felt as contented and at home in any other hotel in the world as I did just at that moment, I should be a very lucky man.

OPPOSITE A detail from one of the banisters. ABOVE The Haerlin family crest in a window beside the staircase; the barman in the lounge.

MAISON
J.F. MILLET
1849 1875
ENTRÉE À 20
LIBRE

CHARMING COUNTRY HOTELS

L'HOTELLERIE DU BAS-BREAU

BARBIZON, FRANCE

EVERY HOUSE IN the main street of the village of Barbizon, it seems, bears a plaque commemorating its occupancy at one time or another by a painter or sculptor of the Barbizon school. After a while you have become so accustomed to stopping every five or ten yards to read yet another fascinating inscription that you run a grave risk of finding yourself, as I did at one point, reading with enormous interest a small plaque on a street lamp informing you that the lamp in question had been erected there by the commune in 1969.

There is one sign, however, that is guaranteed to stop every literate English-speaking visitor in his tracks. This one nestles between the timber frames on the front of the Hôtellerie du Bas-Bréau. It reads: "R. Louis Stevenson while at this hotel wrote *Forest Notes.*"

From there your eyes will undoubtedly travel downwards to take in two more modern signs—one announcing that the house has been awarded **** Luxe by the Commissariat Général au Tourisme, and the other that it is a member of the Relais de Campagne—Châteaux Hotels organization.

You may previously have decided against going down the road to visit the Atelier de Rousseau (Théodore, that is) and avoided the crowds milling round Millet's studio and passed on, but you will almost certainly find it far more difficult to resist the combined attractions of those three signs outside the Bas-Bréau.

Passing through the low archway into the little courtyard you will begin to understand what it was that attracted that peripatetic man of letters, Robert Louis Stevenson, to this neck of the Fontainebleau woods and to this hostelry in particular. For one's first reaction will almost certainly be of having stumbled upon a corner of a foreign field (or village anyway) that is forever England—particularly in the yard, which does very much look at first sight like that of some coaching inn in Gloucestershire or Somerset, with its cobbles, its outside wooden staircase, its tubs of flowers and its collection of ornate fire-backs that lie propped casually against the walls. The impression of Englishness is further increased in the bar. Hunting horns, copper, bits and pieces of pewter, wooden beams and deep leather armchairs abound; a perpetual smell of wood smoke emanates

OPPOSITE The main street of Barbizon. Every few yards there is a reminder of the artists of the Barbizon school.

from a great open fireplace; and the reception desk is tucked away cosily and unobtrusively in one corner of the bar.

It is doubtful if, when RLS first poked his head through the door and asked dourly, "Any chance of a room for the night?" that a nice receptionist hurried out to ask him to sign the book before accompanying him to his room. Nor that, when he got to it, he found it filled with antique furniture and decorated with the finest fabrics and tissues. Nor, in all probability, did he sip at an aperitif and toy with a gull's egg while running his eyes over the menu and trying to choose between *le filet de Charolais en feuilleté sauce Perigourdine* or the *foie gras chaud aux raisins*. Such sophisticated delights only began to be introduced in 1935, when the Fava family took it over and devoted their lives to making it one of the most charming and delightful country hotels in Europe. Even so, he obviously found Monsieur Siron, who owned it at the time, a pleasant enough host, and the hotel itself sufficiently comfortable and conducive to the practice of his art, for he returned on several occasions over a period of some seven or eight years.

It requires little detailed knowledge of the Barbizon school of painters to understand what it is that from 1830 onwards attracted (and still attracts) so many artists to the area. The extraordinary combination of forest and flat plain was irresistible to painters like Millet and Rousseau, Diaz and Barye, Daubigny, Daumier, Courbet, Corot; ánd later, Sisley, Monet, Pissarro, and Renoir.

In time Monsieur Siron's inn became an exhibition hall for local work, and there was great excitement when, in 1869, Napoleon III and his Empress stopped for a while at the Hotel de l'Exposition (as

Monsieur Siron had by then renamed it) and bought a few paintings.

In Charlemagne's day, over a thousand years ago, wolves roamed the forest of Fontainebleau, and continued to do so until in the seventeenth century it became a royal domain, much prized for its wealth and variety of game. Today the hunt is no longer for deer or partridge, but for fresh air and the pleasures of the countryside that lie, in the words of the hotel brochure, *"á trente minutes des portes de Paris par l'autoroute du sud."* It is for these, as much as for the comfort of the twenty-five rooms and the food and wine, that Parisians drive out to the Bas-Bréau at weekends and tourists break their journeys on the way to the south. (Although, in the case of the Englishman who every year on his birthday flies over by private plane for lunch with a few friends, it is clearly the food that has the edge on the climate.)

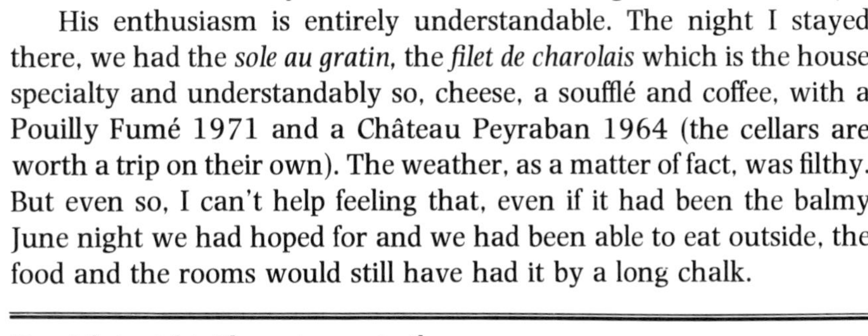

His enthusiasm is entirely understandable. The night I stayed there, we had the *sole au gratin*, the *filet de charolais* which is the house specialty and understandably so, cheese, a soufflé and coffee, with a Pouilly Fumé 1971 and a Château Peyraban 1964 (the cellars are worth a trip on their own). The weather, as a matter of fact, was filthy. But even so, I can't help feeling that, even if it had been the balmy June night we had hoped for and we had been able to eat outside, the food and the rooms would still have had it by a long chalk.

Top, left to right: The entrance in the main street; the courtyard from a bedroom; the dining room. *Bottom left:* The balcony corridor of the bedroom annex in the garden, with the main building in the background. *Center right:* A fire·back in the yard.

Dîner offert en l'honneur

DE SA MAJESTE LA REINE ELISABETH II D'ANGLETERRE

Le 17 Mai 1972

EN L'OUSTAU DE BAUMANIERE

Loup farci en croûte sauce crevettes

Baron d'agneau

Petits pois frais du jardin

Mousseline d'artichauts

Plateau de fromages

Sorbet au citron

Fraises à la crème

Millefeuilles

Friandises Baumanière

CHEVALIER-MONTRACHET "LES DEMOISELLES" 1964

CHATEAU MARGAUX 1955

PIPER HEIDSIECK CUVÉE FLORENS LOUIS 1964

L'OUSTAU DE BAUMANIERE
LES BAUX-DE-PROVENCE, FRANCE

ON WEDNESDAY JUNE 25, 1975, at 6.30 in the evening, the medieval village of Les Baux-de-Provence was struck by a plague in comparison with which, even Pharaoh would have agreed, frogs and lice would come as a welcome relief.

One minute the narrow, winding streets were almost deserted, the stone walls echoing with nothing more than the odd exclamation of delight from the occasional sightseer. The next moment the whole place was swarming with children, who within seconds had insinuated themselves into every crack and crevice of the old village. Everywhere you looked there were children: clambering over walls, rushing in and out of shops, settling briefly at café tables to consume soft drinks and biscuits, and then rushing away to buy souvenirs or chocolate from the little shops with which the village is honeycombed. It was through a seething swarm of one such group that I forced my arm to seize a colored postcard from a revolving rack of cards. It was a view, taken from the village, of the Baumanière, nestling amid the green foliage of the valley below. On the back of the card was written, *"L'Oustau de Baumanière—célèbre hostellerie où Sa Majesté la Reine d'Angleterre a passé la nuit du 17 au 18 mai 1972."* Or, as we say in England, "Queen Elizabeth slept here."

One cannot help wondering how much, if anything, Her Majesty can recall of that night. After all, she must have stayed in quite a few choice spots in her time. On the other hand, one palace must seem very much like another after a while, and it probably came as a refreshing change, if nothing else, to spend a few hours as a guest in a little country hotel.

One thing is certain: with a restaurant as famous the Baumanière just down the road, the inhabitants of Les Baux have seen many famous and distinguished people coming and going in the last thirty years—including the entire crew of the film *Caravan to Vaccares*—but never will they forget the day that La Reine d'Angleterre and le Duc d'Edimbourgh and le Prince des Galles and the British ambassador in Paris, Sir Christopher Soames, and some dozen officials and courtiers spent a night in their village.

It was all Sir Christopher's idea. He had known the Baumanière for years—and since it is one of the few three-star Michelin restaurants in France, the royal party would at least get a good meal.

The rooms may not be exactly sumptuous, but they are all extremely comfortable and homely. One or two of them have the most marvelous views over the Carmargue, and the whole situation of the place is extraordinarily beautiful, surrounded on three sides by curious, primitive-looking pale gray rocks, on the top of which sits the village of Les Baux. In fact, having spent twenty-four hours myself there, I cannot believe that Her Majesty, for all the wonderful places she has stayed in the world, could forget her visit to the Baumanière any less than the villagers could.

The dinner on its own would surely constitute a high spot in anyone's life. But of course the great thing to remember about a

Top left: Raymond Thuilier. He began life in the insurance business and took up cooking when he was over forty. *Bottom left:* L'Oustau nestling among the primitive rock formations of Haut-Provence—seen from the village of Les Baux. *Top right:* The dining room during dinner. The Baumanière has kept its three Michelin stars since 1953. *Bottom right:* The swimming pool.

restaurant like the Baumanière, and the reason it has its three-star rating, is that whether you are the Queen of England, the Shah of Iran, or plain C. Matthew, your food will be equally fresh, equally well-cooked, equally graciously served, and you will be sure of an equally memorable evening. And when it comes down to it, it is not for the view or the weather or the pool or the rooms or the medieval village that people drive miles into the depths of Haut-Provence, but for the food. The other things are merely garnishing—very beautiful garnishing, to be sure, but garnishing all the same.

From about five-thirty in the afternoon onwards, as the rays of the setting sun begin to paint the rocky landscape an unbelievable pink, life at the Baumanière is devoted entirely to preparing for the evening meal.

In one corner of the terrace the sommelier, already dressed in his regalia of office, is sorting through his enormous *Cartes des Vins*. Cars are beginning to draw up, bringing last-minute kitchen staff and waiters. On the terrace itself a number of waiters in shirt sleeves are preparing the tables for pre-dinner drinks.

And then suddenly a white-coated figure appears in the doorway announcing that all is well in the kitchen and that Maître Thuilier is ready for his first drink of the evening.

It is as though one were in a theater, long before curtain-up, watching the preparations for the evening performance, when suddenly the star of the show comes out on to the stage just to sit and contemplate for a while before the audience arrives.

He was in great form that evening as we sat over a glass of champagne while he reminisced about the days before the First World War when he first came to England. "I was at Horley, in Surrey. Do you know Horley?" He has never forgotten the time some girls, realizing he was French, called out "Hallo, Froggy-boy," to him; nor of how shocked one nicely brought-up Home Counties girl was when he gave her her first taste of continental kissing; nor of how cross some people had been at the fact that he was not wearing khaki, and how amused the Queen had been at the story.

Although he is over eighty now, Monsieur Thuilier has lost none of the enthusiasm and sense of adventure that persuaded him, at the age of fifty-one to give up a successful career in insurance to devote himself to cooking and hotel-keeping.

He had bought the Baumanière originally in 1941. It was just an abandoned farmhouse then and remained so for the rest of the war, and not until 1946 was the restaurant declared open by a young man from the local *Office de Tourisme* named Georges Pompidou.

In 1947 Thuilier was awarded his first star by Michelin; his second came two years later and his third in 1953. He has kept all three ever since—no mean achievement when you hear stories about restaurants losing a star simply because it takes more than ten seconds for a waiter to produce a light for the inspector's cigarette.

The problem, as Monsieur Thuilier's grandson, manager Jean Chariol, explained, is twofold.

> On the one hand, just because we have three stars we have people coming here from miles away expecting far too much. I mean, they've heard so much about it they think they're going to be given things to eat that they've never eaten before. On the other hand, the staff have to do the same things day after day—cutting up the meat and serving at table—and yet somehow make every guest believe that the whole thing has been laid on specially for him. The miracle is that it happens. The point is that what we offer here is not just the food so much as a combination of good food, beautiful surroundings, the personality of my grandfather, the slowness of pace at which you eat, the whole experience. There are plenty of good eating places in France, but many of them aren't pretty at all.

Having wondered up to that moment whether I was gastronomically up to the evening ahead, it was with a far lighter heart that I sauntered into the dining room a few minutes later.

The *canard aux citrons verts* did succeed, as Monsieur Thuilier had promised it would when we discussed the menu earlier, in making me rethink entirely my whole attitude towards the duck family. The Châteauneuf-du-Pape was a brilliant suggestion by the sommelier, and the *tarte aux pêches* was unimpeachable.

No course came too early or after too long a delay. I never had to gesticulate at a waiter, all of whom seemed to have been born with some telepathic device whereby they knew at once the instant I needed some more wine in my glass or an extra dash of cream on my tart. The room we ate in was rustic, cosy, illuminated to perfection and totally without pretentiousness. I particularly admired the plates, which were designed at Limoges at the end of the eighteenth century for the Comte d'Artois.

Outside I paused for a while to let the scents of the warm Provençal night air drift into my nostrils, and to watch the moon dancing on the water of the pool.

The following morning, between dips in the pool, I spoke again with Monsieur Thuilier. He was telling me how his mother had cooked for thirty-eight years at two *Buffets de la Gare*. Why in that case, I asked him, had he ever decided to take up insurance? "You always need to have a profession in order to find out what it is you really want to do in life," he replied. "My boss, when I told him that I was going to leave to become a cook, said, 'It is a great adventure you are undertaking.' I replied, 'So is life.' And if you have the passion, you must succeed. Don't you agree?"

Left: The door to one of the bedrooms.
Right: A light lunch.

LE MAS DES SERRES

ST. PAUL-DE-VENCE, FRANCE

Le Mas des Serres is the French equivalent of that English country pub that I have been dreaming about and looking for in vain for the past twenty years. You know the one—tucked away in lovely countryside with wonderful food and just a few rooms, and a host who comes and joins you after dinner for a drink and some good conversation; and not too many people know about it, so that it is still unspoiled. You know the sort of place. . . .

It was about three o'clock on a warm Sunday afternoon in late June that I first came to the Mas des Serres, after half an hour's automobile derring-do that had begun in Cannes and ended at the crossroads at Cagnes-sur-Mer, where a signpost to Vence leads you gently off the RN7 (Route Nord de la Mer) up through the little town of Cagnes and into the Provençal hills. The address of Le Mas being St. Paul, our spirits were already starting to sink in anticipation of the traditional crowds of Sunday sightseers, when about two miles above Cagnes we turned off to our left down a narrow, winding, leafy lane, through cool woods and between high hedges until we began to think we were lost. And then, breasting a small hill and rounding a final bend, we were there.

At first glance it was nothing special—just another Provençal farm house, smarter than some perhaps, but easily missable were it not for the little clutch of plaques and awards on the wall at the bottom of the drive that hinted at all manner of gastronomic delights. From the brilliant sunlight of the little cobbled courtyard we plunged into the cool darkness of the house, through the bar and out into the garden where, beneath the green shade of a vine-covered terrace, lunch was still being lingered over to the accompaniment of clinking coffee cups, tinkling wine glasses and muted conversation.

We were informed by a fifteen-year-old waiter that Madame Saucourt, the owner, was occupied for the time being, but if we cared for something—some coffee perhaps? A black currant sorbé? Some wine?

We had some of all three and sat looking contentedly across what was almost an English garden—thick green lawn. herbaceous border bursting with color and a fine cypress hedge within which it is all contained. In the midst of the flowers a young man in a blue bathing costume and enviable sun tan was hoeing.

The waiter produced three thick scrapbooks, two of which contained a variety of press clippings, and the third a number of photographs showing what the place was like when Madame Marie-Therese (Marité, to her friends) Saucourt, an interior decorator by profession, first found the place fifteen or so years ago: terrible, basically. Just a broken-down, deserted farmhouse. Impossible to imagine now, even with the help of the photographs. Later we were joined by Madame herself. To this day she cannot explain entirely what it was that attracted her to a virtual ruin, and persuaded her to restore it and make it into a little gem of a country hotel.

Her taste and personality are reflected everywhere—in the olive-

OPPOSITE Clinking coffee cups, tinkling wine glasses and muted conversation in the green shade of the terrace.

Upper left: The lounge with the little bar in the corner. Fifteen years ago it was a broken-down abandoned farmhouse. *Center left:* The dining room. The lamp shades are made from banana leaves; the ashtrays are made

for the house. *Lower left:* Every bedroom has its private garden. Fresh iced water, fruit and flowers are provided as a matter of course. So are the books. *Above:* Marité Saucourt. "C'est pour l'amour des choses bien faites."

wood furniture and rattan chairs, in the Picasso and Braque lithographs, in the tiny stone bar in the corner of the sitting room, in the lampshades in the dining room, made by Marité herself from banana-tree bark.

If you press her further about her motives she will probably reply: *"c'est pour l'amour des choses bien faîtes."* It is a point of view that finds expression in every aspect of her work.

The Mas des Serres has six bedrooms, all of them different and all named, with one exception, after the flowers which the designer Paule Marrot chose as subjects for her designs—Jacinthes, Margeurites, Guermantes, Gais Soucis, Tournesols and Acacias. Every room has its own private garden hung about with sweet-scented flowers and in every one guests will find bottled water, fruit, flowers and shelves of books in all languages. Everything has been carefully chosen to make you feel you are staying with rather good people in the country. Everything fits. Even the ashtrays are made specially for the house.

It's worth staying a night just for the breakfast, so they tell me, with the four little pots of homemade jam and honey, the pat of butter on a single vine leaf and the passport wrapped in a napkin.

This time it was not to be. "But you can come to dinner," she said, more as a statement of fact than a question. And so we returned happily the following night.

Dinner, like lunch, is taken on the terrace whenever possible, to the accompaniment of the crickets and tree frogs.

The great thing about the food at the Mas is that Marité has more or less ignored Provençal dishes ("You can get that anywhere round here," she explains) in favor of things like *boudin paysan du Limousin fourré au chataignes et pommes fruit,* and *gibellotte de lapereau* (wild rabbit) *à l'estragon et aux nouilles fraiches.* Once again, enormous care and attention is paid to detail. With your order of *les trois terrines et pâtés de la maison* come instructions from your waiter as to the order of ascending flavour in which they should be eaten.

As for the rabbit, did I prefer to kick off with a shoulder or a leg, so that they would know which piece to put back in the oven? It is carefully explained also that the chutney for the chicken curry is home-made from melon, plum, mango and papaya. The *salade de mesclun* really does come from the garden and the Château Grand Picque Caillou 1971 is Marité's personal discovery.

And so the evening progresses, delight after delight: *fromage frais* and *yaourts faits á la maison,* wild honey ice cream, coffee in little individual pots—and at the end of it all, Madame joins you at your table for coffee, brandy and a little light badinage.

I have absolutely promised to return next year. I must, if only to find out if it's true what they say about those breakfasts. I only hope I remember to book early enough. Some American clients had written in May to reserve a table for the following August 23rd. Just to be on the safe side.

SHARROW BAY
ULLSWATER, ENGLAND

OPPOSITE It all began with £500, a red setter bitch and a suitcase with a kettle tied to the outside.

Of all things, it was the lights that struck me most. We had had a tiring drive from Scotland. Motorways, while undoubtedly reducing the time taken over journeys, have their own special ways of taking it out of you—the need for constant attention, crosswinds, noise—so that by the time we had pulled off the M6 at the Penrith junction and begun to relax a little along the winding, tree-lined, comparatively empty road to Pooley Bridge and Lake Ullswater, we were keenly looking forward to a welcoming end to three or so hours of nerve-wracking motoring. The sight of the distant mauve hills, very reminiscent of the Highlands we had only recently left behind, and, very soon, of the calm flat expanse of Lake Ullswater, the second largest of the lakes in the Lake District, could hardly have failed to induce in us a sense of peace and tranquillity. But it was not until we had finally turned into the gateway, some two miles along a narrow lakeside road the other side of Pooley Bridge, that we were able to feel that our journey was over. Between the stone gateposts, past the little lodge on our right just inside, then on down a long drive, lit every ten yards or so by little lanterns, past a field of cows on our left, then round a final bend and down a short slope and we were at the front door of the hotel, right on the water's edge.

I said at the beginning that it was the lights that struck me most, but in fact that was after the young man in the white coat, who at the time was busily struggling with luggage belonging to two other recent arrivals, had stopped to greet us, to ask if there was anything he could carry for us, and to wave us in the direction of the front door. It was a promising start. I did notice, I remember, the two stone cherubs that sat on either side of the door dangling bunches of grapes, as well as the doll on the chair just inside, and the Victorian dried-flower arrangement covered with a glass dome. But then we were through the second door into a small sitting room, and it was at that stage that I remember being particularly struck by the fact that every single lamp in the room, and there must have been seven or eight of them, was on.

It is perhaps some measure of the indifference with which one is received into the majority of hotels, both large and small, that the mere fact of switching on all the lights in the main reception room should have struck me as anything out of the ordinary. Certainly the owners of Sharrow Bay, Francis Coulson and Brian Sack, would be astonished at my astonishment. Their aim in life is and always has been to welcome visitors and make them feel at home. And since there is no more welcoming sight for a weary traveler than a brightly lit room with lots of comfortable chairs to sit in and a great number of pieces of china and glass and copper and flower arrangements to look at while he recovers his breath over a tray of tea and cakes, then it goes without saying that that is the least they can provide.

Being the excessively generous people they are, however, the least could never be enough. Thus, when we had finally summoned

enough strength to totter up to our room, we found not only the most charming decorations (soft pink carpeting, good antique furniture, pretty curtains), and all the lights blazing, but also a couple of welcoming glasses of sherry, a small selection of books, a portable radio, a hair dryer, a Scrabble set *and* a dictionary, and everywhere, everywhere, flowers.

It was with a sense of deep contentment, tinged with just a dash of bemusement and slight disbelief, that we unpacked, bathed and changed in preparation for dinner.

Dinner is the social highlight of the day at Sharrow Bay. The Lake District being one of the best areas in Britain for walking and touring, most guests prefer to set off for the day after breakfast with one of the hotel's prodigious packed lunches, rather than waste precious time coming back for lunch. Breakfast, although undoubtedly a gastronomic event attended fully and enthusiastically by the entire guest list (and with the prospect of a plate of eggs and bacon, Sharrow-style, who can blame them?), tends to be something of a silent, dead-pan affair. So it is not until the evening that guests, exuberant after yet another day's exploration of the lakes and mountains, and anxious to compare notes about each other's discoveries, really come together for the first time. Then the hotel is at its liveliest.

Not wishing to encourage the casual passer-by to drop in for a quick one, thus destroying the essential privacy of the place, the hotel has no bar and only a table licence. The result is that before

dinner the two sitting rooms rather take on the air of doctors' waiting rooms, with every chair occupied by guests sipping gins and tonics and dry sherries which have been brought to them by a waiter, leafing through magazines or murmuring together, all eyes fixed firmly on the door in eager anticipation of the moment when the little gong will sound, at which they all leap to their feet and hurry into the two dining rooms to eat. Unpunctuality, one feels, will not be overlooked.

But I suppose that anyone who has taken the trouble to produce food of the variety and ingenuity with which one is then confronted could be forgiven for worrying slightly about guests who do not seem to be taking one's efforts as seriously as one might wish. The night we stayed, for example, the dinner menu consisted of just the twenty-one different sorts of first course, including carrot and orange soup, peach in cream curry sauce, and chicken livers cooked in cream with mushrooms and marjoram; then *sole en croûte* with Mornay sauce, followed by a choice of roast lamb, roast wild duck, roast pheasant or *allumette de boeuf*, ending up with fresh fruit Pavlova, chocolate and brandy cream roulade, vanilla Bavarois, gâteau Alcazar, cherry cream cheesecake, cheese, coffee and *petits fours*. The wine was a Vosne Romanée 1970 from Louis Latour, and absolutely delicious it was too.

After a meal like that it seems churlish to complain about anything, and certainly not the generosity of the helpings. Francis Coulson, I know, is a great believer in the importance of presentation. He has always prided himself on being something of an artist in the

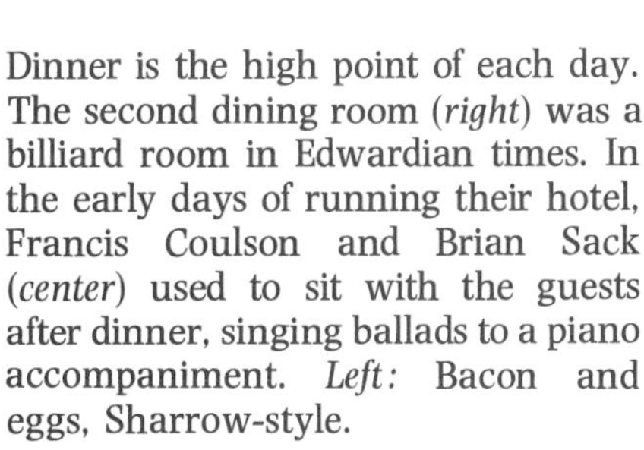

Dinner is the high point of each day. The second dining room (*right*) was a billiard room in Edwardian times. In the early days of running their hotel, Francis Coulson and Brian Sack (*center*) used to sit with the guests after dinner, singing ballads to a piano accompaniment. *Left:* Bacon and eggs, Sharrow-style.

way he arranges the food on the plate, and Brian Sack speaks admiringly of his partner's love of "painting with food." Thus a plate of roast pheasant is served with no fewer than ten different items: the meat itself, roast potatoes, half a tomato with a sprig of parsley on top, breadcrumbs, game chips, a lettuce leaf, mustard and cress, bacon, peas, and braised celery. And that is before one has even begun to tackle the matter of vegetables: cabbage, more potatoes, cauliflower, zucchini and swedes. It is hard to avoid feeling, even before one has begun eating, that one is more of a glutton than one realized. And as for afterwards. . . .

But then, to be fair, we had spent most of the day sitting in a car, unlike the majority of the guests who, I imagine, had had the benefit at least of the exhilaration of looking at some of the finest mountain scenery in Britain and enough fresh air to guarantee a healthy and well-deserved appetite.

The Lake District, quite apart from its obvious attractions for walkers and climbers, is also, of course, famous for its literary associations.

One of its most famous authors was Beatrix Potter, who, after her amazing success with her children's stories, lived quietly at Sawrey with her second husband, a solicitor from Hawkshead, and became one of the most successful sheep breeders in the whole area. One person who remembered her well is Mrs. Ruddick, a charming and extremely well-read lady who, after the death of her husband, offered to help Coulson and Sack in the hotel and is now one of the cornerstones of the establishment, performing every possible task from receptionist to sommelier. As a child she used to go to tea with the old lady at Sawrey. It can't have been an altogether easy experience since Miss Potter really did not care for small children at all, and could only tolerate them when they sat still in a corner without uttering a word.

But the literary figure with whom the Lake District is most closely associated is Wordsworth. He was born at Cockermouth, lived for many years with his sister Dorothy at Dove Cottage in Grasmere, and derived much of his inspiration from his awesome surroundings.

In fact it was at Ullswater, not far from Sharrow Bay, that he was wandering lonely as a cloud that floats on high o'er vales and hills, when all at once he saw the crowd, the famous host of golden daffodils. And in your hotel room you will find, as likely as not, a copy of Dorothy Wordsworth's journal on your bedside table.

One of Coulson and Sack's favorite guests is the great Australian soprano Joan Sutherland. They once decided to honor her, as her fellow countrywoman Dame Nellie Melba had been honored many years previously by the Savoy, with a special dish. It remains to be seen whether *Joan Sutherland Bavarois* goes down in gastronomic history in the same way as *Pêche Melba.* All we do know is that Miss Sutherland was delighted with it. When the boys brought it all the way from the Sharrow Bay and presented it to her in her dressing

The lounge overlooking Ullswater. *Top:* Pre-dinner drinks. *Bottom:* Tea is served.

room at Covent Garden shortly before the curtain went up, instead of taking a small mouthful and politely declaring her appreciation, she ate the whole thing and then went on stage to give one of the best performances of her career.

The story of Sharrow Bay is full of romantic, dramatic tales, but none can quite compare with the one about how it all began in the first place.

It was in 1948 that Francis Coulson saw an advertisement in the *Manchester Guardian* for a rather ugly Victorian house on the edge of Ullswater. For some time he had been nursing an ambition to run a hotel, thought it sounded promising and hurried up to have a look. The two old ladies who owned the house invited him to stay with them and they quickly decided that he was just the person to whom they would feel happy selling their home. And so it was that soon after that, with only £500 in the bank, a red setter bitch called Peggy for a companion, a suitcase with a kettle tied on the outside and great determination, Coulson moved into the house. For a while he slept on the floor, but gradually over the next few months, by dint of enormous hard work, he succeeded in making the place sufficiently habitable that by Easter 1949 he was able to welcome his first guests to Sharrow Bay. According to Brian Sack, who joined him three years later, almost everything went wrong in those early days. On the very first night the cook broke her arm, and for a long time such money as Coulson did make came from the huge quantities of teas that he served every afternoon to casual passers-by. Fortunately, however, he was blessed with three great gifts. One was that he was a natural homemaker; he knew instinctively how to arrange a room so that it looked its most attractive. "Give Francis one piece and an empty room and he'd know at once the right place to put it," says Sack. The second gift was a love, born of a Lancashire upbringing, of good food. The third was an absolutely genuine desire to welcome people into his home and give them everything that he possibly could to make them happy.

Brian Sack, who was trained as a chartered surveyor but had always wanted to be in the hotel business, heard about Sharrow in the summer of 1952. He arrived, thought the place "absolutely devastatingly beautiful," found that he and Coulson shared a common belief in what made a very good hotel, and they have been together ever since.

They must have had great fun in those early days, baking madly every day for teas, sitting round the piano after dinner with the guests singing Victorian ballads, and afterwards preparing hot drinks for everyone.

Despite its strikingly Victorian appearance, the house is basically a three-hundred-year-old cottage onto which a number of additions were made—the first being the present frontage in 1840 and the last being the billiard room which was built on in Edwardian times and is now the second dining room. In keeping with the Victorians' horror of empty spaces, Coulson and Sack, who both suffer from an incurable desire to purchase almost anything that takes their fancy, have filled every available bit of space with more items than you would believe it possible to fit into one house: porcelain, table lamps of all shapes and sizes, pots of flowers, bits of copper and brass, candelabra, dolls, gilt mirrors, gilt wall lamps and, above all, cherubs. Cherubs reclining, cherubs flying across the wall, cherubs suspended from the ceiling, cherubs in the heavy wallpaper design.

On one table alone in the dining room I counted a Foinisetti duck, two bronze and ormolu candelabra, a vase of crysanthemums, a Georgian commemorative mug, a pair of green Dresden figures, a bronze candlestick, a silver tobacco jar and an Italian gilt cherub.

The bedrooms, which all have Victorian names like Abigail, Phoebe, Charlotte, Hermione, Simplicity, and Charity are, on the whole, a good deal less cluttered. They come as something of a relief after the richness of the downstairs rooms—rather like a plain omelette after a week of Cordon Bleu cooking. Coulson and Sack themselves are the first to admit that they ought to think about throwing out some of the furniture and decorations. But of course if they did, and if they were to cut down on the elaborate food, or change the pink carpets for blue, or take the Scrabble sets out of the bedrooms, or start economizing on the lighting, then it wouldn't be Sharrow Bay any more. And anyway, I cannot imagine either of them having the heart to chuck anything away.

Above: "A rather ugly Victorian house on the edge of Ullswater." *Left:* Cat posing with one of the many cherubs. *Right:* The annex.

TRESANTON
ST. MAWES, ENGLAND

OPPOSITE THE HOTEL Tresanton, on the other side of the bay, stands one of the very few lighthouses in history to have changed sex.

In the eighteenth century it was known as St. Anthony's Lighthouse (which is how Tresanton first came to get its name, the ubiquitous Cornish prefix Tre- meaning house or dwelling).

Then, for reasons which are obscure, and upon which I shall not even begin to speculate, the name of the lighthouse was changed to St. Anne's.

Stand on the hill above it, as I did on a clean September morning last year with a brisk wind keeping the lowering black clouds at bay, and you have before you the best view possible of that section of the Cornish coastline. Away to the left is the old shipping town of Falmouth, its docksides bristling with cranes that stand at all angles like stick insects. Further to the right, a clutch of sailing dinghies seems to be guarding the little village of St. Just-in-Roseland, out of sight around the corner. And directly before you, extending for a mile or so to your right, shining brightly in the September sun, lies St. Mawes. A jumble of houses, cottages, hotels, pubs, piled one on top of the other up the steep hillside, and supported by a solid-looking wall beneath which huge gulls, white and speckled-brown, sit dozing on the seaweed-covered rocks.

It is as difficult to distinguish Tresanton from that distance as it is easy to drive straight past the front door when you first arrive. The hotel is as much a jumble as the rest of the village, consisting as it does of three different buildings of varying shapes and sizes and all situated at different levels.

The original house is a long, low eighteenth-century building with white walls and pale blue window frames. It sits overlooking not only the narrowest section of the main street of St. Mawes but arguably one of the narrowest main streets anywhere in Britain. Parking your car nervously you make your way through a small arch, past a little sign saying "We do not serve tea to non-residents" and along a tiny, flagstone path until, with luck, you find a sign saying "Entrance." If, like me, you fail to do this, you will almost certainly find yourself turning sharp left and climbing some stone stairs, past the bar and on up until you are standing in a most lovely terrace full of flowers and shrubs and plants in tubs and more steps leading down on to a smaller terrace, which in turn looks out over the main street and the bay toward St. Anne's Lighthouse. Behind you is Avalon, the second house that makes up the main part of Tresanton. The third house, Anchorage, is two doors farther along the street. If you have not yet had the distinct feeling that you are in someone's private home, you will certainly have it the moment you walk into Avalon and find yourself face to face with a small Corot.

On the whole, this is not something that happens often in small country hotels. If it did, one cannot help feeling the picture would be

OPPOSITE Standing on a terrace full of flowers and shrubs and plants in tubs, looking out over the main street and the bay.

given a rather more ostentatious setting than just inside the front door. At Tresanton, however, such considerations are unimportant. Like the Chippendale scenes on the wall in the bar, that is where the owner put the painting when he first bought it, and that is where he wanted it to stay. The owner in question, the man who created Tresanton over thirty years ago, was an extraordinary figure by the name of Jack Silley. He had been born in the East End of London, done well for himself, and ended up by owning the Falmouth Docks. At one stage in his career he had also owned the Saville Theatre in London, and had sold it for a million pounds which he managed to spend in a year . . . but that's another story. He loved Cornwall, but being unable to find a hotel in the area that pleased him, he bought himself a nice little house called Tresanton. That was in 1944.

Being a gregarious sort of fellow, he soon began inviting his pals down to stay; they in their turn would ask if they could borrow the place when he was not in residence. At that time there were only three rooms in the house, which was supervised by a housekeeper and, as one man who has known Tresanton from the start explained to me, the whole place was run rather on the lines of an army officers' mess: people simply wrote down in a book whatever they wanted in the way of food or drink and when they left, they also made a note of what they had consumed.

In 1947 Silley bought the three cottages just above the hotel with a view to extending the premises. Unfortunately, that same year, there was a fire and all three were destroyed. Before long, however, he had rebuilt the house in a style that was thoroughly in keeping with Tresanton, and began to fill it with fine pictures and furniture. He had a great passion for ceramics, and guests who were around in those early days remember how packing cases were forever arriving filled with beautiful pieces of china, as well as pictures, furniture and goodness knows what else.

Often Silley himself was not fully aware of the real value of the things he bought. Only last year Mrs. Oliver, the hotel's present owner, was somewhat surprised when Arthur Negus, the well-known antiques connoisseur, who happened to be staying in the hotel, congratulated her on the quality of what had always been considered a very ordinary chest of drawers.

Silley loved Cornwall and he loved Tresanton. It was not so much a business for him as a hobby, and the enthusiasm with which he ran the hotel infected everyone who stayed there. It was more like a permanent country house party than a hotel, and guests returned regularly at the same time every year in order to ensure that they would be there at the same time as their friends.

Jack Silley was killed in an air crash in 1973. But his spirit lived on in Tresanton, and the atmosphere remains today very much what it was when he was there. That the tradition should have continued unbroken in this way is due largely to Yvette Oliver, a young woman who has been with the hotel from the beginning, and is now herself

Far right: Tresanton is a long, low eighteenth-century building with white walls and pale blue window panes. In atmosphere it is more like a private country house (*top left*) than a hotel; every bedside table (*center left*) has a tin of biscuits and a flashlight.

the proprietor. With much help, both moral and financial, from a faithful band of old Tresanton hands, Mrs. Oliver has succeeded in running Tresanton just as Jack Silley had run it. She keeps it small and homely, maintaining the standard of food and service in the dining room, and above all paying constant attention to tiny details—things like the umbrella behind the door in every room in Tresanton and the Anchorage, for use on the way to the bar and the dining room; the small flashlight and the tin of biscuits on every bedside table; and the unfailingly helpful porter who appears to spend a considerable part of each day tearing up and down to a parking spot up above the hotel, fetching and returning people's motor cars.

There are many other things besides that to add to the country house atmosphere: the huge teas that are laid out every day, the sensational bread-and-butter pudding for a taste of which people have been known to cross continents, the coffee on the sideboard in the sitting room after lunch and dinner, the warmth of the fire in the big open grate, a barman whose talent for mixing drinks is exceeded only by a quite astonishing skill in flower-arranging, and the bar itself—where everyone in the house, plus two tortoises, gather every night before dinner to swap stories of the day's activities.

And if, by chance, you should come back with a couple of nice fat sea bass you have picked up on a fishing trip, the chef will be only too happy to cook them for you for dinner.

Marvelous New Ones

THE BERKELEY
LONDON, ENGLAND

OPPOSITE One of the Gibbons cherubs in the Lutyens Writing Room.

OF ALL THE hotels in London, I doubt if there is one that arouses quite such strong feelings of affection and nostalgia in quite so many people as the Berkeley. I am talking now about the old Berkeley—the one that stood for years on the corner of Piccadilly and Berkeley Street until it was pulled down about five years ago to make way for the Bristol—and not to its splendid successor down the road in Knightsbridge. For in order to understand what sort of hotel the new Berkeley is, and how it came about in the first place, it is important to have some idea of what the old place was like.

The story of the Berkeley really begins, for our purposes at any rate, at a party given in 1901 by the Savoy Hotel Company to launch Claridge's, which they had recently acquired. One of the guests was a young man by the name of George Reeves-Smith. managing director of the small, comparatively unknown Berkeley. Upon being introduced to him, Richard D'Oyly Carte, the founder of the Savoy, who had recently lost César Ritz to the Carlton and was very much in need of someone to take his place, knew immediately that he had found his man. The only drawback was that Reeves-Smith had a contract with the Berkeley that he did not wish to break. D'Oyly Carte pursued the only course of action possible under the circumstances: he bought the Berkeley, Reeves-Smith and all. Although Reeves-Smith moved his office to the Savoy, he continued to live at the Berkeley, which, under his guidance, quickly began to acquire the very special character it was to maintain until the day it was pulled down some seventy years later.

If there was one feature for which the Berkeley was known more than for any other it was its restaurant. Even before the First World War, the Berkeley Restaurant was one of the most popular and fashionable meeting places in town for the young and well-to-do.

Its success was undoubtedly due to a large extent to the fact that it was one of the few places in London a chap could take his girlfriend for a spot of dinner and dancing, completely unchaperoned.

Night after night the little Berkeley Restaurant with its funny, old-fashioned décor and its little round dance floor was packed with breathless debutantes and their attendant "Deb's Delights"—actors

and socialites, racing drivers and peers of the realm, race-horse trainers and politicians, and the ubiquitous, inevitable Prince of Wales—later Edward VIII.

The Berkeley Restaurant was equally popular at lunchtime with debutantes and their mothers, up to town for a spot of shopping, and with that now apparently extinct breed of Englishman, the Man About Town. I am not sure that I ever met one of them face to face, but I always pictured them as looking somewhat like P. G. Wodehouse's Bertie Wooster, toddling in to the Berkeley to toy with some fish.

But although the dance bands and the cabaret were undoubtedly a big attraction, it was as much to see Mr. Ferraro as anyone else that the young, and not so young, flocked to the Berkeley in the years between the wars. Filippo Ferraro was manager of the Berkeley Restaurant from 1922 to 1939 and from all accounts he must have been an extraordinary man.

It was at the Savoy Grill, where he was assistant to the great Sovrani, that he began to acquire his following; and when he moved to the Berkeley in 1922 many of his old clients moved there with him. He had been very impressed by the hand-written menus he had seen in the top Parisian restaurants, and not only introduced the idea to the Berkeley but even took to discussing a meal with guests and *then* writing out the menu they had chosen so they might have the pleasure of contemplating it while they waited. It was this extraordinary brand of personal service more than anything else that gave the Berkeley Restaurant its name.

Ferraro always tried to make the food he served as seasonal as possible. During the summer there would always be plenty of sea food and salads on the menu, while in the winter months, not only would the frozen guest be confronted with piping hot stews and curries, but even the color of the light bulbs and the upholstery were changed to produce a warm, cosy atmosphere.

The Berkeley Restaurant can also claim to be the first in London to be air-conditioned in summer—thanks again to Ferraro, who simply placed a huge lump of ice on a tray in the middle of the room (suitably disguised with flowers, needless to say) and turned a fan on it.

In addition to all these qualities, Ferraro had a reputation for being a very kind man, and it was his kindness that attracted many of his loyal clients. Women with debutante daughters always knew they could trust him to keep an eye on them and to assess the situation of the latest young man in tow.

His generosity knew no bounds. Often he would present young clients, whom he liked and knew to be hard up, with bills for half the true amount. The rest would come out of his own pocket.

He also took a close personal interest in their happiness and welfare. The Berkeley Restaurant was a great place for proposals of marriage, and there was one table—Number 29—that had a reputa-

PRECEDING PAGE *Clockwise from upper left-hand corner:* The Wilton Street entrance; lunch in Le Perroquet; the top-floor swimming pool; the entrance hall. ABOVE One of the suites.

tion for producing particularly happy results, largely because Ferraro gave this table only to young couples he thought genuinely suitable for each other. Needless to say it was Ferraro who looked after the Duke of York (later King George VI) the night he is believed to have become engaged to Lady Elizabeth Bowes-Lyon (now the Queen Mother). "A maître d'hôtel," Ferraro once said, "must be an actor, a magician, an ambassador, a ready reckoner and a psychologist."

The day he left to go to the Mayfair was a sad one in the history of the Berkeley.

Another great Berkeley figure was Gino Galbiati, Mr. Gino to his friends, who took over the restaurant in the fifties and was in many ways just as famous and popular to later generations of Berkeley regulars as his predecessor.

During the Second World War, the Berkeley opened a new bar. It was called the Perroquet and it attracted a large number of dashing young officers who used it as a meeting place while they were in town on leave.

Mr. Bonesi, who was general manager of the hotel during the thirties and forties, remembers them all well. "They were always in there," he told me once, his gravelly Italian voice cracking with pride; "the Guards officers, the boys home from the front, the Battle of Britain pilots, all the young bloods of society. I remember one night we had three new V.C.'s in at once. Ah, the champagne flowed that night, I can tell you."

Tea at the Berkeley was always very much a part of the London social scene in the old days, especially during the Season, when debs and their mammas would nip in for a breather before hurrying home to change for yet another cocktail party/dinner party/coming-out dance. So strong a center of debutante activity had the Berkeley become over the years that when, in 1953, the hotel thought up the idea of running its own Debutante Dress Show—a tea-party cum mannequin parade in aid of charity—the event was an instant success. Those heady days are, alas, now no more than a series of fond memories. All the same, a pale imitation of the old London Season does still take place between May and August every year, and one of the high spots, so I am assured, is still the Berkeley Debutante Dress Show.

Well, the Debutante Dress Show may be something of a relic from a byegone age, but the place in which it is held certainly is not. Nor is it a pale, modern imitation of its namesake. The new Berkeley is arguably the best and most elegant hotel to have been built in Europe since the war. And it has succeeded in incorporating so many of the characteristics of the old hotel and so much of its charm and atmosphere, that people who knew the Berkeley well have the feeling, when they walk into the new Berkeley, that they are coming back home. As Mr. Fornara, the general manager of the old Berkeley from 1955 and the man who helped with the move, put it to me: "We brought our soul from the old Berkeley; from the day I moved in here, I felt

I had lived here all my life. It is not so much a new hotel as a continuation of the old."

But why, you may very well ask, if you have not yet had a chance to see the new hotel for yourselves, was it necessary to move at all? The answer, quite simply, is that even Rolls-Royces reach a stage when they begin to show signs of wearing out, and the owner finds himself spending so much in spare parts to keep it going that finally he is faced with two possibilities: either put in a whole new engine and interior, or buy a new model.

It was soon after the end of the war that the Berkeley directors realized the old hotel had reached precisely that stage.

At first it was thought possible that the hotel might be rebuilt on the same site. However, not only would that have involved closing the business down for a number of years, but it was becoming clear that with more and more traffic pouring along Piccadilly and Berkeley Street every day, the Berkeley Hotel was never going to be the same as it had been anyway. Apart from anything else, it was becoming increasingly difficult for cars and taxis bringing guests to the front entrance to stop long enough even to allow their passengers to get out. One way and another the concept of the Berkeley as a private house was going to make less and less sense as the years went by. And so a search began for a completely new site.

On November 23, 1960, it was announced that the company had acquired a site of more than one acre in Knightsbridge, overlooking Hyde Park. Building began in the spring of 1968. The architect was Brian O'Rorke, a Royal Academician. On August 3, 1969, the old Berkeley closed its doors for the last time.

As Mr. Fornara explained, the business of moving out of one hotel and into another over a period of two and a half years had to be planned with all the care of a delicate military operation. The first task was to deploy those members of the staff who wished to stay on into Claridge's or the Savoy or Stone's Chop House or Simpson's-in-the-Strand. Some, like the chef, went abroad to gain useful experience.

As for the old Berkeley clients, it was proposed that they should stay at one of the hotels in the Savoy group for the same price that they had been paying at the Berkeley. It says something both for the hotel and the loyalty of its guests that when the new hotel was opened in February, 1972, only two out of all the old Berkeley regulars decided they were quite happy to stay on at Claridge's. The rest returned to their beloved Berkeley.

As the guests drew up outside the front entrance in Wilton Place, the only thing that told them it was a hotel at all were the words "The Berkeley," three or four inches high, carved into the pale Clipsham stone in which the entire hotel had been built.

Any doubt they might have been harboring by then would have been instantly dispelled the moment the door of their car was opened by one of the carriage attendants from the old hotel in his familiar fawn trousers, fawn topcoat with brown buttons, and brown derby.

In the front hall they would have felt they were in a magnificent private house rather than a hotel, what with the friendly log fire burning in the huge marble fireplace, the big leather armchairs, and the great bowls of daffodils and catkins. Glancing to their left, they would see something else to make them feel thoroughly at home: the famous Lutyens Writing Room, reconstructed exactly as it was in the old hotel with its pale gray paneling, carved cherubs and all.

In time they would doubtless have found more and more familiar features that had been rescued from the old Berkeley and incorporated into the new hotel: fireplaces, banisters, furniture, mirrors. . . .

In a marble corridor leading off from the hall is the one and only sign in the hotel. *To Le Perroquet*, it says. Not a bar this time but a restaurant, split into three levels—entrance, bar and dining room—each divided by water and sculptured glass sheets, with a ceiling of what look like inverted egg boxes, and at the far end a dance floor and discotheque.

The new Berkeley has another restaurant on the other side of the building and very good it is too, if you like rooms that are decorated entirely in lilac. Yet I have the feeling that it is in Le Perroquet more than in the restaurant that the atmosphere of the old Berkeley is most nearly captured.

Walk into the Perroquet at lunchtime any day of the week and you will find a very English, rather young and on the whole upper-middle-class clientele: young businessmen in good suits and Gucci shoes drinking Campari and soda; mothers talking earnestly with their daughters; young wives and mothers in Dior scarves and Jaeger skirts, up from the country for a day's shopping, popping in for a spot of lunch and a quick natter with their friends before moving on to Harrods and Peter Jones and thence home to their manor houses in the Cotswolds.

There is so much to talk about in the new Berkeley that it would take an entire issue of *Architectural Review* to do full justice to it all—to the pink and gray ballroom with its marble and chrome columns, and its chandeliers like melting icicles hanging from the mirrored ceiling; to the lobby of the ballroom entrance, like a striped tent at an Oxford Commemoration Ball; to the light, bright bedrooms with their white wickerwork headboards and enormous marble bathrooms; to the twenty-five suites, each one of which is decorated in a different style; to the spacious seventh-floor studio rooms with their terraces and views over Hyde Park and Knightsbridge; to the swimming pool on the top floor with its roof that opens in the warm weather; to the carpet in the corridors that was made specially in Bayeux, as well as to the numberless examples of British craftsmanship at its best. One room I am particularly fond of (and here the Queen and I have something in common, for it is reputed to be her favorite too) is the Tattersall Room, built to commemorate the foundation of Tattersalls, the famous bloodstock agency, in premises only yards away from the Berkeley. The theme of the room is, needless to say, equine. On

the walls hang portraits of such great nags as Orville and Phosphorus and Highflyer; an old print depicting the famous scene of the Flying Dutchman beating Voltigeur in the Great Match at York in 1851; and an old bas-relief of the Norfolk Gelding Golden Reaper, winner of three consecutive races at Barham Downs in June, 1804. No wonder Her Majesty feels so much at home in these surroundings. Having said which, it is well known that the first time the reigning English monarch was known to eat in a public restaurant was one day when the Queen, quite unannounced, walked into the restaurant of the new Berkeley with some friends, sat down and had lunch. From all accounts she very much enjoyed the experience and has been back several times since. I do not believe it is just because of the impeccable service upon which the Berkeley, quite rightly, prides itself, nor just because of the food, nor yet because it is so conveniently near the Palace that she enjoys coming there. I bet that this is about the only hotel in London where she can walk in with a few friends for lunch and no one behaves as though anything extraordinary has happened. And really, in a way, that says more about the new Berkeley than anything.

Top left: The ornamental gates at the entrance to the restaurant. *Center left:* A detail from the restaurant. *Bottom left:* This mirror in the lounge came from Windsor Castle. *Top and center right:* Two details from Le Perroquet. *Far right:* The Tattersall Room, said to be the Queen's favorite.

California
Streets

STANFORD COURT
SAN FRANCISCO, U.S.A.

JAMES NASSIKAS, PRESIDENT and general manager of the Stanford Court Hotel, is very fond of quoting these lines from an article written by the *New York Times* architecture critic, Mrs. Ada Louise Huxtable:

> I never approach a trip requiring an overnight stay without a sinking heart. It's not that I won't be reasonably comfortable . . . basic things like beds and ice and Coke machines are the preoccupation of the American hospitality industry. It's that I will be so depressed. It is not the impersonality or anonymity of a hotel room . . . it is that one is forced into a banal, standardized, multi-billion-dollar world of bad colors, bad fabrics, bad prints, bad pictures, bad furniture, bad lamps, bad ice buckets, and bad wastebaskets of such totally uniform and cheap consistency of taste and manufacture that borax would be an exhilarating change of pace.

He is fond of quoting these lines because they put into words everything that he deplores about the vast majority of hotels throughout the United States and, I daresay he would argue, throughout the world. How is it possible, he asks, for a great or even a good hotel to be created by a committee? "All committees can do is to check out what has been proved successful in the past and repeat it. For over two decades now a wedge has been driven between the professional architect who is designing or renovating a hotel and the professional hotel administrator who is going to have to operate the hotel." And it has been his life's ambition ever since he left the Hotel School in Lausanne twenty years ago to be a professional hotelier who "would not have to become a member of a committee and who could take risks in making the kinds of decisions which enable the participating consultants to design a hotel with individuality and character."

Which is all very well, but how many hoteliers ever get the opportunity to build and run their perfect hotel?

Well, Jim Nassikas for one. He was managing the Pontchartrain in New Orleans in the late sixties when he was approached by Edgar Stern, grandson of the founder of Sears Roebuck, with a project for buying up a swish apartment house. The building stood on the site of the old Leland Stanford Mansion on Nob Hill on the corner of Powell and California, the only point in the whole of San Francisco where the cable cars cross. Nassikas must have had difficulty believing his own ears when Stern put the proposition to him: he, Stern, would provide the money, and Jim Nassikas would be responsible for the creation of the finest hotel possible.

The job began in 1969 with the total demolition of the interior of the building.

Nassikas's first object was, as he put it later, "to bring San Francisco to San Francisco . . . by giving the hotel a sense of place." This is something he feels is rarely captured in American hotels. "How many times have you stood in the lobby of a hotel in Chicago

OPPOSITE The hotel was created out of an apartment house that stood on the site of the old Leland Stanford mansion on Nob Hill.

Fournou's
ovens
BAR &
RESTAURANT

Clockwise, from upper left-hand corner: The covered forecourt is reminiscent of the old days of the Palace Hotel; Fournou's Ovens, the splendid hotel restaurant; Chef Marcel Dragon, standing at the oven with one of the long sticks he uses to manipulate the various roasting meats; this clock near the reception desk was a personal gift from Napoleon to one of his generals; the Stanford Court does not go in for big, flashy showcases; one of the beautifully designed suites; part of the entrance hall.

and felt you could just as easily be in Cleveland or Detroit or Kansas City? How many hotel rooms have you found yourself in in the United States where you have to look at the book of matches to be sure of which hotel you're in?"

In the face of such widespread uniformity, the very idea of keeping the low eight-story building (which San Franciscans had known and loved for years) was in itself something of a hotel revolution. In addition, the construction of a great stained-glass canopy over the open court of the old building and the building of a fountain in the middle, reminded guests of the old days of the Palace Hotel, when its glass-enclosed court rang to the sound of horses' hooves and carriage wheels.

Nassikas's second aim was to create a hotel that in no respect reminded a guest of anything he had ever seen or experienced in a chain hotel. So, the first thing he notices as he enters the lobby is that there are no signs telling where he should go to check in, have a meal, spend a penny or make a telephone call. He will also observe that no matter how busy the hotel is, there is a marked lack of noise or raised voices, and that paging is done in the old-fashioned way by a page boy carrying the pagee's name on a board. There are a few shops, to be sure: a tobacconist, a newsagent, a beauty salon, a shirt-and-tie shop, a Scotsman called John Small who sells military accessories connected with the British army; but these are discreetly tucked away round the corner.

The newly arrived guest might also notice the rather fine French clock that stands near the reception desk, and if he looks more closely he will learn that it was a gift from Napoleon to General Comte Jean François Aimé Dejean, Ministre de la Guerre. As the assistant manager leads him toward the elevators across the Carrara marble floor he may be pleased, as I was when I first arrived, to notice that the floor of the elevator is also covered in the same marble. Along the small corridor that leads to his room he may pass some unusual antique Chinese prints. Nassikas is particularly proud of the various antiques he collected on his travels while the hotel was being built—many of which he found on Royal Street in New Orleans as well as in France and London.

At first sight the room appears to be modest, both in proportions and furnishings: a large double bed, some small armchairs round a simple white marble-topped table, a pleasant color scheme. Only with a slightly closer investigation do those little details, which provide that little bit of luxury and over which Mr. Nassikas pondered for so many hours, become evident: the television set hidden in the top of a rather fine cabinet, the pretty writing paper of various shapes and sizes, a sign by the telephone that points out that guests may make as many telephone calls as they wish within the San Francisco area free of charge, the large bar of scented soap *and* the neutral one in the immaculate marble bathroom, the second television set by the sink (Nassikas himself hates to miss a second of the *Today* program

Top: One of the double rooms, with the TV set tastefully concealed in the wardrobe. *Bottom:* The manager sees no reason that any of his guests should have to miss a second of the *Today* show.

when he is getting up in the mornings and sees no reason that his guests should either), the amusing little DO NOT DISTURB! and DISTURB! signs for hanging on the door, the fact that when you telephone room service, the person who picks up the phone knows your name without having to be told. . . .

As Nassikas reiterated to me later, "I was determined not to have anything that looked like anything anywhere else."

One part of the hotel that is certainly like no other that I have seen is the restaurant, Fournou's Ovens.

Time was when the reputations of the great hotels of the world were built on their restaurants. For years now, however, hotel restaurants have become less and less popular, and people going out for the evening have preferred independent restaurants. It was for this reason that Jim Nassikas determined to make *his* hotel restaurant compete with other top restaurants in the town by not mentioning it in the hotel publicity, by giving it a separate entrance on California Street and its own phone number, and, most important of all, by giving it a style that has no connection whatever with anything in the rest of the hotel.

Fournou's Ovens is built on two levels, on the lower of which are situated seven ovens—the largest one of which is called Fournou (which itself means oven in many languages) and six smaller ones. In these are roasted every night four marvelous dishes: roast rack of lamb with *saux aux aromates,* roast duckling with green peppercorn and kumquat sauce, roast fillet of beef with *sauce Perigourdine,* and roast chicken with *sauce morilles*. The whole operation is supervised by the chef Marcel Dragon, who must lose pounds every evening as he manipulates the various roasting meats with a long stick. Like everything else in the Stanford Court, Fournou's Ovens show what it is possible to achieve in a new hotel, given that the man responsible for designing it and running it has taste and imagination and, above all, cares that his guests should enjoy the best available. Good taste does not cost any more money, but it does cost a very great deal more time and energy and thought. The Stanford Court has 402 rooms with 34 suites, all different, all elegant, all as comfortable as one could wish.

Three years before the hotel was opened, Jim Nassikas bought a disused warehouse on the outskirts of the city in which he built four rooms, three bathrooms, and forty feet of full-scale corridor—just to make sure that when the real thing was made, even the switch on the bedside table light should be as conveniently placed as possible. As he put it, "If we in the hotel business would only spend sufficient time to look deep within ourselves we would find a vast storage of capability from which would flow the needed creative considerateness to meet our guests' needs in newer, diffierent and more innovative ways. We are, after all, a business of monumental magnificent trivialities."

GREAT RESORTS

BRENNER'S PARK
BADEN-BADEN, GERMANY

THE FIRST TIME I saw Brenner's Park-Hotel was in some of the early sequences of Joseph Losey's film, *The Romantic Englishwoman*. Some of you who saw the film too may, like me, have the opportunity to visit Baden-Baden and view these particular scenes from the film at first hand. Others may very well decide to go purely on the strength of the film alone, just as thousands of holiday makers every year head for Salzburg to see the locations for *The Sound of Music*, to Casablanca to hunt for Rick's Bar, or even—who knows?—to New York in the hope of catching a glimpse of Kojak tearing past, his teeth clamped round a lollipop, his hand round a beaker of coffee.

That is not to say, of course, that tens of thousands of people do not go to Salzburg for the Festival or to visit the birthplace of Mozart; or to New York for the shopping; or to Casablanca for . . . any number of reasons. The things that intrigue and excite people about cities or countries are as many and as various as those that intrigue them and draw them to hotels—historical associations, beauty of situation, marvelous restaurants, a package deal at the right price, friends nearby—anything you like to think of. But nothing seems to fascinate us all quite so much as the knowledge that our hotel (or seaside resort or alpine village) was once used as the setting for a feature film.

Few towns in Europe can boast a more glorious, glamorous, romantic history than Baden-Baden. The very mention of the name alone conjures up images of narrow streets thronged with all the nobility of Europe; of top hats and eyebrows being raised, and parasols and eyelashes being fluttered in return; of Edward VII in the casino losing his shirt, and Dostoievski his sanity; of music, elegance, beauty and wealth, gathered together from all corners of the world in this one little town on the edge of the Black Forest. Yet I confess quite unashamably that what fascinated me most of all about Brenner's Park and Baden-Baden was how the out-of-season atmosphere that Joseph Losey had succeeded in capturing in his film corresponded exactly to the atmosphere I found there the afternoon I arrived—damp, murky, slightly mysterious and infinitely sad. That a place could live up to my expectations so exactly filled me with an inexplicable sense of wonder and delight that has not quite worn off to this day.

OPPOSITE The hotel seen across the River Oos—damp, slightly mysterious and infinitely sad.

On the other hand, I should be the first to admit that, had Mr. Losey (or for that matter the author) chosen as his location a hotel with a less romantic history, situated in a less charming spot, my fascination at the place might well have been considerably less.

The story of Brenner's Park-Hotel began in 1872, when Anton Alois Brenner, a "garment-maker for the court" bought for 171,200 florins the Hotel Stephanie-les-Bains and its grounds. For two thousand years Baden-Baden had been famous throughout Europe for its thermal springs. Romans, recognizing the healing properties of the warm waters that spring from the Florentinerberg and contain ionized minerals and salt, were the first to build baths at their source. By the early nineteenth century, Baden-Baden had been discovered by the rich French who flocked there in such numbers that it soon became known as "le faubourg de Paris" and "La Ville d'été." And then suddenly, it was all over; in 1870 the most fabulous era in the history of Baden-Baden came to an abrupt end with the outbreak of the Franco-Prussian War. Had it not been for the efforts of Anton Brenner, and later his son Camille, to whom in 1883 he sold his hotel—now known as the Stephanienbad—it seems very likely that the fortunes of Baden-Baden would have declined disastrously. As it was, Camille Brenner quickly set about turning his hotel into an establishment of a quality high enough to attract such guests as the Grand Duke Michael and the Grand Duchess Olga of Russia, the Emperor Dom Pedro of Brazil, the Sultan of Lahore, the Maharajah of Kapurthala, and King Chulalonkorn of Siam.

On the whole, at this time, members of ruling houses preferred to be housed separately from the lesser mortals who had begun to patronize the grand hotels of Europe, and it was largely for their benefit that Brenner built two annexes to the hotel—the Villa Stephanie and the Villa Imperiale. In 1898 he purchased the property next door to his own, and two years later a five-story wing to the hotel was opened. From then on, more and more visitors, particularly Americans, began coming to Brenner's Stephanie-Hotel.

Emulating his friend César Ritz, who had for a while leased the hotel next door to the Stephanie, Brenner installed private bathrooms in all the rooms facing the gardens and the River Oos, as well as furnishing them with antique furniture, valuable rugs and good pictures.

In 1913 Brenner added a Grand Ballroom, and of course the hotel was equipped with all the latest technical conveniences: telephones in all the bedrooms, refrigeration, electric clocks, pneumatic posts—even its own electrical plant. He also anticipated the arrival of the motor car by building what were probably the first hotel garages to be seen in Europe, and organized elaborate outings for his guests into the nearby Black Forest.

In 1912 Brenner bought the Hotel Minerva (the one that Ritz had managed), tore it down, and in its place built the Sanatorium Stephanie—the first establishment of its kind in Europe to offer medical

attention and cures *and* all the conveniences of a first-class hotel.

But in 1914 Camille Brenner died of pneumonia while on holiday in Nizza. Then came the First World War, and it was not until 1919 that his son, Kurt Brenner, was able at last to put into practice some of the ideas he had been turning over in his mind for so many years.

The first thing he did was to convert the Sanatorium Stephanie into a 160-bed hotel, which he named Brenner's Park-Hotel. Five years later he acquired the little Villa Knorring which lay between the Stephanie-Hotel and the Park-Hotel. This villa, known today as the Park Villa, was rebuilt in 1924 as the Casino Stephanie and decorated in Japanese style by the artist and puppeteer, Ivo Puhonny. It was soon to become the hub of Baden-Baden social life in the 1920's.

It was only a matter of time before the whole thing blew itself up. In 1930 came the crash that was to put an end to full houses for ten years or more. Times were hard but not so hard that the rich and famous were unable to pay their annual visit to Baden-Baden—men like Henry Ford, W. L. Mellon, Carl Duisberg, William H. Vanderbilt, and John Jacob Astor, who wrote in the hotel guest book on October 4, 1932, "I can truthfully say that I have never liked any hotel better than Brenner's Kurhof"; the Rothschilds and the Thyssens; artists like Mary Pickford, Lillian Gish, Elizabeth Bergner, Yvonne Printemps, and Caruso; composers like Irving Berlin and Franz Lehar; politicians like Neville Chamberlain and Gustav Streseman. Princess Alexandra of Greece wrote warmly of her visit to Brenner's in 1932 and Gustav V of Sweden was to be found on the courts first thing every morning.

When war broke out again the hotels had to close since Baden-Baden was unfortunately in the area of military operations. In 1941, however, when the theater of war had moved away from the west, they were both able to open again. In the same year, knowing that the family on its own would never be able to keep the hotel going after the war, Kurt Brenner sold the majority of shares to the wealthy manufacturing family of Oetker.

But it was not until another fifteen years had passed that the hotel was in a position to carry on business in the normal way, let alone make money for its owners. In 1942 it found itself housing members of the American embassy in Berlin; from 1944–5, Vichy politicians used it as a temporary refuge; and the moment the war was over, all hotels in Baden-Baden were requisitioned by the Moroccan vanguard of the French army. For eleven miserable years the Stephanie-Hotel suffered the humiliation of being used as an office building. By the time it was finally handed back at the end of 1956, it was in such a bad state of repair that the Brenner corporation had no alternative but to sell it to the people who ran the baths and springs who in turn pulled it down and built in its place a modern Kongresshaus.

Certainly by the late fifties, tourism was beginning to be re-established all over the world as a major industry; but who wanted

to spend a fortnight in a little wooded town in southern Germany when for the same money, or less, they could be swanning about on the beaches of Spain or the Caribbean? Of course the rich and the exotic continued to come to Brenner's Park: Gulbenkian, the Windsors (naturally), Zsa Zsa Gabor, David Selznick, J. Paul Getty, who declared in the guest book in a moment of unwonted high spirits and a terribly shaky hand, "Brenner's Park is the top," the Kings of Greece and Denmark, Adenauer and de Gaulle, Rosalind Russell, Jean-Claude Brialy, the French actor who wrote poetically in the book, *"Quand j'étais enfant je passais devant le Brenner en rêvant, et voilà que je me suis reveillé dans une chambre au Brenner!!"* ("When I was a child I used to walk past Brenner's dreaming, and suddenly I have woken up in a room in Brenner's!!") Having had the experience myself, (only of waking up in a room there, you understand—not of walking past as a child), I appreciate Monsieur Brialy's sense of wonder and delight. If he had anything like the room I did (an enormous suite of rooms to be more exact—slightly larger in area, I should guess, than my apartment in London), with a balcony overlooking the park and the sound of the river Oos tinkling through my half-open window in the early-morning together with the rays of the sun, he must have wondered if he was still dreaming.

Of course, Brenner's Park-Hotel is not what it was; but then again, what is? Kurt Brenner's brother, Alfred, is still alive, but has taken no active part in the running of the hotel since Rudolph August Oetker assumed total control in 1959. Kurt Brenner himself died in 1953. When he was alive he lived like a king in Baden-Baden, driving through the narrow streets, waved on by policemen who invariably held up the traffic until he had passed by. In his own hotel he was a dictator. If he did not care for the look of a new guest, he told him the hotel was full; every evening before dinner he walked through the elegant pink-and-white drawing room warmly greeting old guests, being coldly polite to those who he did not know; he did not care much for young people. His arrogance toward them all knew no bounds. They say that one evening he paused at a guest's table on his way through the restaurant, tasted the unfortunate man's soup, decided it was not good enough and ordered it to be taken away from him forthwith and changed for something else. What he would have made of it all today—the publicity, the advertising, the glossy brochures, the conferences, the working with travel agents, the sales promotions, people like me writing about the hotel—all the usual hardware of modern hotel-keeping—I dare not imagine. When I asked his brother Alfred if he knew of any books in which the hotel was mentioned, he replied, "In my days we did not care about publicity."

No, Brenner's Park is certainly not what it was. But, my goodness, it is still a marvelous hotel. And I am not referring just to the grandness of it all—the huge bedrooms, the great corridors, the indoor swimming pool (without question the most beautiful I have ever seen in any hotel anywhere), the great carpet in the entrance hall to

the Red Room which was originally ordered by Hitler. (I can think of no other hotel to which the well-known maxim that luxury is space could be better applied.) I am thinking more of that attention to detail, those small touches that have disappeared from most hotels today—even some of the best—and that give one a small hint of what it must have been like once upon a time to stay in a place like Brenner's: the two types of shower in my bathroom, the long-handled shoe horn in my hallway, the little note in my sitting room that informed me that my maid's name was Elisabeth and my valet's Helmut, the fact that every time I used a towel it was automatically taken away and a clean one put in its place, the fact that the hotel will happily store your own special bed until your next visit, the fact that one rich guest still comes there in order to have his laundry done the way he likes it . . . things like that. And then, just occasionally, something big happens: a group of people arrive, an event takes place—for example, the famous Racing Week at the end of August—and suddenly the years slide away, and one has the impression that one might be looking at a scene that took place half a century ago. I remember one cold November morning, a year or so ago, walking out into the street for a breath of fresh air before breakfast. It was early, the sun had not yet risen over the mountains, the trees were still full of mist and there was no sound of cars. There, standing on the pavement and on the steps of the hotel, was a group of rich men about to set off for a day's hunting. They wore knee breeches and thick stockings and jackets with leather patches on the shoulders, and high-crowned trilby hats of the sort you often see in the Black Forest. They carried guns in leather cases, and as they stamped their feet and blew on their hands, their breath was white in the frosty air. Later a couple of big Mercedes and a Rolls Royce came and took them away, but just for those few brief moments, it was as though nothing had changed in the world for fifty years.

PRECEDING PAGE *Top:* The dining room. Kurt Brenner would sometimes forbid guests to eat what they had ordered. *Bottom:* One of the suites overlooking the gardens and the river. THIS PAGE *Top left:* Everything at Brenner's Park is rather special. *Top right:* A detail from the Park Villa next door to the hotel. In 1924 it was rebuilt in Japanese style and called the Casino Stephanie. *Center right:* A messenger boy on one of the hotel's delivery bicycles. *Bottom:* The recently completed indoor swimming pool with its Tuscan-brown walls is one of the most beautiful in the world.

THE BÜRGENSTOCK ESTATE
BÜRGENSTOCK, SWITZERLAND

The legendary private domain of Fritz Frey with its three hotels—the Grand on the left, the Palace in the middle and, next to it, the Park. Below, the Lake of Lucerne; in the distance, the town of Lucerne.

As a day for paying one's first visit to Bürgenstock—or for doing anything more enterprising than staying in bed with an apple and a good book—it could have been bettered. It was a stinker of the sort that only the Swiss and the Scots are capable of inflicting on innocent people. I had left Locarno only two hours earlier in bright sunshine, but for some reason by the time the train pulled into Lucerne station, a mist had descended over the lake and surrounding mountains, giving one the distinct impression of having stepped into a particularly gloomy Impressionist painting.

On the other hand, simply knowing that somewhere in the midst of that swirling grayness lurked massive peaks and towering rocks lent an air of mystery and adventure to what is normally nothing more than a forty-five-minute touristic jaunt by jolly steamer from Lucerne across to Kehrsiten, the little landing point for Bürgenstock. For the first twenty minutes or so, however hard one peered ahead, one could see nothing: the mist and the lake had joined together, and after a while one seemed to be chugging along in a ghastly limbo of gray nothingness. And then, suddenly, looming menacingly out of the mist was this enormous mountainside, wooded and steep, on the very top of which one could just make out the indistinct shapes of three buildings perched precariously on the very edge. This was the legendary Bürgenstock.

I do not doubt that the view of the hotels on a fine clear day is equally impressive. Yet somehow the weather that day, depressing though it was, had imbued the place with a mysterious grandeur that warm sunshine would dissipate along with the clouds.

This romantic feeling of inaccessibility was further heightened by the long ride up the mountain side on the funicular railway, through dripping woods and beneath clammy crags. In the end one had become so carried away by the wonder of it all that one's arrival at the little piazza, with its lawns and herbaceous borders and souvenir shop and restaurant and damp tourists in plastic raincoats, was bound to prove something of a disappointment.

At first, Bürgenstock is all rather muddling, consisting as it does of three hotels—the Grand, the Palace and the Park—plus a large swimming pool, various chalets tucked away in the trees, a golf club, restaurants, a night-club, roads, vegetable gardens, a church, office buildings and goodness knows what else. And all of it stretched out along the top of the mountain, looking down arrogantly—smugly almost—on the city of Lucerne way below.

Is this a hotel one has come to? A group of hotels? A resort? A private village, perhaps? Or, even more far-fetched, a privately owned canton, quite separate from the rest of Switzerland?

And then there are all the paintings—the Rubens and Snyders, the Breughel and the Tintoretto, the Boucher and the Northcote—with which the walls of the Grand and Palace Hotels are casually adorned; and the tapestries, and the fifteenth-century German wood carvings in the Gothic Chapel. And that extraordinary, vertiginous lift that carries you up the outside of the mountain—where does that come into it?

Luckily in my case, most of the questions were soon answered by the owner, Mr. Fritz Frey. Having pictured a small, dull Swiss gentleman in a light gray suit, it came as some surprise that the only gray things about him were his hair and his Rolls Royce. The slacks were fawn, the pullover green, the open-necked shirt checked and the loose raincoat shabby. Whether he really is as big as I remember him I am not sure; perhaps he is just the sort of man who gives you that impression of enormous size and power. Certainly I can recall being quite nervous of him when first he ushered me into his office, hurled himself into a swivel chair behind his desk (piled high with plans and scale models for the new complex he is planning) and told me the story of Bürgenstock.

At the same time as Niklaus Riggenbach was building the Rigi railway on the opposite shore of Lake Lucerne, a shepherd's son from Obwalden by the name of Joseph Bucher-Durrer, inspired by recent conquests of the Swiss Alps, decided to build a great hotel on the wooded ridge of the Bürgenberg. He set to, leveling the rock, constructing artificial terraces, and building a road from Stansstad to the top. Finally, on June 24, 1873, the hotel was opened. It was a magnificent luxury affair and he called it the Pension Bürgenstock. The hall was hung with silk tapestries originally intended for the salon of the Empress Eugénie in Paris, a touch that appealed to the upper middle classes of the time, who by now had become used to the idea of each new hotel being larger and more sumptuous than the last. Down in Lucerne, César Ritz had taken over the National Hotel with Escoffier as his chef, and they say that visitors would be quite content to stay there with their servants for three weeks at a time until rooms became vacant at Bürgenstock.

And thus it was that the legend of the green mountain began. In 1888 Bucher-Durrer opened the Park Hotel and, in 1904–5, the Palace. He also built the Bürg funicular railway and the astonishing Hammertschwand lift, which is reached by a most lovely woodland path round the side of the hill. Intrepid visitors can go to the very top of the mountain and look down on the truly fantastic view of the Bürgenstock, with Mount Pilatus behind and the lake and Lucerne away to the right.

Soon Bucher-Durrer had begun to create for himself a hotel empire consisting of the Grand Hotel de la Mediterranée at Pegli near Genoa, the Europe in Lucerne, the Grand and the Palace in Lugano, the Quirinal in Rome, the Euler in Basle, the Palace in Milan, the Palace in Lucerne and finally, in 1906, the Semiramis in Cairo. He died the same year, leaving behind not only his hotels but also power stations and funiculars and tramway systems in half the countries of Europe, a wood-processing plant in the Balkans, and the Stanserhorn railway.

Sadly, the First World War saw a great decline in the hotel

business, and when Friedrich Frey-Fürst, an electrical engineer from Lucerne, first came to the Bürgenstock in 1925, determined at any price to prevent the place falling into foreign hands, he found a ghost village and three hotels all in bad need of renovation. To this day Fritz Frey can remember vividly the sight they beheld on walking through the front door of the Grand Hotel.

> There were no pictures anywhere, the ceilings were covered with hideous frescoes, the corridor windows were of stained glass, wherever you looked there were potted plants and stuffed chamois and wicker chairs and plush curtains and stamped brass fittings. All the wiring was exposed, the rooms were freezing cold, without any running water, and there were very few bathrooms. The place had no style; it was a mixture of ponderous Victorianism, misconceived classicism, roccoco trimmings on the façades plus a dash of orientalism. There was no room service and no bar; the gardens were a mass of picturesque follies and mazes with romantic-sounding names. The general impression was of a convalescent home for the decadent sons of demented millionaires.

Frey-Fürst knew a great deal about electrical engineering and very little about hotels, but he was a man of enormous determination, imagination and energy, and before long he had completely modernized the Bürgenstock, its railways, its water and electricity plants. In 1928 he cleared a whole area of forest and built a golf course. He put in a beach down at Kehrsiten where the steamers put in (the cantonal boundary goes through the middle of it, and when the Nidwalden government put out a decree that no one in the canton should be allowed to wear bikinis, ladies who wished to sun bathe simply walked to the other end of the beach).

Nothing deterred Frey-Fürst once he had set his mind on something—not even the Wall Street crash. ("Well, in those days there were very few buyers for huge Rubenses and Snyders and Tintorettos, and he had somewhere to put them.") When local peasants refused to sell the man from town a piece of land he had his eye on, he sat down and milked a cow, and once they saw he was one of them they agreed to sell at once. He was a fearless man. Once during the war his car went off the road and crashed 150 feet to the rocks below, but he climbed out quite unhurt and walked home.

Friedrich Frey-Fürst died in 1953, leaving his son Fritz Frey to carry on the tradition he had established of constant renovation, creation and imagination, a task he has been pursuing with obsessive zeal ever since, and which has been made possible by the very fact that, with the family firm still very active in Lucerne, he can afford to plow any money he makes from the hotels straight back in again. "I have to keep going and spending money," he says, "because if I don't the whole thing will collapse. I have to fight against the tide of commercialism which has already washed over many once great

hotels, and so I have turned the Park over for conferences and so on, and I can afford to run the Palace and the Grand for people who appreciate peace and quiet in beautiful surroundings. How many other hotels can you name where you can eat a sandwich and drink a beer in front of a Rubens? And then of course I have a very good partner in the mountains. Everything is quite untouched, just as it has been for centuries. Have you noticed there's not a single new building in those meadows behind the hotel?" I had, and asked him why. He grinned. "I own the road," he said. "Up here I have one of the last genuinely feudal enterprises left in Europe where no one can interfere. There is no government money whatever in this place. You know, someone once compared Bürgenstock with a ship—funnily enough the mountain is shaped like the prow of a ship—and it's true we have everything here: our own bakery, our own sawmill, our own electricity, our own church, our own water, our own doctor, our own post office, our own roads. So you see, we don't need anybody or anything."

What sort of people, I ask him, eyeing a photograph on his desk of Sophia Loren hugging him in the snow, stay up at Bürgenstock?

"Famous people have stayed," he replied with a shrug; "film stars, businessmen, the man who assassinated Rasputin, the Queen of Spain, but I don't keep a guest book. I'm not impressed by famous names. One of the things about being a hotelier is that one no longer has any social ambitions. All that concerns me is that I should be seen as the host of a large, well-managed house where guests, famous and otherwise, are relieved of all their worries. All hoteliers in the future are going to have to come round to that way of thinking. Up here we run counter to all the modern trends of speed and short cuts. Hotels may try on brilliant stunts which will dazzle for a while, but in the long run they fail to satisfy, because the thing that counts in the end is quality."

He walked with me over to the Grand Hotel. The mist was beginning to lift, and all around us the peaks of the mountains were beginning to show through the clouds. Apart from the occasional clank of a cowbell down in the meadows there was silence.

Two pieces from the Bürgenstock art collection. *Top:* A decorative allegory by Jean-Baptiste van Loo. *Bottom:* An Italian-inspired Gobelin tapestry, c. 1700.

LE CAP ESTEL
EZE-BORD-DE-MER, FRANCE

It is perfectly possible to be biffing along the Corniche du Littoral from Beaulieu on your way to Monte Carlo and, without realizing it, sail gaily past what is arguably one of the best hotels on the south coast of France. Most people know Eze-Village, that once-magical medieval village perched on a rock just above the Moyenne Corniche which developers and restauranteurs and pseudo-art gallery owners and souvenir salesmen have turned into a trendy bit of nonsense. It is one of those sights that everyone who visits the Riviera for the first time feels compelled to go and see—hence its sad fate. But Eze-sur-Mer, the coastal village that lies more or less directly beneath Eze-Village, is less compelling—merely a collection of shops and villas to be driven through, with or without a traffic jam, on one's way to Monaco, Menton and the Italian border. Le Cap Estel is on the Beaulieu side of the village, and the reason it is so easily missable is that its entrance is on a rather tricky bend, with precipitous rocks towering on one side and a slightly less precipitous, though no less unnerving drop down to the sea on the other. The average foreign driver, for whom that road is never less than a nightmare at the best of times, finds he has better things to look out for than a plain white building on a little wooded promontory some sixty feet below, which, even if he looked very closely, he couldn't see particularly well anyway. But of course in a world in which everything is made as accessible as possible to everyone, there is nothing like a little inaccessibility to deter the average tourist and thus ensure a certain degree of privacy and exclusivity. That the present owners of the Cap Estel, the family Squarciafichi, are able to enjoy such rare advantages is due entirely to the flair, vision, persistence and not least the enormous personal wealth of a Russian Count named Stroganoff (of *boeuf* fame, one likes to think). It is he who was struck by the lunatic conviction that a bare, shapeless, and apparently useless lump of rock sticking out into the sea between Beaulieu and Monte Carlo could be transformed into the most wonderful garden on the whole coast.

The rock belonged to a Mr. Frank Harris, the English author of a now-notorious collection of autobiographical reminiscences, and the then Princess of Monaco. They had bought it with a view to building on it an intellectual residence where writers could withdraw from the world whenever they felt like it. The project had come to nothing, however, and in 1892 the rock was sold to Count Stroganoff, who, to the amazement of the local inhabitants, covered the rock with vast quantities of soil that he had specially brought in. On top of this he built his villa and also planted a small wood, thus creating one of the few spots along the whole coast that combine sea and forest.

And so it remained until 1937, when it was bought by an eccentric American millionaire from Estonia called William Zimdin, who, because he had never learned to swim, was in the habit of receiving friends while seated naked in a large bathtub in the garden.

Zimdin at once set about pulling down the Stroganoff villa and putting up in its place a large house modeled after those he had lived

OPPOSITE The hotel viewed from the Corniche Littoral, with Cap Ferrat behind.

in during his younger days in Yugoslavia and Austria. Even then he was not satisfied, and in the two years that he owned the property he demolished and rebuilt no less than three houses—which must surely qualify Le Cap Estel for some sort of entry in the *Guinness Book of Records*. In 1939 he was on the point of blowing up the tunnel of the main railway line that runs beneath the property, with a view to building yet another villa, when the French counter-espionage people stepped in and Zimdin stepped out to America, leaving behind just four walls which the Germans were later to find more than useful as an observation post.

After the war, the place remained abandoned until 1952, when Robert Squarciafichi, whose family had owned a restaurant in Beaulieu before the war, bought the property and began to transform the empty shell into a small hotel. It took him and his wife a year to put in seventeen rooms, each with a bathroom. From the beginning Le Cap Estel was, because of its competitive rates, extremely popular with English tourists. Indeed, up to only three or four years ago something like seventy per cent of the clientele came from England, and it is easy to see why. There is nothing the English enjoy more than the homely, informal, slightly haphazard atmosphere that is so characteristic of family-run hotels both in Britain and abroad. The building itself is grand and impressive, with a wide elegant terrace and splendid stairs that sweep down to the gardens; yet everywhere there are curious, anomalous touches that appeal very much to the English love of the eccentric—like the parrot called Can-Can that sits either in or on top of his cage beside the reception desk; and the funny little collection of three rooms known as "le Bâteau" built into the wall over the sea, with their little port holes and railings and nautical décor that make you feel as though you are on board a cruise ship; and the furniture in the rooms, all of which is thoroughly comfortable but none of which quite matches; and the fountain in the middle of the garden which, as you dine out at night, changes color from red to blue to white; and Auguste the gardener who is never seen without Yuki, his pedigree King Charles Spaniel; and on the far side of the garden against a high wall the rather dilapidated cages that house Mrs. Squarciafichi's pet pheasants, hatched originally from eggs brought over by guests from Scotland. The pheasants used to wander around the gardens until they took to flying out to sea and trying, always with fatal results, to land on the water. "They're very stupid birds," Mr. Squarciafichi explained with a shrug of the shoulders.

But perhaps the thing that over the years has attracted not only the English but also such distinguished international figures as Adlai Stevenson, Georges Pompidou, Paul-Henri Spaak, Joseph Kennedy, Anthony Quinn, the Sultan of Oman and many others is the extraordinary combination on the one hand of first-class service, marvelous facilities, extreme comfort and delicious food; and, on the other, the constant presence of the family—Robert Squarciafichi and his wife, their son Stephan and his Japanese wife and little daughter,

and their son-in-law Hervé Durand—which gives the whole place an air of great informality. Their office beside the reception desk is always open and guests are encouraged to wander in whenever they feel like a chat.

I remember sitting in the lounge one morning, talking with Mr. Squarciafichi about the history of the hotel. Suddenly, in the middle of the story, his two grandchildren burst into the room, shouting and laughing, and leapt onto his knees. And there they stayed for the next quarter of an hour while we talked. Perhaps they were rather noisy, I cannot really remember. I daresay they interrupted their grandpapa from time to time in the middle of a rather complicated story. But if they did, he certainly showed no signs, apart from the occasional "Ssh, ssh," that their presence seriously disturbed him. And, as far as I was concerned, it seemed the most natural thing in the world that they should be there—even during a business meeting.

A beautifully run hotel in a superb situation is always attractive, but one that is blessed with that degree of charm as well is irresistible.

Top left: Dinner on the terrace. *Center left:* There is also an indoor pool built into the rock beneath. *Center right:* Lunchtime in the garden. *Left:* The hotel is very grand, yet everywhere there are anomalous touches. *Far right:* Le Bâteaú.

CARLTON

CARLTON
CANNES, FRANCE

OPPOSITE The main entrance viewed across La Croisette from the sea front.

Legend has it that the twin domes on either end of the Carlton Hotel were modeled on the breasts of a famous beauty of the day, and looking at them one can see why she was famous. If the legend is true then I take it that the ornate and elaborate façade supporting the domes was based upon the same lady's lacy, not to say substantial, brassiere. Whichever way you approach Cannes, by land, sea or air, chances are the first thing to catch your eye will be that glittering façade, and those pointed pink domes which established for the whole town a tone of cheerful vulgarity that has lasted for over seventy years.

Which is quite right and as it should be. Cannes is after all a holiday town, relaxed, sunburnt, always in a bikini; a far cry from Nice, which is much more serious and commercial and *mondaine* and always seems to be wearing a silk scarf around its bare shoulders.

Never for one moment do you feel that the Carlton takes itself too seriously. Bathing wraps and shorts and bare, wet feet never look out of place in a lobby that in its grandeur and formality reminds one more of the Ritz in Paris than a seaside hotel. If someone gave you ten francs for every tie you spotted in the grill of a summer's eve, it would barely cover your drinks bill. Sporting types would do better to put their money on the bronzed, bare bosomry that winks and glistens at you wherever you look on the Carlton beach.

Yet never for a single second has it allowed its standards to slip, which is why it is still the great hotel it always has been.

The waiter in the grill, who has lived on the coast all his life, from time to time pulls his customers' legs by trying to persuade them he is really an Irishman who just happens to speak very good French. But at the same time every portion of butter he serves comes on ice, garnished with a little parsley, and woe betide him if it doesn't. As the manager said, "We *have* to have little dramas from time to time. You forget the parsley one night, and the next you'll find the ice missing. . . ."

On the beach, clothing may be casual to the point of non-existence, but the moment you arrive, a little brown man in pure white vest and shorts hurries out bearing towels and escorts you to a brown wooden *chaise longue* of your choice. And as you pad back through the lobby in the last rays of the setting sun, the sand sticking between your toes and the salt making a fright of your hair, you won't be required to lift a finger to make the elevator work, because the Carlton is one of the few hotels left in France, and I'd dare hazard in Europe, with a brace of *liftiers* in white jackets with matching gloves to do the finger-lifting for you.

I would also guess that it is this curious mixture of casual informality and highly efficient formality that has, ever since the hotel was first opened, attracted what used to be known as High Society. What an old-fashioned term that sounds now! Images of Nubar Gulbenkian standing in the kitchens, personally supervising the preparation of his favorite dish—*hure de sanglier truffé aux pistaches*;

Clockwise, from upper left-hand corner: The entrance hall where shorts and bare, wet feet somehow never look out of place; the domes were modeled after the breasts of a famous beauty; the Cristoforo Colombo off the Carlton Beach; the lacy facade; the dining room; the Carlton Beach viewed through the front door.

CARLTON

LIFTIER

of oil sheiks dishing out gold lighters as liberally as others would dish out visiting cards; of retired cat burglars in immaculate dinner jackets, bearing a striking resemblance to Cary Grant, attempting to secure the good favors of elegant women looking like Princess Grace of Monaco; and of King Farouk of Egypt rolling in at four in the morning and calling for one of the freshly roasted fowls the hotel kitchen cooked every half-hour, day or night, so that he could always be sure of being able instantly to sink his teeth into a breast roasted *à point*.

Mind you, had it not been for his enormous wealth, one wonders whether the ex-king would have been welcomed anywhere along the coast in his gross, declining years. Stories are still told at the Carlton about his bizarre behavior, and not without a certain degree of malice. One night in the Palm Beach Casino a young woman opposite him at the gaming table needed a light for her cigarette. Farouk casually tossed a gold lighter across the green baize, indicating that she should keep it. She picked it up, turned to one of the waiters standing near her chair and handed it to him, saying, "I imagine this was meant for you." But nothing really shocks or insults the Carlton. If it did, it would not have remained for thirty-three years the hub of the Cannes Film Festival—during each day of which something in the region of five hundred million dollars changes hands over drinks on the hotel terrace. It was up the steps of the Carlton that a starlet rode one year on a large horse in an attempt (unsuccessful, as it turned out) to be noticed. It was at the Carlton that a photographer one night made a picture in which a starlet stood at every window holding a lighted candle. "It could only happen," as the locals are forever remarking, "at the Carlton."

Not a bad motto for a hotel in many ways.

OPPOSITE *Top left:* During the Cannes Film Festival, millions of dollars change hands over drinks on the terrace of the Carlton. *Top right:* A corridor leading toward the dining room. *Bottom left:* A window beside the main staircase. *Bottom right:* One of a team that is on duty day and night. ABOVE Lunchtime at the beach.

THE CLOISTER
SEA ISLAND, U.S.A.

BEING A EUROPEAN and being used to seaside resort hotels which consist basically of a hotel, a garden, a swimming pool and tennis courts, I never fail to be astonished at the sheer comprehensiveness of American resort hotels and the sheer quantity of activities that are laid on for guests all day and every day.

Of course, this is not to say that in Europe if you want to play golf or go riding or water-skiing or bicycling or clay-pigeon shooting, such diversions cannot be laid on in a trice by the hotel management. But somehow, in resort hotels of the sort I am talking about, the understanding is that guests make their own plans.

Yet arrive at a swish American resort hotel like The Cloister, Sea Island, Georgia, and you are confronted with goodness knows how many booklets, leaflets, maps and slips of paper giving you a wealth of information about tennis tournaments, golf competitions, special meals, organized outings, welcoming get-togethers and farewell parties, film shows and bridge contests. You begin to wonder if you haven't let yourself in for some sort of initiative test rather than a relaxing few days away from it all.

Take, for example, the special Thanksgiving festival which The Cloister laid on last year under the general title "The Goose Hangs High at Sea Island."

No fewer than ten separate activities were scheduled during the first day of the holiday alone, beginning with an "Orange Blossom" welcome in the Colonial Lounge at noon—"A fine time to greet old acquaintances and make new ones." A Get-Together and Ping Pong Tournament for young people at the Beach Club Gazebo when junior hotesses, Candee Caroll and Doree Jones, were on hand to greet you and make sure you were introduced to other young arrivals. Holiday Tea-Time with Laura Dunn in the Solarium from 4.00–5.00. A "Gather Round" in the Fountain Room from 6.30–7.30 in order to get acquainted at the Harvest Table, tasting wines, sampling cheese, sipping "Pilgrim's Punch" and browsing among paintings and sculptures from the Left Bank Art Gallery. Cocktails and dancing in the Cloister Clubrooms from 7–7.45 and 9.30–midnight. After-dinner coffee in the Spanish Lounge. An illustrated talk entitled "This is Sea Island" by Mary Burdell in the Solarium at 9.15. A Dutch Treat Teen Table ("for teens and college") in the Clubrooms at which the junior hostesses continued to introduce young people who had not yet met anyone. A Champagne Interlude in the Clubrooms at 10.30 p.m.—"Nancy and Tom Gallagher will dance for you and with you. Champagne for the lucky couple." And finally, for anyone who still had an ounce of energy left in his body or a square inch of room in his stomach, a Holiday Nightcap in the Colonial Lounge of milk and gingerbread "'til bedtime."

And that was only the first day. Four more like it were to follow. Hardly a moment seemed to pass without something special going on somewhere—from a Demonstration of Gourmet Cooking and a Nature Lover's Tour of the Cloister Grounds to a Horseback

OPPOSITE A cloister window in the Spanish Lounge.

Breakfast ("See the sun come up over the water") and a Coke 'n' Popcorn Movie Party ("Come join the crowd").

But of all the events laid on by The Cloister during their various special celebration holidays the one I am most sorry to have missed was the Midnight Raid-the-Kitchen Party on New Year's Eve, described somewhat cryptically as "Lots of good food in the Cloister Kitchens." And all this is on top of the golf, swimming, sailing, riding, skeet shooting, sitting about, eating, drinking, going for walks, having a bit of a think, sightseeing, shopping and the hundred-and-one other frivolous pastimes that go to make up a seaside holiday. I simply do not know how people manage it all.

And as for the battalions of staff waiting only for a phone call to leap into action and play their part in making your holiday a non-stop whirligig of pleasure. . . . At the Golf Club alone there is a director of golf operations, a professional, a staff and touring professional and three assistant professionals, not to mention assorted caddie masters, caddies, head starters, under-starters, a course superintendent, and a clubhouse manager.

There is also a tennis professional and two assistants, a tournament director, a sports director, as well as different people in charge of swimming and diving, riding, fishing and skeet shooting.

Then there are the shops, supplying everything—well, more or less everything—the most demanding of guests could wish for, from guns and fishing rods to pullovers and bathing costumes.

Far left: The dining room. *Above, top:* The Spanish Lounge. *Above, bottom:* The beach—a mere five miles long—and the Cloister beach houses.

Far right: Bicycling, riding and golf: three of the main sporting activities at the Cloister.

From my description you have almost certainly gained an impression of a place literally seething with people. Yet nothing could be further from the truth. For the extraordinary thing about The Cloister is that it covers such a wide area that even though the resort may be completely full (which it is, incidentally, for at least nine months of the year), you would believe, when you first arrive there, that you are there by yourself.

In fact, The Cloister has 236 guest rooms altogether, both in the hotel building itself and in various guest houses, beach houses and cottages. The original section of the hotel was designed by the famous Palm Beach architect, Addison Mizner, and opened on October 12, 1928, under the managership of Mr. Irving Harned, who has been known to many generations of Cloister folk and is still there at the reins to this very day.

This smallest of the Golden Isles of Georgia was something of a resort over two hundred years ago when Fifth Creek Island, as it was then known, was granted by George III to one James Mackay, a captain in the South Carolina Independent Company of Foot. Mackay had fought with Colonel George Washington and his Virginia Militia in 1754 against the French and their Indian allies. He retired to his island in the same year, after resigning his commission, but he never made much use of the place and finally sold it to John Couper of Cannon's Point Plantation, St. Simon's Island. Long Island, as Sea Island was then known, finally became the property of Couper's

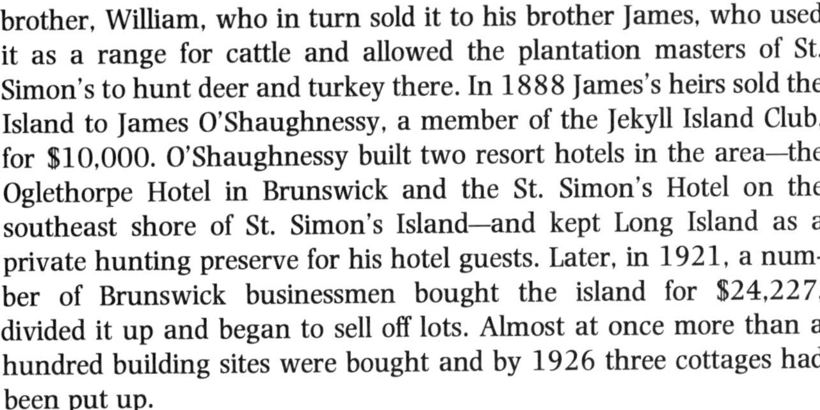

brother, William, who in turn sold it to his brother James, who used it as a range for cattle and allowed the plantation masters of St. Simon's to hunt deer and turkey there. In 1888 James's heirs sold the Island to James O'Shaughnessy, a member of the Jekyll Island Club, for $10,000. O'Shaughnessy built two resort hotels in the area—the Oglethorpe Hotel in Brunswick and the St. Simon's Hotel on the southeast shore of St. Simon's Island—and kept Long Island as a private hunting preserve for his hotel guests. Later, in 1921, a number of Brunswick businessmen bought the island for $24,227, divided it up and began to sell off lots. Almost at once more than a hundred building sites were bought and by 1926 three cottages had been put up.

The same year they sold out for $300,000 to a development company called Long Island Beach Properties who soon afterwards sold again to one Howard E. Coffin. He changed the name to Sea Island Beach and, seeing the resort possibilities of the place, set about realizing his dream. Expansion began to take place almost as soon as the hotel opened and has continued, along with the construction of many beautiful private homes, to this day.

Today there are some three hundred private houses on the island, belonging to such people as the chairman of Exxon, Mr. McGraw of McGraw-Hill, and the chairman of the Singer Corporation. All of them are managed by the Sea Island Company, which controls everything on the island, and a hundred of them are available for letting as holiday homes during the year. Anyone renting one of these private homes automatically becomes a member of the Cottage Club, which enables him to play golf and tennis at a reduced rate, and to become a

member of the Beach Club—all of which is free for hotel guests.

Managing a resort the size of Sea Island is hardly a picnic, and in the hands of people with less concern for human happiness the place could easily have become a huge, impersonal holiday camp. However, as Mr. Harned himself explained. "We are more concerned here with the creation of atmosphere than in the running of the operation."

He believes that people come to Sea Island to enjoy the sea, the sun, the open air and some good healthy exercise. They do not come there to mooch about in their rooms and watch TV. In fact, there are no TV sets in any of the rooms.

Other hotels may appeal to café society, to dressy people, to the jet set, but The Cloister appeals to clean-cut middle-class families from places like Back Bay or Westchester County, who enjoy being together and taking advantage of the beautiful surroundings and good weather, and who also apparently, enjoy getting up early and enjoying an enormous breakfast, since breakfast is in many ways the best and most abundant meal of the day.

Such sitting about as there is indoors takes place more often than not in one of the great lounges—the Spanish Lounge perhaps, with its three cloister windows, its high wooden ceilings, its big fireplaces where wood fires burn in winter, and its gigantic chairs, designed by the architect to conform with the baronial dimensions of the rest of the room, which are wide enough and deep enough to accommodate two or three normal-sized people. In them sit the older and less energetic, clustered attentively around a table of cards, happy to leave round robin tennis parties and putting tournaments to the more physically competitive, until the time comes to change, often into evening dress, for dinner. And after that . . . who knows? Another rubber possibly? At all events, probably not foxtrotting round the clubroom floor to the strains of "Dancing in the Dark" from the five-piece orchestra whose leader has been at The Cloister long enough to be able to remember many of the great figures who have been there since the war—Lord Beaverbrook, James Stewart, Irene Dunne, William Boyd, Sir Eric Bowater (once Lord Mayor of London), Queen Juliana and Prince Bernhard of the Netherlands.

He would almost certainly remember too the occasion when President Eisenhower was staying and put on his uniform and all his medals and went into the kitchen to receive a special commemorative dish from the chef. And the time Winston Churchill's daughter came there to marry the photographer Anthony Beauchamp.

Mind you, he is not the only one with a long memory. Cloister staff have a reputation for staying on. Five of the bellboys have been there for over twenty years, and a room waiter by the name of Stretch, although he has been in retirement for some time now, still comes back to help out when he knows certain old guests are coming who would be deeply disappointed to find he was not there.

Far left: General manager Irving Harned, and the honeymoon register and picture book. *Center top:* The Constitution Oak, planted by Calvin Coolidge in 1928. The species of oak was used to build the frigate, *The Constitution* ("Old Ironsides"). *Center middle:* One of the lounges. *Center bottom:* Dancing after dinner in the Clubrooms. *Top right:* Part of the lawn. *Bottom right:* Tea in the Solarium.

GLENEAGLES
AUCHTERARDER, SCOTLAND

I UNDERSTAND NOW, for the first time, how Casanova must have felt every time he clapped eyes on a beautiful woman. It came to me in a moment of wild inspiration on the first tee of the King's Course at Gleneagles Hotel. I was talking to the professional at the time, a soft-spoken, gentle man named Ian Marchbanks, and we were bemoaning the apparent disappearance from the earth and in particular from Gleneagles of that species of man known as The Character. Even the great caddies, it seems, are now more or less extinct; the last one having died only the other year—an Irishman for whom every day was his birthday, to which his clients rarely failed to contribute anything less than a crisp fiver. It was all good nostalgic stuff; and yet I have to confess that throughout it my concentration was wandering disgracefully in the direction of what is arguably the most alluring sight I have ever experienced in over twenty years of golf.

I refer to a great deep bunker, 350 yards or so away, at the end of the softest, greenest, most voluptuous fairway I have ever seen, beyond and on top of which lies the green of the hole they call Dun Whinny. And at that moment I realized that what women were to Casanova, so a great golf hole is to millions of golfers all over the world; and I knew that until I had indulged myself in the pleasure of playing that first hole—no, not even that, just one good tee shot would be enough—I would not be in a fit state to think seriously about anything else. To make matters worse, I was due to leave at the end of the morning and it was already past ten. Rarely have I felt such an overwhelming desire to take possession of a golf course—if only a small part of it. I can only suppose that it was due to over-excitement that my tee shot, when it finally came ten minutes later, was pushed so drastically out to the right. My second to the green (or, more accurately, to the bunker) was little better. It must have something to do with the northern light, because everything up there seems to be much nearer than it really is.

The approach to the green from inside the bunker is only slightly less difficult than that to the summit of the Eiger via the north face: very steep and apparently insurmountable.

Having finally holed out some three strokes later, my earlier frustration was relieved sufficiently for me to be able to return to the clubhouse and continue my conversation with Mr. Marchbanks. But of course I did no such thing, and it will come as no surprise to anyone even faintly acquainted with the game of golf to learn that it was not until after two o'clock that I finally drove away from the front door of the hotel.

There are three courses at Gleneagles Hotel: King's, which is probably the best known and certainly the most testing; Queen's, which makes up in beauty what little it lacks in difficulty; and Prince's, which was converted only last year to an eighteen-hole from a nine, and, although it really cannot compare with the other two on any score, is nevertheless charming and satisfying.

ABOVE The main entrance. OVERLEAF *Top:* A hotel in the Highlands to rival

The names of the holes on the King's and Queen's courses, so redolent of history and legend, plus the fact that most of the greatest names in golf over the last fifty years have trodden the greens and fairways (and bunkers), are enough to send a tingle down the back of the neck. But to arrive on Braid's Brawest (the hole that the great James Braid, British Open Champion several times over and the man who laid out the course, considered the most testing of all), knowing that you have to carry the ridge with your second shot to stand the slightest chance of a 4; to tackle the Par 3 Het Girdle where your tee shot is death or glory to a green that falls away sharply on all sides—that will really set your blood racing. And as for the fourteenth on Queen's, the Witches' Bowster, I feel certain that even the most dedicated player would be tempted to pause for a second or two from his game to enjoy the beauty of the setting.

After a day on courses like these, many a reasonable golfer might be content to settle for accommodation in the most modest inn or hotel. But to walk off the eighteenth at King's, "King's Hame," with the prospect of a night in the only hotel in Britain outside London to be classified *de Grand Luxe* by the Michelin Guide, is to experience a sense of luxury and well-being that is unique in the world.

At first glance, Gleneagles Hotel looks like one of those splendid country houses one glimpses from time to time in Scotland, through the trees or between a fold in the hills, and asks oneself how on earth anyone could possibly have afforded to build such a place, or afford to live there now. And in a way, that is exactly what Gleneagles is—or at least was when it first opened in 1924.

Although the hotel's insignia is a fierce-looking eagle with wings outspread, the name Gleneagles is actually a corruption of *glen de l'église*, a reference to the kirk of St. Mungo which was believed to have existed down in the glen. Above the glen was a plateau commanding extensive views of the Grampians, the Ochils, Strathearn, Glendevon and the distant Carse O'Gowrie.

One day before the First World War, a man called Donald Matheson, the general manager of the Caledonian Railway, was traveling past. For some time he had been nursing a secret ambition to build a great hotel with a golf course and grounds that would in size and splendor rival the famous spas of Europe. As soon as he set eyes on Gleneagles he knew that this was the place. His enthusiasm quickly infected the owners of the railway and in 1913 work began on the hotel. This had to be abandoned a year later when war broke out, but work continued on the golf course, which opened in 1919. It was not until five years later that the hotel was completed. Nothing like it had been seen in Scotland before and newspaper headlines on the day after the opening ran the gamut of superlatives in their efforts to express the general amazement of everyone who saw the place: "New Wonder Hotel," "Golf de Luxe," "Opulence and Elegance," "A Fairy Palace," "Luxury among the Mountains," "Tourists' Perthshire Paradise." One compared it with Kubla Khan's

the great spas of Europe. *Bottom:* Across the hall and into the ballroom.

palace, another called it the Eighth Wonder of the World and went on, "And the greatest wonder of all. The Gleneagles Orchestra under Mr. Henry R. Hall, which supplied the music to the dance, was broadcasted every Tuesday and Friday. Broadcasting from the Scottish Highlands! Ma conscience . . . ! Aladdin and his wonderful lamp never accomplished anything more wonderful than this."

After such a glittering debut, it was inevitable that Gleneagles should, in the years that followed, have attracted the very best clientele.

Scotland in those days was a major landmark in the social round; but whereas previously the upper classes had rarely headed North at times of the year when there was nothing to kill, now they found in Gleneagles all sorts of excuses to stay in Scotland in the spring and summer months too. Not only did the hotel offer some of the best golf to be found anywhere in Europe, but there was also croquet, bowls, walking, trout fishing, and first-rate tennis courts.

It is some measure of the distinction the hotel quickly acquired that the branch line of the London Midland Scottish railway (as the Caledonian became known after the First World War) came right to the back door, and passengers wishing to travel to London by the night train simply stepped directly from the hotel onto their sleepers. On the other hand, some daredevils with less time on their hands preferred to take advantage of the hotel's airplane landing station, and glossy society magazines of the period include various photographs of young men swathed in greatcoats and scarves and gauntlets and sporting flying helmets and goggles, standing beside their little biplanes.: "Mr. J. G. Crammond flew from Croydon to join his parents at the hotel." Three quarters of the guests photographed in those days appeared to be, if not titled, then certainly distinguished in some form of public life. Lady Margaret Douglas-Hamilton and the Marquis of Clydesdale; Lord Joicey, aged eighty, driving off from the first tee; Lord and Lady Maud Carnegie, who were staying with the Princess Royal and Princess Arthur of Connaught; Lloyd George swinging wildly with a long iron and so forth.

Needless to say, all that sort of thing came to an end in 1939, when the hotel was taken over as a convalescent home for officers. After that it was never quite the same again. But although Gleneagles, like almost every other big hotel in the world, has had to resign itself to the fact that it can no longer depend upon a rich clientele to keep it going and has therefore had to resort to incongruous commercial techniques (conferences, groups, etc.) for its survival, the hotel has somehow succeeded in retaining its social cachet. From time to time the great house still rings to the sound of dancing and laughter just as it must have done in the days before the war—especially when the 51st Highland Division have their reunion there in October, with Highland dancing in the ballroom and everyone filling up their dance cards as fast as they can.

"This is one of the few occasions on which the ballroom is used

properly these days," Mr. Bannatyne, the general manager, told me gloomily. "Well, you see, the whole style of dancing has changed, and people nowadays don't need a great ballroom just to stand opposite each other and jiggle about."

Those who do wish to dance after dinner nowadays have to make do with the thin sounds of a small orchestra and the carpet rolled back in the main sitting room. Still, I suppose it is better than nothing.

Like Mr. Marchbanks up at the club house, Mr. Bannatyne worries about the strange disappearance of the great characters of yesteryear.

> I've seen four hefty young men at a wedding bend down and lift the bride and bridegroom's car up off the ground just as they were setting off, and of course the wheels spun round and nothing happened. You never see anything like that any more. There are no more great parties like there used to be, either. And then of course, one of the reasons the dancing finished was that everyone dines so much later these days. In the old days, if a man was entertaining guests to dinner he ordered for them in advance so that everyone got through dinner in time to do something afterwards. Nowadays everyone arrives in the dinning room at 8.30 and starts ordering different things off the à la carte and consequently the meals take nearly three hours to finish.

Still, if you have to spend time over your dinner for want of anything else to do, I cannot think of a more pleasant dining room to spend it in; nor have I come across better food anywhere in Europe that is worth lingering over longer than I have at Gleneagles. Unfortunately, I did not have the opportunity to try any of the real Scottish specialities like Cabbie Claw (poached white fish, flavored with horseradish) or Timbale of Scampi Uisgh-Beath, which is scampi in a whisky-flavored sauce, or Pear Butterscotch. I was there rather late in the season, in October, and in order to try these examples of Scottish gastronomy you really need to be there in the summer when the Malmaison Restaurant from Glasgow take over the bow-windowed Glendevon Room. Nevertheless, everything I ate in the main dining room, with its wonderful views across green lawns and gray balustrades to the distant hill shrouded in mist, was without exception simply delicious.

Afterwards, I wandered aimlessly through the great house—into the Terrace Lounge, once the men's smoking room, with its huge black and gold Empire sideboard, its heavy pink curtains fringed with green, and its two facing fireplaces of positively baronial proportions; along endless high-ceiling corridors, past old maps showing the layout of the hotel and golf course as they were fifty years ago; past the little wood-paneled post office, and Lawrie's gift shop; along more corridors and through a brightly lit blue and white shopping arcade with more gift shops offering shirts, pullovers, and ties at a ten per cent discount; until finally I came to an illuminated sign hanging

from the ceiling pointing the way to the swimming pool, squash courts, billiard room and cinema (which doubles as a non-denominational chapel). A ping pong table occupied most of the squash court, the pool was closed, so was the billiard room (you need to ask specially for a key these days), and in the cinema Burt Lancaster was swashbuckling his way through *The Flame and the Arrow* to an empty auditorium. The season was very nearly over.

In the lounge a couple strode bravely round the little floor in a spirited quick step. Would I, I wondered, even if I were by chance to spot a likely partner, be able even to remember the steps? The hotel may not be quite what it was, but then neither am I. Nothing to do but head for my bedroom and the TV and a long lie in the pale whisky-colored water and think about how I was going to carry that big bunker on Dun Whinny the following morning.

GRAND HOTEL DU CAP
ANTIBES, FRANCE

OPPOSITE The hotel from the Eden Roc pavilion.

I WAS IN the middle of a plate of *fraises des bois* on the terrace of the Eden Roc pavilion at the Grand Hotel du Cap at Antibes when the lady at the next table picked up the remains of a bottle of Puligny Montrachet and poured it over her companion's trousers. He seemed mildly annoyed but not surprised; neither were the waiters, one of whom handed the man a clean white linen napkin. He dabbed at himself in a half-hearted fashion for a second or two, then turned to the person sitting on the other side of the table and continued the conversation as though nothing had happened. Was this the early stage of a crumbling marriage that I had just witnessed, or a way of telling the waiter that the wine was corked?

Whatever it was that had caused it, it fell, I was glad to see, within the tradition of extravagant gestures for which the Grand Hotel du Cap has become famous over the years.

There is the story, for example, of the Russian Prince Apraxine who, while wintering at the Grand Hotel, was in the habit of having fresh strawberries delivered to his suite every morning at enormous expense. And every morning he would crush the fruit with a fork, then ring for his Cossack servant who would enter, eat the strawberries, click his heels and retire. The routine never changed. When asked to account for his bizarre behavior the Russian nobleman replied, "As a matter of fact I can't bear strawberries but I do so adore the perfume they give off when they are crushed."

Then there was the famous evening in 1927 when Scott and Zelda Fitzgerald threw a farewell party at Eden Roc for Alexander Woolcott and Grace Moore and her fiancé, Chato Elizaga. A great many toasts were drunk, and a great many speeches made, until finally Zelda shouted, "Words, mere words. Can't we give our friends a real present, like this. . . ." Whereupon she leapt onto a chair, whipped off her panties, and threw them at Elizaga. He, not to be outdone by this gesture, bowed gravely at Zelda and vaulted over the balcony fully clothed into the sea. After that Alexander Woolcott took all his clothes off and marched into the hotel, through the lobby and up to his room.

Why such a beautiful, restful hotel as the Grand Hotel du Cap incites people to such exuberant behavior I cannot imagine, unless it is something to do with the sheer exuberance of the place itself. Fitzgerald's description of the hotel, which he used as the model for Gausse's Hotel des Etrangers in *Tender is the Night*, does not do it full justice. "On the shore of the French Riviera, about halfway between Marseilles and the Italian border, stood a large, proud, rose-colored hotel. Deferential palms cooled its blushing façade, and before it stretched a short dazzling beach. Now it has become a summer resort of notable and fashionable people; in 1925 it was almost deserted after the English clientele went north in April. . . ."

Large it certainly is, even though it does only have eighty bedrooms; and proud. But far from being rose-colored it is gleaming white with blue shutters and yellow blinds. And before it stretches not a beach but a wide sweeping graveled pathway, carpeted in places, that stretches away down to the rocky promontory on which stands the elegant little Eden Roc pavilion, looking for all the world like the stern of a cruise ship that has berthed at the bottom of the garden. But the most striking thing of all is that in this day and age, in a place like the Riviera where land is like gold dust, the Grand Hotel should still be able to afford to sit there in twenty-five acres of private grounds. Turning in through the gates of the hotel after an hour or so on the N7, or even five minutes in Antibes during the height of the season, is like arriving in the Garden of Eden. Much has changed over the years, to be sure, but there is a timeless quality about the hotel which is infinitely reassuring. On the other hand, life has not always been easy for the old lady.

The Villa Soleil, as the hotel was first called, opened in 1870 with a fabulous banquet consisting of sixteen courses, a ball, and lavish celebrations in the garden. But then almost at once came the Franco-Prussian War and the hotel nearly went bankrupt. It re-opened in 1889 and for the first few months the sole occupants were two English spinsters who paid twelve francs a day each. It didn't seem quite enough to support forty employees, five horses and a private bus. But then Gordon Bennet of the *New York Herald Tribune* took a fancy to the place, put ten million francs into it and his sister into the second floor. From then on the hotel nudged along (with the help of half a million from Lord Onslow) until 1914. The years following the war were slow ones for the Grand Hotel, as they were for the rest of the coast. And then came Juan-les-Pins.

Before the First World War, the Parisians had always spent their holidays on the sandy beaches of Normandy—at Cabourg or Houlgate or Deauville—or else in the north at Le Tréport or Le Touquet. The furthest they had ventured was Biarritz. But Juan-les-Pins could offer not only sand, but sun too—all summer long.

The man responsible for launching the summer season was Edouard Baudoin, who got the idea from a film about Miami that had featured a number of ladies in beach pyjamas. He bought the casino in Juan, built a restaurant next door, hired Pascaline to do the cooking, and in the very first year well-known names were to be seen everywhere—the Dolly Sisters, Bentley the car manufacturer, and many others. Soon afterwards, hotel developer Frank Jay Gould appeared on the scene and joined Baudouin at the casino and Aletti at the Hotel Provençal.

Gradually the Grand Hotel too began to change its habits. Up to 1922 Antoine Sella, the hotel's owner, had been running a winter resort that opened in November and closed in Easter. But then two favorite guests, Sara and Gerald Murphy, asked if they could stay on through the spring. Sella agreed. The Murphys brought the Picassos with them. By 1925 Scott Fitzgerald was writing to a friend, "No one at Antibes this summer except me, Zelda, the Valentinos, the Murphys, Mistinguet (sic), Rex Ingram, Dos Passos, the MacLeishes,

Charles Bracket, E. Phillips Oppenheim, Mannes the violinist, Max Eastman, ex-Premier Orlando—just a real place to rough it and escape from all the world."

By the time Antoine Sella died a few years later, not only had the seasons been altered, but so too had the clientele. Just as the Russians had come in 1914, so now the literary and artistic world of Fitzgerald and Murphy gave way to the beach pyjamas and the martinis. Glossy magazines of the time were filled every week with pictures of the smart set at play at the Eden Roc. *The Graphic*, for example, in August, 1930, showed "an attractive glimpse of Eden Roc at Cap d'Antibes, the summer rendezvous on the Riviera where many well-known English people gather to lunch and bathe in the sun." The photographees were nearly always the same: Lady Ashley and her sister, Miss Vera Hawkes; Mr. Cecil Beaton (in French matelot outfit) and his sister Nancy; the Rajkumar of Pudukota with his mother and Miss Mimi Burke; Ian Hay, the popular author; Miss Dorothy and Miss Cicely Debenham; the Marchioness of Milford Haven; Mrs. Reginald Vanderbilt, Miss Tallulah Bankhead (seen repairing her make-up) and a friend; Beatrice Lillie and Noël Coward; Mr. George Bernard Shaw. . . .

Whether in forty years' time the sort of people you meet around the pool of the Eden Roc, or pass while walking in the cool of the evening through the scented pine woods, or jostle at the cold *hors d'oeuvre* table at lunchtime, will evoke quite the same feeling of nostalgia in our children it is impossible to tell. Certainly I did not recognize a famous face on any of the occasions I visited the hotel; but that does not mean a lot these days. Even so, of all the great hotels I know, I can think of none that has succeeded better than the Grand Hotel du Cap in retaining the atmosphere that its founders were attempting to achieve and that they enjoyed in their heyday.

The hotel looks more beautiful than ever. Thanks to the far-sightedness of the new owners, a small fortune has been devoted to turning the rather *louche* back entrance into a spanking front entrance, with great glass windows leading out on to a grass-covered terrace with stone balustrades, and inside, a whole new reception area, far larger, lighter and more elegant than it was when I first went there. The high-ceilinged corridors, too, are forever being re-lined with the most charming tissues of pastoral scenes—so cool to come into after the shimmering afternoon heat of the garden.

And for those, like myself, who relish the idea of those golden pyjama-clad, martini-sipping days of before the war, there are still plenty of reminders—like the collection of little white gravestones under an olive tree in the corner of the rose garden on which are inscribed the names of Poppy, Poony, Tchou-Tchou, Dou-Dou, Mouflon, Flock, Olympia, Skipy, Siria, Patou and Chick, 1922–39, for seventeen years faithful friend to C. & H. Izrastoff.

Top left: The pool at Eden Roc. *Top right:* The hotel is set in 25 acres of its own grounds. *Center left:* Part of the dogs' cemetery. *Bottom right:* F. Scott Fitzgerald's Hotel des Etrangers in *Tender is the Night*. *Bottom left:* The staircase to the garden.

1858 - 1922

HERE STOOD A FAMOUS HOSTELRY
AFFECTIONATELY KNOWN AS

·THE·OLD·WHITE·

ONCE THE PRIDE OF THE OLD DOMINION

WHOSE GRACIOUS HOSPITALITY, BEAUTIFUL SURROUNDINGS AND HEALING WATERS GAINED NATIONAL RENOWN AND MADE IT THE OBJECT OF MANY A PILGRIMAGE.

HERE GATHERED FROM THE NORTH AND SOUTH GREAT GENERALS, FAMOUS STATESMEN AND PHILANTHROPISTS, LOVELY LADIES AND REIGNING BELLES "WHO LEFT UPON THE SILENT SHORE OF MEMORY IMAGES AND PRECIOUS THOUGHTS THAT SHALL NOT DIE AND CANNOT BE DESTROYED".

ERECTED BY ITS SUCCESSOR
THE GREENBRIER
1940

THE GREENBRIER
WHITE SULPHUR SPRINGS, U.S.A.

NEAR THE CORNER of the piazza at The Greenbrier is a plaque on which are inscribed the following words: "1858–1922. Here stood a famous hostelry affectionately known as THE OLD WHITE. Once the pride of the old dominion whose gracious hospitality, beautiful surroundings and healing waters gained national renown and made it the object of many a pilgrimage. Here gathered from the North and South great generals, famous statesmen and philanthropists, lovely ladies and reigning belles 'who left upon the silent shore of memory images and precious thoughts that shall not die and cannot be destroyed'. Erected by its successor THE GREENBRIER. 1940."

That successor is today one of the most elegant, charming, gracious, relaxing and grand resorts in the world. Set among 6,500 acres in the beautiful Allegheny Mountains of West Virginia, there is almost nothing you cannot do in this extraordinary place.

You can play tennis, under the watchful eye of professional Vic Seixas, on one of the fifteen outdoor and five indoor courts. You can play golf on a course that has sorted them all out in its day—from the Duke of Windsor to Sam Snead. You can go swimming in the huge indoor pool or the huge outdoor pool. You can go riding through two hundred miles of woodland and mountain trails or trot round the grounds in a carriage and pair. You can practice your bowling in one of the eight bowling lanes, your shooting on the trap or skeet fields. You can spend a profitable afternoon in the President's Cottage Museum, originally one of the first private cottages built at White Sulphur Springs in the early 1800's and so called because of the many Presidents who have used it as their Summer White House. You can browse around the Little 5th Avenue Shops. You can sit about and do absolutely nothing at all. Or you can do the thing for which so many thousands of people have been coming to the Springs since the dawn of history: take the mineral waters.

The Greenbrier is, as they say in the literature, "Where the vacation season never ends," and it promises the lucky visitor, as they also say in the literature. "Life as it should be."

Well, that of course depends on how you think life should be. Michael Bowyer, a farmer, lawyer and general-store keeper in Fincastle, Virginia, obviously thought it should be healthy, for in 1784 he acquired the 950-acre White Sulphur Springs property on Howard's Creek about five miles up from where it joins the Greenbrier River.

In 1788 Bowyer, his family and two friends, Mr. and Mrs. Wiley, arrived and began to build themselves cabins and stables. Bowyer's was a single cabin; Wiley, realizing the amount of money that could be made by catering to invalids and passing travelers, built one twice as large and offered half of it as rented accommodation. Soon a second, milky-white spring was discovered and trade began to grow at a brisk pace.

One day in the early 1790's, three young city men from the

East rode up to Bowyer's log cabin; by the end of the decade they had married all three of Bowyer's rosy-cheeked, barefooted daughters, Fanny, Polly and Betsy. When Bowyer died in 1808, the property was divided between his son James and his three daughters, the husband of one of whom, James Calwell, immediately set about building ten new cottages, which were ready for guests by 1810. Soon he had assumed the management of the whole estate and in 1817 he enlarged his father-in-law's tavern and built a wooden spring-house which was in turn replaced by today's elegant white-domed structure with a statue of Hygeia, Goddess of Health, perched on top.

By this time, White Sulphur Springs was playing host to a number of distinguished visitors, including President Andrew Jackson who came there shortly after the Battle of New Orleans, and Henry Clay, then Speaker of the House of Representatives and very much a nabob, whose presence undoubtedly attracted a great many more useful guests.

And it was not only the nabobs who were beginning to patronize White Sulphur Springs by the 1830's. Young lawyers, anxious to make useful contacts with wealthy clients, would stay for several days on end, while in the summer of 1837 President Van Buren and his advisers met there to discuss whether they should re-charter the Bank of the United States. It was from this meeting that the modern monetary system and today's U.S. Treasury were evolved. Three other Presidents who benefited from the healing properties of the Springs at that time were President Pierce, President Fillmore, and President Zachary Taylor.

By 1850 it was becoming increasingly clear to James Calwell that a proper hotel would have to be built at White Sulphur Springs if they wished to take full advantage of the increasing number of visitors.

A year later however, Calwell was dead, his dream still unrealized. For six years negotiations for the sale of the property continued, until finally, in 1857, it was bought for $200,000 by eight Virginians. In June of the following year, the Grand Central Hotel, the largest hotel in the United States, so they said, was opened in White Sulphur Springs. The parlor was reckoned to be half as large again as the East Room in the White House, and legend had it that the dining room was so vast that waiters had to serve the food on horseback.

Despite its impressive title, the Grand Central was known to its regular guests as The White, and no matter how adamantly the proprietors insisted on calling it by its proper name, the guests continued to refer to it fondly by its nickname.

Hardly had the paint dried on The White's skirting boards than sounds of discontent began to be heard in the South. For four summers a firebrand pamphleteer by the name of Edmund Ruffin stayed at White Sulphur Springs in an effort to persuade influential Southerners to support secession. The scent of war seemed to be in everyone's nostrils. Even young Charley Bonaparte, great-nephew of Napoleon

PRECEDING PAGE *Clockwise from upper left-hand corner:* Historic Alabama Row—once cottages owned by Southern nabobs, now the Greenbrier Art Colony; part of one of the original White Sulphur Springs buildings; the new indoor tennis courts; the swimming pool; part of the main dining

room—one of the paintings is by Samuel Morse, inventor of the telegraph; the Spring House, built in the early 1800's; the 15th tee on one of the Greenbrier's three courses.

ABOVE The lounge—George Washington by Gilbert Stuart.

and the man who was later to found the FBI, spent a great deal of time drilling his fellow youngsters outside the hotel front door.

Yet, despite the gathering gloom, the seasons at The White during the late fifties were more brilliant than ever, and even during the first year of the war the season took place as usual, though at reduced rates "owing to the embarrassed state of the country."

By the later summer, however, there was too much military activity in and around The White for the season to continue and on August 23, a month earlier than usual, the hotel closed its doors.

On June 18, 1867, a little more than two years after Appomattox, The White opened for the first time in six years. "We cannot expect to see there," the *Richmond Dispatch* commented gloomily, "the society that once gave life and gaiety and grace to that incomparably delightful summer resort." But then, on the afternoon of July 24, a man wearing a wide-brimmed hat, an old army greatcoat and a white beard, rode up to the front door of The White and from that moment on life at the Springs took a marked turn for the better. The man was General Robert E. Lee. With him were his wife, who was suffering badly from rheumatism, his son Custis, his daughter Agnes, her friend Mary, and Mrs. Lee's maid Milly.

At first his appearance caused great confusion, largely because no one was quite sure how to treat the great man. The young men in particular found him deeply uneasy. As a young friend of his observed, "he seemed to test them with an Ithuriel spear, and they were inclined to shrink from the lofty standard he maintained." The young girls, however, got on with him splendidly. According to his chronicler, "he loved to see the girls surrounded by cavaliers and merry in the dance, and many a young Southerner owed his acquaintance with the belle of the season to General Lee's stately presentation."

In 1882 the property was acquired by a wealthy cattle farmer named William A. Stuart and restyled the Greenbrier White Sulphur Springs Company. He put in a racing track, built a new kitchen wing and hired Napoleon III's chef, Adolf Zetelle. But by the late eighties he was in financial difficulties, and for several years ownership of the hotel passed through various hands until in 1888 it was finally bought by the Chesapeake and Ohio Railway. Despite the prevailing uncertainty, however, The White had never seen so much romance, so many dashing cavaliers and such beautiful Southern belles as it did in the eighties and nineties. One newspaper commented, "The Lord made the White Sulphur Springs and then the Southern girl, and rested, satisfied with His work."

There was Mary Triplett, over whose hand the last duel in Virginia was fought; Mattie Ould, a wit as well as beauty, who after waking from a doze with her head on General Young's shoulder remarked that she was "just trying an Ould head on Young shoulders"; Mary Handy, Sally Watson Montague, Lillie Norton, Nellie Hazeltine and Irene Langhorne whose sister Nancy married Waldorf Astor and became the first woman ever to take her seat in the English House of

Top: The Greenbrier. *Bottom:* Busts of presidents line this corridor leading to the lounge.

Commons. (She once told Winston Churchill that if she were his wife she would flavor his coffee with arsenic. To which he replied that if he were her husband he would drink it.) Irene later married Charles Dana Gibson and became the archetype of his Gibson Girl.

Another belle, Bettina Ordway Padelford, shocked everyone by appearing in public in transparent Egyptian lingerie and encouraging young men to drink champagne from her slipper, a habit that, in the words of one Major William Hale, "almost demolished the moral and social structure of the famous resort."

It looked as though belledom was in serious danger of getting out of hand. One day in 1884 a group of belles and beaux were returning from a "tally-ho" picnic when they came across five men playing a most extraordinary new game. "I played marbles when I was a child," remarked one of the beaux, "but this is the first time I've seen men play!" The game was golf, recently imported from Scotland, and it was being played on a nine-hole course on the estate of Russell W. Montague.

The end of the nineteenth century was an age of great affluence, which at White Sulphur Springs manifested itself in a number of ways. Guests had been arriving in trains "with sleeping palaces attached" since 1871, but by 1890 more and more were turning up in private railroad cars. William K. Vanderbilt owned two, the Astors, the Dukes, the Drexels and the Biddles had one each. Some even went so far as to attach a special carriage containing their own furnishings. Fancy dress balls and champagne suppers were more elaborate than ever, and the newspapers devoted column after column to the glamorous goings-on.

But by the turn of the century, The White was beginning to look rather shabby, and it was obvious that major changes would soon have to be made. The New York architect Frederick Julius Sterner was called in and he suggested a brand-new 250-room building in the Georgian style. His plans were accepted and in September, 1913, The Greenbrier was opened alongside The Old White. One guest described it as "a fairy palace set amid the lights and shadows of the Allegheny Hills."

A nine-hole and an eighteen-hole golf course were constructed, and tennis courts and more cottages were built.

In 1912 The Old White failed to pass the state fire inspection and the historic structure had to be pulled down.

The Old White boasted many great visitors, and The Greenbrier clearly had every intention of maintaining the tradition. In 1916 President Woodrow Wilson came with his wife; General John J. Pershing wrote his Pulitzer Prize-winning history of World War One there; and in 1919 the Prince of Wales spent four days there. What he did not know at the time was that the woman for whom he would later renounce the throne of England had not only stayed in a cottage in Baltimore Row with her Aunt Bessie, but had also spent the first of her three honeymoons at The Greenbrier.

The twenties and even the thirties were a time of great expansion for White Sulphur Springs. The old buildings were added to, new ones were built, and a second eighteen-hole golf course—as well as facilities for polo, fencing and indoor archery—was put in. In 1936 a young golfer who had just won the Cascades Open was taken on as a professional at White Sulphur Springs. His name was Sam Snead.

During World War Two, The Greenbrier became home for a while for some 1,400 interned German and Japanese diplomats and newspaper correspondents. By 1942 they had all been replaced by normal guests, but only for a month. On September 1 the army bought a place as a hospital, and when Ashford General Hospital, as it became known, closed its doors on September 5, 1946, the property was declared surplus and put up for sale.

The man who bought it was Robert R. Young, controlling stockholder in the Chesapeake and Ohio Railroad Corporation, and with Dorothy Draper as decorator and designer he set about making the hotel as beautiful as it had been before the war.

Where possible, historic furnishings from the old hotel were used —the Sheffield chandelier, the Queen Anne table in the President's Parlor, the antique girandole mirror in the Victorian writing room, the five Czechoslovakian chandeliers in the Colonnades dining room. To these were added the nine-foot chandelier in the Cameo Ballroom, and an Aubusson rug for the President's Parlor.

The grand opening party took place for four days in April, 1948. Fourteen private railroad cars, a number of private airplanes and countless limousines brought such international figures as the Duke and Duchess of Windsor, Prince and Princess Hohenlohe, the Marchioness of Huntington (Kathleen Kennedy), Winthrop Aldrich, the John Jacob Astors, the Anthony Biddle Dukes, and the Winton Guests. Among the political fraternity was the young representative John F. Kennedy, whose parents had honeymooned there in 1915. Elsa Maxwell was there, of course, as were William Randolph Hearst, J. Arthur Rank and Bing Crosby, who always claimed that his room-maid used a mink mop and wore lorgnettes.

Ever since it was reopened after the war, The Greenbrier, under the supervision first of Robert R. Young and now Truman Wright, has undergone numerous changes and improvements. The three golf courses have been brought to a peak of excellence, the Greenbrier Clinic was established, and the kitchens have acquired a nation-wide reputation. The standard of personal service, it goes without saying, is as high as any in the United States.

The decision of whether life today at The Greenbrier is "Life as it should be" is, of course, up to the people who go there. Certainly the quality of life there is, apart from one or two obvious differences, very much the same as it has been for nearly two centuries.

HOSTAL DE LA GAVINA
S'AGARÓ, SPAIN

OPPOSITE The main entrance.

LA GAVINA IN both Catalan and Castilian means "The Seagull," and for over half a century this hotel has been surging forward on its serene flight. Architecturally, gastronomically, and from any other point of view you care to think of, it is way way above any other hotel along that part of the Spanish coast known as the Costa Brava.

Looking at S'Agaro now, it is hard to believe that just after the First World War it was nothing more than a large, very beautiful but totally barren tract of land, separated from the sea by an irregular strip of pine trees and a collar of rocks, and inhabited only by lizards. The nearest sign of life came from the herds of goats from the farm-houses on the plain of San Pol.

The beach of San Pol was well known to the fishermen of the region, and some of them were in the habit of setting up tents on it as long ago as the turn of the century. A few important families from nearby San Feliu had built themselves luxurious seaside chalets and surrounded their properties with high walls, but apart from them there was nothing and nobody.

It was in this inhospitable spot, on the eastern corner of San Pol beach, that in 1924, a man by the name of José Ensesa Pujadas, the father of the present proprietor of S'Agaro, decided to build a house for his son, Ensesa was born a peasant, discovered he had a talent for business, and over the years had put his gifts to good use. Perhaps he foresaw the day when tourism would come to the area, perhaps he just wanted to build his son a nice house by the sea. In any event, on July 24, 1924, his son José Ensesa Gubert spent his first night in his house at S'Agaro. It was he who would eventually create out of that barren, solitary stretch of land a place of great beauty, with fine buildings, elegant gardens, squares and avenues where like-minded people could come and meet each other and relax in total comfort.

Unlike his father, José Ensesa was a man of artistic temperament who had a wide acquaintance of artists, including the architect Rafael Masó y Valenti. It was the determination of Señor Ensesa's vision and the brilliance of Señor Masó's imagination that together made S'Agaro possible.

Inspired by the landscape. Masó found no difficulty at all in picturing the pergolas, balconies, squares, avenues and staircases that might or might not one day become realities. The execution of those drawings was a slower and more difficult process, but gradually the houses and gardens began to appear and grow in number. The houses were based largely on typical Spanish country houses, in which roofs and galleries, porticos and terraces, towers and eaves combine to take full advantage of the sky, the surrounding country-side and the sea.

S'Agaro was originally planned as a colony—a group of houses to which the sort of people who felt at home there would return year after year. And yet, even at the beginning, there was some idea in the minds of José Ensesa and Rafael Masó that that colony might one

Left, top left, top right: The hotel abounds with statuary. *Right:* The lounge. *Bottom left:* The sitting room of a suite. *Bottom right:* The Empire Suite.

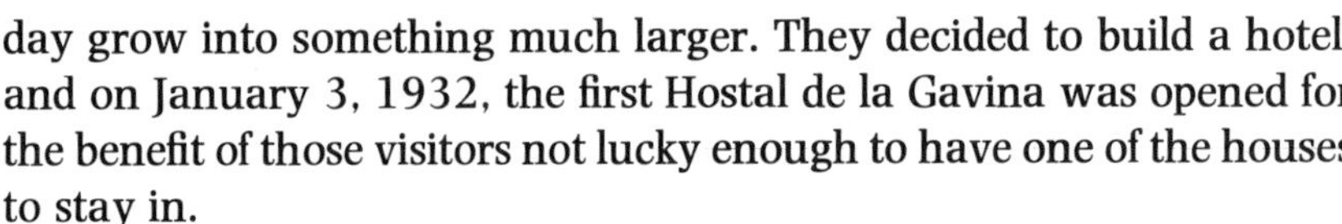

day grow into something much larger. They decided to build a hotel, and on January 3, 1932, the first Hostal de la Gavina was opened for the benefit of those visitors not lucky enough to have one of the houses to stay in.

This first Hostal consisted basically of two houses, attached on either end to form two sides of a square, like a pair of architectural Siamese twins. The atmosphere, as the word *hostal* implies, was that of an old-fashioned inn where guests felt thoroughly at home and received personal attention from the landlord himself. In the words of the advertisement announcing the opening, "As from the First of the New Year, in the Hostal de la Gavina, the manager, Manuel Nonell, will offer you an open-armed welcome, healthy food and attractive, comfortable rooms." Ten of them, to be precise, every one of which was designed by Masó himself and filled with local antique furniture, Catalan ceramics, old ships' bills of health and so on. So successful was La Gavina's first season that the following year another fourteen rooms were added, the dining room was enlarged and a tea lounge was constructed. All were filled with old, classical and local decorations. And the cost of a room? Twenty-eight pesetas for full board. Complete tea, including orchestra: five pesetas. By 1935 La Gavina was beginning to attract the official world of Spain, as well as a number of important foreign visitors. One of these, a high society figure named Prince M'Divani, happened to be killed on one of the Gerona coast roads near S'Agaro. Unfortunate for him, but

fortunate for La Gavina, which suddenly became known, through sensational newspaper reports, as a highly exclusive resort for the famous and wealthy. The Costa Brava was hardly known outside Spain in those days, and to those anxious to try a new vacation experience, the name S'Agaro sounded exotic and exciting.

In 1935 Masó died, whereupon José Ensesa immediately called in the architect Francisco Folguera to continue the task that the great man had left unfinished. It cannot have been easy for a man of Folguera's talent to be confronted with a half-completed work, but he quickly became imbued with the spirit behind the creation. One of his first works was the Church of the Virgin of Hope, which fits perfectly into its surroundings as though it had been meant all along.

Under Folguera's direction, S'Agaro changed enormously. New houses arose among the trees, new avenues were laid, a ring road was constructed, and the whole place assumed a quite remarkable splendor. To achieve this, Folguera would often use old architectural units —windows, passageways, arcades and so on—which he removed carefully from buildings about to be demolished, and then incorporated into his own constructions, either alone or attached to plain or whitewashed walls. It was under Folguera that the Hostal de la Gavina assumed its present shape, its mixture of extreme simplicity and great comfort, and many of its most outstanding features. Among his most notable achievements was the oak-paneled, gold-leafed Royal Suite in the style of Louis XV; a suite with an awe-inspiring headboard from which two gold swans keep watch over the Empire furniture and the enormous double bed; the superb Italian-style loggia of Senya Blanca, whose balconies and high, graceful arches look directly out onto the waves of the Mediterranean; the long, vaulted corridors; and the huge lounge, overlooked by a vast Flemish tapestry, a wide chimney decorated with Catalan tiles, and a wooden-beamed ceiling. Seated here in one of the large armchairs one really has the feeling, which all the architects of La Gavina were trying so hard to achieve, of a great Spanish country house; and Folguera's idea of arranging the whole thing into a series of totally separate but at the same time interconnected Mediterranean buildings adds to this sense of intimacy.

By the fifties the tourists had begun to pour on to the Costa Brava in numbers that no one could ever have foreseen. It would have been easy enough for La Gavina to turn its attention from the comparatively small, select clientele that it had hitherto enjoyed toward a mass market. But by then the tradition had rooted itself far too firmly for any shift of ideals to be possible. So although the place grew considerably during this period, its soul remained intact.

In 1960 Folguera died, and once again someone was at hand to carry on the work. His name was Adolfo Florensa, and he had just retired as head of the Municipal Buildings Group of Barcelona. Among his many notable achievements had been the Hospital of Lerida, the Nautical School of Barcelona and the rebuilding of the Palace of Perelada. He was tired and his health was not particularly strong, but he accepted José Ensesa's offer to come to S'Agaro, and the years up to his death were some of his most industrious and fruitful. His last work was the Garbi swimming pool—arguably one of the most elegant in the world, with its Balearic porticos, its spacious porch open on four sides and its statue of the Venus of S'Agaro by the famous artist Rebull. The hotel's large, cool entrance hall was also Florensa's work.

It was almost inevitable that S'Agaro would sooner or later start to become the center for formal artistic events, and in 1956 José Ensesa launched the first S'Agaro Music Festival. Spain is not short of such affairs. And yet I would doubt if, of all the beautiful settings in Spain where music is performed, any is more enchanting than the gardens of Senya Blanca at S'Agaro.

As always, it was to his own country that José Ensesa turned first for the artists and talents he wished to attract to S'Agaro, and in many ways the greatest compliment that could be paid to the place is that not only the country's three greatest lyrical artists—Victoria de Los Angeles, Teresa Braganza and Montserrat Caballé—came there to perform, but also such notable figures as the cellist Gaspar Cassado, Nicanor Zabaleta, Narcisco Yepes, Antonio, Lucero Tena, Eduardo Toldra, and such orchestras as the City of Barcelona, the Barcelona Symphony Orchestra, and the Chamber Orchestra of Madrid.

From abroad came such outstanding artists as the singer Elizabeth Schwarzkopf; the violinists Szeryng, Kulka, and Campoli; the pianists

Top left: Arches over the main entrance. *Top right:* The entrance hall with Florensa's marble floor. *Center right:* The hotel on the S'Agaro peninsula. *Center left:* A corridor with carved antique chests. *Bottom right:* The front door.

Kempff, Waats, Magaloff, and Cziffra; the Hamburg Chamber Orchestra, the Rome Quartet, the Opera Giocosa of Genoa and the State Ballet of Vienna.

Over the years S'Agaro has also attracted many great sporting events—from regattas and tennis tournaments to hockey matches and horse shows. And of course, there have been the guests. The list is endless: ex-King Umberto of Italy, the Queen Mother of Belgium, Prince (now King) Juan Carlos and his wife, Sophia of Greece, British ministers Selwyn Lloyd and Reginald Maudling, Cole Porter, Joan Fontaine, Fairbanks, Sinatra, the bullfighter Luis Miguel Dominguin, Clare Booth Luce.

But these are, after all, only names drawn from a hat. Thousands more not so well-known and some not known at all have enjoyed the peace and beauty of S'Agaro in the fifty years since José Ensesa's father first began to build that house on that barren piece of land.

Josep Plà, the distinguished Catalan writer, once said this about S'Agaro: "It is the most intelligent and most comfortable development phenomenon that has been carried out on the Costa Brava. S'Agaro is a lesson and an example. A lesson in good taste, and an example of order and tenacity at the service of the dignity of the country."

HOTEL DE PARIS
MONTE CARLO, MONACO

THE FIRST TIME I went to the Hotel de Paris was with a party of friends for dinner about five years ago. The little square, with the casino next door and the Café de Paris opposite, was all lit up and looking its absolute best as we drew up outside the front door of the hotel.

Alex, the famous voiturier, hurried forward, spectacles and teeth flashing, to open the car door and wave us up the steps with the great brass railings on either side. As I strolled through the lobby, so grotesquely ornate that it's rather like a bad dream of the sort you get after eating a particularly unwise combination of rich foods, and into the bar, I was confronted by a number of people at various tables and in various attitudes who looked as though they had been placed there forty years before as part of the décor by some mad designer (possibly a relative of the man who designed the lobby). Here, leaning against the bar, staring out across the tables with an air of calm superiority born of enormous wealth, a drink permanently clutched in his pudgy hand, was a mountain of a man in a white suit with a hooked nose and massive jowls looking rather like Sidney Greenstreet in his prime. There, at a table, sitting bolt upright and staring straight ahead with unblinking eyes, was a woman—she could have been any age between 50 and 100—with hair like threads of stainless steel, done up in an elaborate bun over one ear and hanging straight down to her waist over the other. What she was doing there I couldn't say. She spoke to no one and no one spoke to her; she never smiled, never moved her position. Like the man in the white suit, she belonged there, and that was all there was to it.

Later we moved into dinner in the Salle Empire, a room slightly smaller than St. Peter's in Rome, whose elaborate gold decoration, heavy tapestry and massive columns did little for our digestion. High above us on a stage, a three-piece orchestra tiptoed its way through "Charmaine" and "The Indian Love Call." Later the violinist walked among the tables asking for requests. Finally he reached our table near the window. Outside on the pavement, pedestrians paused to stare at the scenes of luxury so near to them and yet so far. The violinist bent a polite ear to my raised finger. Would he be kind enough to play "The Man Who Broke the Bank at Monte Carlo"? He straightened up, frowned, shook his head and said he was sorry but he didn't know that one. He moved on to the next table. Whether his apparent ignorance meant that he had never heard of anyone breaking the bank at Monte Carlo, or simply that he was rather hard of hearing, I couldn't say. Perhaps he thought I was trying to make fun of him. The fact remains that Charles Coburn's song was probably responsible more than any other single factor for creating a popular vogue for Monte Carlo at the very beginning of its career. What is more, the song was based on a real man called Charles Deville Wells, who broke the bank not once but several times. He was an Englishman, a common little fellow by all accounts, who claimed to have found an infallible system. He succeeded in three days in turning his

Monaco, with the new Sporting Club in the lower left-hand corner.

original stake of $800 into $80,000, which was a lot of money at the turn of the century. In those days each roulette table carried the equivalent of only $8,000 in gold coins, and when Wells, through a combination of luck, courage and a personal adaptation of the Martingale system, broke the bank, this meant that he denuded the reserves of his particular table, a black crepe sheet was laid drastically over it, and a fresh supply of gold coins had to be sent for.

Wells went on playing for eleven hours a day, for three days, and finally, on his way out, as if to add insult to injury, casually broke the *trente et quarante* table too. That was in May.

"They always come back," said François Blanc, the casino's founder. Wells did, six months later, and won $20,000, a quarter of which he spent on Casino shares. In January the following year he was back again with his mistress, a former artist's model named Jean Burns, and a palatial yacht called Palais Royal. This time he lost heavily and was forced to wire to England to his friend Catherine Phillimore—sister of the famous judge—for funds, which she promptly sent. These he also lost. A year later he was arrested on the yacht by the French police in Le Havre and accused of obtaining money by false pretenses. The truth was that The Man Who Broke the Bank at Monte Carlo was a confidence trickster, posing as an engineer and inventor, whose only invention was a musical skipping rope. The yacht he had obtained on the grounds that he was testing a fuel-saving device for coal-burning ships.

The entrance hall.

Wells was never permitted to return to Monte Carlo again, yet he remains today the principality's most famous visitor.

It might also be argued that it was on account of people like Wells that Monte Carlo was dubbed "The Sunny Resort for Shady People."

Before we rush ahead too far and too fast, let us pause for a moment and reflect on how it all began.

In the middle of the nineteenth century, the little principality of Monaco was in deep trouble. It was blessed with few natural sources beyond fish; it was virtually inaccessible except from the sea; it was on the verge of bankruptcy; and its prince, Charles III, was at his wits' end. It was his mother, Princess Caroline, who, aware of the growing fashion for sea bathing and spas, sent her secretary Eynaud to Baden-Homburg to investigate rumours of the *succés fou* of a casino that had been opened by a man named Benazet.

Eynaud hurried back with the news that the reports were well-founded. It was his considered opinion, moreover, that anyone wishing to open a casino would be well advised to do so under the guise of a spa.

And so it was that in 1858 a thirty-year concession was given to Napoleon Langlois and Albert Aubert to build and manage the *Bains de Monaco*. To this end they acquired the Villa Bellevue, which, though well named, was unfortunately extremely difficult to reach. (An etching of the period shows the casino staff peering anxiously through a telescope at an approaching boat that may or may not have contained prospective gamblers.) In addition to this, there were no decent hotels in Monaco, and it was only a matter of time before Langlois and Aubert went bankrupt and the whole enterprise fell apart.

Watching with great interest from Nice was François Blanc, the man who had been responsible for the success of Baden-Homburg. He knew very well that there was a fortune to be made on the Riviera in the winter months when Homburg and the German casinos were closed, and he was determined to be the one who was going to make that fortune. The long and short of it was that Blanc was granted the concession for the casino. The company he set up was called the *Société des Bains de Mer et Cercle des Etrangers*, and an early shareholder was the cardinal who later became Pope Leo XIII. The site he chose for the casino was a deserted hill across the harbor from the place called Les Spelugues ("the caves"), which he at once renamed Le Mont Charles—hence Monte Carlo.

The casino was opened with great pomp on February 18, 1863. In the same year, work began next door on the Hotel de Paris. The architect was Dutrou, and his design was based largely on that of the Grand Hotel des Capucines in Paris. On January 1, 1864, the hotel was opened. At that moment the Hotel de Paris and the casino became firmly and irrevocably entwined, and have remained so to this day.

Anyone of note who has come to Monte Carlo to gamble over the past century has almost certainly either stayed at or spent time at the hotel. In all the dramas—big social events, romances and bankruptcies—the hotel has usually featured at some point.

For instance, in 1910 a demonstration was staged by some militant Monegasques who were protesting against the employment of too many foreigners by the casino. Prince Albert, fearing for his sovereignty, not to say his safety, appealed for assistance from the British Naval Fleet which happened to be moored in Villefranche harbor. A contingent of sailors thereupon converged upon Monte Carlo with orders to watch the flagpole of the Hotel de Paris, to which a large number of cases of wine had recently been delivered. The moment the flag was hoisted they were to rush into the hotel, tear open the cases (which were in fact filled with arms and ammunition), and take up a position to defend British property. As it turned out, such drastic moves were not required: the prince retained his supreme power and the hotel continued along its path of success.

Again, it was invariably in the Hotel de Paris that the great cocottes of the nineties were to be seen night after night, dining quite openly and always undisturbed with dukes, princes, and sometimes even kings. Their manners were as beautiful as their faces, their behavior at the gaming tables was impeccable and their jewelery rivaled that of royalty itself. Yet never once did they cross the dividing line between the *monde* and the *demimonde*. One of the most famous was La Belle Otero, the gypsy girl who could boast at the end of her life that she had shared the beds of some of the most illustrious men

Top: Dinner on the hotel terrace, with the Casino in the background. *Bottom:* A quiet moment in the Casino.

in Europe. Only once was she ever upstaged by another woman—an honor that has been attributed to many women but which in my version goes to Liane de Pougy. Liane, having seen Otero arrive one night glittering with jewels, herself arrived the following night wearing a plain white dress and no jewels at all, accompanied by her maid who was hung about with jewelery far above anything that Otero had ever worn.

Lily Langtry, the famous actress and friend of Edward VII and Judge Roy Bean, was another beauty who graced Monte Carlo in those golden days before the First World War. So too was Gaby Deslys, the dancer, who was the mistress of King Emmanuel of Portugal and died tragically at the age of twenty-nine. Harry Pilcer, once her dancing partner, recalled a story of how at the Hotel de Paris she had been presented with a cask full to the brim with gold pieces by a rich admirer. The gift impressed her only mildly, since she was at that moment wearing a seventeen-string pearl necklace, each pearl of which was roughly the size of a small grape.

The briefest glance through the society magazines of the early years of this century is enough to convey the glamor, the talent, the wealth and the beauty that Monaco attracted: the King of Württemburg, the Aga Khan, Lloyd George, W. J. Vanderbilt, Saint-Saëns, Massenet, the Rajah of Pudukota, Noilly Prat, Lily Langtry, A. J. Balfour, the Duke of Norfolk, Paderewksi, the Grand Duke of Luxembourg, the Duchesses of Marlborough and Roxburgh . . . and always, always at least half a dozen Russian Grand Dukes. A dozen of them patronized Monaco during that time. The senior quartet—Michael, Boris, Andrew and Cyril—were the sons of Tsar Alexander III; the juniors included Nicholas, George, Serge, Dmitri, Vladimir and several more. Many of them had their own homes, others stayed with friends, but all of them patronized the Hotel de Paris.

So, after the First World War, did stars like Dietrich, Chaplin and Swanson; millionaires like the Duke of Westminster and James Henessy; best-selling authors like Maugham, E. Phillips Oppenheim, Margery Allingham, and Colette; statesmen like Clemenceau and Churchill.

The war years were humiliating ones for Monaco. With refugees crowding in from France, the Summer Sporting Club closed, as too for a short time did the Casino. By way of adding insult to injury, the Hotel de Paris was taken over by the Gestapo as their headquarters. Monte Carlo, however, was made of stern stuff and succeeded in maintaining her dignity throughout. But although in 1945 the old girl made every effort to carry on where she had left off six years before there is no doubt that in the years that followed she went visibly downhill. Many of the old clients had died off or lost their money, and it was not until 1954, when Aristotle Onassis arrived on the scene, that she began to regain some of her former glory. At first he acquired only forty per cent interest in the *Société des Bains de Mer*; but later he increased his holding until he had full control. It was well known that he and Prince Rainier did not get on, but it was impossible to deny that Onassis's extraordinary personality was responsible for persuading great men like Churchill to return to Monte Carlo, thus restoring to the principality some of its former prestige and glamor.

Onassis was also responsible for installing in the hotel a new sea-water indoor pool to replace the old thermal baths that had been destroyed at the end of the war by a stray RAF bomb, as well as adding four new floors including a sensational grill room on the very top. "It will be the greatest view in the world," he was reputed to have replied to a nervous, penny-pinching colleague. "What does it matter how much it costs?"

But all the wealth in the world cannot ensure the continuing greatness of even the greatest hotel without the expertise and reputation of a great manager. The Hotel de Paris was fortunate indeed in having at that time a man who is acknowledged to be one of the greatest managers of them all—Jean Broc.

But of all the people responsible for Monte Carlo's continuing success over more than a century, none have played a greater part than the gamblers themselves—from the famous Nicolas Zographos, the head of the so-called Greek Syndicate who once won nine million francs on two cards at baccarat, to the most modest vacationer who, with a handful of francs in his pocket, pauses by the front door of the Hotel de Paris to give the traditional rub to the knee of Louis XIV's horse.

One would have given a lot to watch Zographos playing baccarat. They say he was very like a bank manager in his behavior and the way he dressed. Every day he would arrive after lunching off a grilled cutlet, fresh fruit and mineral water. He would play for a while, then return to the hotel where he would relax in his room before going back at midnight along the underground passage that connects the hotel with the casino, arriving just as the big game was about to start. By 1939 he was worth anything between ten and fifty million dollars, and yet the year before he had lost thirty-six million francs in one week. "Well, you see," he explained calmly, "Monsieur Citroën, the Aga Khan and Mr. James Hennessy were staking about five million francs on each hand."

There are so many great gambling stories associated with Monte Carlo and the Hotel de Paris: like the one about the man who, back in the days when gold coins were still in use, tore a gold button off his coat, put it on a number and won the equivalent of $50,000. Then there was the young man who, knowing that if anyone was ever found having committed suicide in Monte Carlo, the Casino authorities always stuffed his pockets full of bank notes just to dispel any unpleasant rumor that gambling losses had led to his death, feigned death and walked away with a small fortune.

And they do say that one immensely wealthy Russian gambler by the name of Nicolas Stakaieff, who lost his whole fortune in 1916,

Top left: Part of the hotel's vast cellars. *Center left:* A wall lamp in the hall. *Bottom left:* A detail from the façade. *Top right:* Louis XIV just inside the

main entrance (gamblers always touch the horse's knee for luck on their way out). *Bottom right:* A chandelier in the hall.

was given a life pension by the casino. King Farouk, of course, was an habitué of the casino, and on one occasion lost $8,000 to an English player who promptly died of a heart attack. Onassis, they say, rarely played the tables, although he would sometimes accompany Churchill, who liked to play a few ponderous hands after dinner before tottering back to the Hotel de Paris and his bed.

The hotel is still as extraordinary as ever it was, and yet however much one may try to persuade oneself otherwise, one knows that life can never again be as glamorous and exciting in Monte Carlo as it was in the old days. The hotel has stayed much the way it was, but the outside world has moved on. The Sporting Club is reputed to be pretty dressy still on Friday nights, but the casino is full of scruffy people in beards and jeans. And when I went to chat with Alex the voiturier one evening about the old times, he told me politely but firmly that he was tired of giving away good stories so that writers and journalists should make money out of them. From then on he was going to keep them all to himself so that when he retired, which he did last year, he could write his memoirs and make a little for himself.

Of course one still enjoys the big rooms in the Hotel de Paris, with their high beds and their tall-ceilinged, echoing bathrooms. And yet the sight of Stavros Niarchos's yacht at anchor below, filling half the harbor, is strangely anachronistic. And to dine on the terrace outside the hotel on a summer's night is to feel like something in a sideshow. As you eat your *langouste au whisky*, and smack your lips over the still champagne and make admiring noises at the soufflé and savor the 100-year-old cognac, tourists and sightseers walking by stop and stare at you as though you are a living tableau representing a byegone age. Their faces show neither scorn nor resentment, and yet I couldn't help wondering if one day someone might not feel moved to lob a small bomb among the tables.

Sensible guests, of course, take no notice at all. Their attention is sufficiently occupied with the food and the wine and the strains of "Love Story" coming from the little orchestra just inside. And I feel quite sure that if I were to reveal to any of them my revolutionary fantasy they would reply, as one wit did when someone mentioned the possibility to him: *"Bombe glacé* or *bombe vanille?"*

PALACE ST. MORITZ, SWITZERLAND

OPPOSITE Like a great Gothic castle, impenetrable to all but the most highly favored.

TEN O'CLOCK ON a bright winter's morning and the resort of St. Moritz is on the move. At the bottom station of the Chantarella-Corviglia-Piz Nair railway the lines of skiers are now at their longest and most impatient. In the square below, more skiers wait for the yellow buses that arrive every half-hour to take them east along the valley to the slopes of Pontresina and Diavolezza or west to Corvatsch and Sils. Below the town, the walkers, riders and cross-country skiers move ant-like across the vast white surface of the frozen Moritzsee lake. Above, the Cresta Runners in their spiked shoes, helmets, pads and knickerbockers stand chatting idly beside the Cresta Club building at Junction, waiting for the last runs of the morning before the sun melts the ice. High above it all in Corviglia and Piz Nair, the ski lifts whirr and hum, the skiers leap and swoop and crouch, and the arms of the waiters on the sun-terraces are already tired from delivering countless cold drinks and cups of coffee. The clothing and jewelery shops are doing brisk business, the cafés are full, and the streets are loud with the roar of car engines.

But in the lounge of the Palace Hotel, little stirs except specks of dust in the sunlight that shafts in through the windows overlooking the lake. The occasional guest, richly tanned, wanders up to the reception desk to leave a message; a Frenchman sits with the hotel's owner, Andrea Badrutt, and discusses the arrangements for a private party he is throwing later in the week; a young waiter gives a final flick of the duster to the already gleaming tabletops; from time to time the rhythmic clump and jingle of open ski boots announces that one guest is actually about to take to the slopes.

Otherwise the enormous room is silent and empty. Later, much later, the place will begin to fill up. Toward lunchtime the beautiful women and their escorts will decide the time has come when they can once again face their friends and the day. They will don their ankle-length fur coats and matching hats and boots and make their way out into the town—on foot for the hairdressers, the shops, and the Corviglia Railway that will take them to lunch at the exclusive Corviglia Club, or in their Rolls Royces and Range Rovers to visit friends. The less enterprising will start brushing up their tans on the hotel terrace; the slightly more energetic may head downstairs for the hotel skating rink or the magnificent indoor pool.

By five in the afternoon they begin to gather once again in the hotel lounge for tea and cakes, and life at the Palace begins to pick up. The backgammon boards come out, the gossip flows, staggeringly beautiful women wander about having their hands kissed, harassed waiters rush about with trays of tea and drinks, and above the noise, a pianist trots out "I've got plenty o' nothing." There isn't a chair or sofa to be had. Now that the place has become a miniature casino, people tend to sit where they want. In the old days, though, before and just after the war, important guests had their own special places in the lounge and woe betide anyone unwise enough to sit down in one of them without checking first. Table Number One, just behind a pillar

Top left: One of the traditional old bedrooms. *Top right:* The Moritzsee Lake. *Center left:* The pool. *Center right:* A door handle in one of the old bedrooms, and a detail from the

ceiling. *Bottom left:* By tea time the lounge is full of people playing backgammon. *Bottom right:* A statue of William Tell and his son and a detail from the exterior woodwork.

on the right as you walk through, was reserved for years for the Duke of Alba—at one time Spanish ambassador in London and King Alfonso's right-hand man—a figure of such enormous wealth and influence that when he was in residence at the Palace the king would come to see *him*.

Hoteliers are the greatest snobs in the world and Andrea Badrutt —who, with his brother Hans Jurg, owns the place today—is no exception. When he talks about the Duke of Alba and the other illustrious people who have spent winters there, he does so with unconcealed delight. When exactly it was that the high society of Europe picked out his family's hotel to be their major headquarters for the winter season is not clear. Presumably on the day in 1896 when Andrea's grandfather, Caspar Badrutt, opened the Palace. By that time, the idea of a winter season was well established, having been introduced by Caspar's father, Johannes Badrutt II, thirty years before.

His father, Johannes I, a peasant from the village of Pagig, had moved to Samedan just down the road from St. Moritz in 1815 and built the Hotel A La Vue de Bernina. Following his death, his son sold the hotel and moved to St. Moritz where he built the Pension Faller, later to become the Engadiner-Kulm and now known simply as the Kulm. Johannes II was something of an innovator. Not content with managing the Cresta Run, building a skating rink and instigating curling in St. Moritz, he also introduced electricity into the Kulm. In 1889 he died and the Kulm passed into the hands of Peter Badrutt, who ran it for thirty years until his death in 1913. Although the famous hotel remained in the Badrutt family for many years afterwards, they finally relinquished control. The same thing happened to the Hotel Caspar Badrutt, which Johannes II's son Caspar opened in 1883.

The Caspar Badrutt was a fine hotel, but Caspar's greatest achievement was unquestionably the construction of the Palace. Viewed now from the middle of the lake it dominates the town of St. Moritz like some great Gothic castle, impenetrable to all but the most highly favored. Approached from the town side, its great stone walls, castellated main entrance and high tower give it an even more forbidding aspect. Caspar Badrutt must have taken great pains to ensure that the exterior was sufficiently impressive, the public rooms sufficiently grand, the bedrooms sufficiently spacious and well-appointed that the rich and titled of Europe would come to look at this amazing new hotel and would return, bringing their friends.

Which, of course, is exactly what did happen. Very soon the Palace had established itself as *the* alpine resort hotel. In 1912, an Englishman named Goldman opened an equally grand and equally well-appointed hotel a mile or two away. He called it the Suvretta House and his clients were, and still are, some of the most distinguished and important in the world. But while the Suvretta offered peace and quiet and an escape from the hurly-burly of the social and business round, the Palace encouraged extravagance and high spirits. It

catered for the sort of people whose idea of a holiday was not to escape from everyday life but to transport it with them wherever they went. They came to the Palace to see their friends, not to get away from them; the annual habit grew, and thus it was that over the years the hotel began to develop the characteristics of a club.

In the years between the wars, Caspar's son, Hans, father of the present owners, never faltered in his efforts to make the Palace even more attractive. He added the fourth and fifth floors, the enormous restaurant and the tennis courts. His greatest hobby was collecting fine antiques, every one of which he put into the hotel. And when there was no more room there, he put them into the Chesa Veglia, the famous restaurant and night spot further up in the town which he opened in 1935 and which is still owned by the Badrutt family.

The Badrutts are still the sole owners of the Palace—no mean achievement in these days of groups and chains and corporations—and they continue to maintain the very high standards that their father and grandfather established eighty years ago. The service provided by the four hundred members of staff is unequaled anywhere; the rooms are without exception magnificent; a guest can order a meal any time of the day or night; and downstairs in the sauna room a lady not only changes your towel every time you so much as dampen it, but there is always a refreshing bottle of mineral water lying in a basin under permanently running ice-cold water.

The family provides the comfort and setting, but in the end it is the guests themselves who are and always have been responsible for deciding what sort of hotel it should be. "St. Moritz is still the resort where the big names come," Andrea Badrutt insists, "and the Palace is still the hotel where they stay." Mr. Badrutt admits that several old guests have built their own homes, but they still use the Palace as much as ever they did—for parties, for meals, for collecting messages and mail. And he insists that the guest list still reveals many famous and important names. "You cannot say, for example, that Herbert

Top, left to right: Dancing in the Chesa Veglia; the approach from the town, even more castle-like and forbidding; part of the lounge. *Above:* Part of the door of the old billiard room. *Left:* Andrea and Hans-Jurg Badrutt, who own the Palace.

von Karajan is not a great name, or the Bismarcks, or any of the members of the Corviglia Club. These are important and powerful people. Have you looked at the list?" I had, as a matter of fact. It is pinned to the wall between the concierge's desk and the elevator doors, and it lists not only the names of all the members of the club, but also the rules governing the introduction of temporary members. The Corviglia Club, although founded in the Palace Hotel in 1930 by the Duke of Alba, belongs to no hotel. The Palace merely handles all its catering. "It is," to quote the printed notice, "the exclusive property of its LIFE MEMBERS. They *alone* allow themselves to introduce *their transient friends* as TEMPORARY GUESTS, by signing for them an application, to be approved by the Committee." And it is only after a formal notification of their membership that the successful contestants are permitted at last to enter the sacred portals of the chalet that stands a hundred yards or so from the top of the Corviglia Railway. The Committee includes Comte Rossi di Montelera, Prince Constantin de Liechtenstein, the Duke of Marlborough and the Aga Khan. Life members include the Earl of Warwick, Herbert von Karajan, Mr. Witney Straight and Stavros Niarchos.

To people who are impressed by that sort of thing the list is doubtless very impressive, and must represent quite a challenge to anyone who feels the need to number such powerful and important people among his friends and acquaintances. The majority of us, however, will remain content to sit in the lounge or eat in the dining room or swim in the pool, or perhaps just spend a night in one of the splendid wood-paneled rooms.

For the ones on the inside, the Palace is just like home. For the rest, it is enough to be in one of the world's most fabulous hotels, surrounded by people who may or may not be somebody, enjoying for a while the strange delight of a totally different world.

LA RESERVE
BEAULIEU-SUR-MER, FRANCE

IT WAS HOT that day, even for the Riviera. Almost certainly, one felt, some statistician somewhere was adding a footnote to the history of temperatures of Mondays in late June on the Côte d'Azur.

Not that that was going to stop the residents of La Réserve de Beaulieu from adding another degree or two of color to skins that already resembled the shiny hind quarters of a chestnut mare after a heavy afternoon out with the hunt.

Mind you, I can think of many worse ways to spend a Monday morning than lying in a mindless torpor beside a swimming pool while waiters move silently among the glistening shapes with trays of ice-cold drinks riveted permanently to the ends of their arms, and tables shaded by gay umbrellary are being laid in readiness for lunch.

Very occasionally, by a superhuman effort of will, one succeeded in forcing one's eyes open to take in the view—the long arm of Cap Ferrat reaching out to sea; the rocky coastline above which a never-ending procession of cars and lorries, their roofs flashing in the midday sun, grind their way to Monaco and Italy; a big motor launch leaping across the brilliant sea on its way to Villefranche. . . .

It was just as well that we enjoyed it all when we did, for a few minutes later the whole scene had been totally transformed.

It began with a welcome breeze off the water, which within moments had turned into large powerful gusts, which in turn quickly escalated into full-scale wind. Umbrellas leaped into the air like young goats on the first day of spring, tablecloths turned up at the edges and sent plates and knives and forks crashing onto the floor beneath, waiters began scurrying hither and thither, and for a moment it seemed that the ordered calm of La Réserve might for once in its long history be shattered. Yet within seconds of the outbreak, everything was under control: the tables had all been cleared and set up again under cover; guests already lunching had been ushered into sanctuary; umbrellas had been lowered; loose mattresses, towels and glasses were gathered up. In a matter of minutes not only had life at La Réserve resumed its normal steady pace, but the wind too had abated, like a bully who sees that the object of his threats is not afraid and so withdraws.

Clearly it takes something a great deal more formidable than a few gusts of wind to rattle La Réserve de Beaulieu.

In fact, it would be hard to think of another hotel that is more self-assured, more capable of maintaining its dignity at all times, and more obviously unprepared to compromise over any point. And if this self-confidence borders at times on complacency, it is only the outward manifestation of the unseen and unceasing efforts of Monsieur Jean Potfer to ensure that at no time do the standards he set himself when he first took over the hotel in 1946 slip one iota. If ever a hotel reflected the tastes and character of an owner in every particular it is La Réserve.

OPPOSITE The hotel from the garden.

Top left: The garden. *Top right:* The crest above the front door. *Center:* The swimming pool, looking toward Monaco. *Left:* Jean Potfer, managing director of La Réserve. *Right:* The dining room.

Originally it was a restaurant. Within a few years of being opened by the Lottier family in 1894, it had become one of the best known and most distinguished meeting places on the Côte d'Azur for the crowned heads of Europe and leaders of high society. While the restaurant of La Réserve was at the height of its fame, just after the First World War, the young Jean Potfer was given a job (his first in the hotel business) at the Crillon in Paris. By 1936 he was manager of the Miramar in Cannes.

La Réserve closed when the Second World War broke out, but in 1942 Potfer was approached by a friend who asked if he was interested in their going into partnership, taking over La Réserve, doing it up and, when the war was over, re-launching it as a hotel. On July 21, 1946, La Réserve opened its doors with twenty-two rooms on two levels. (They couldn't really have opened earlier; the whole property was mined.) Potfer's idea was to maintain the high standards of cuisine for which La Réserve had been known so many years, and at the same time to provide accommodation that would complement the restaurant. From the beginning it was, as he himself explained, a "low-profile hotel." Despite this, it gradually began to attract a clientele of the highest quality. "In those early days," he remembers, "it was the only new hotel on the coast and we had a lot of Hollywood people coming here to rest and be private. People like Clark Gable, Gregory Peck, Orson Welles, Rita Hayworth. . . ." In 1955 he added a third story and another eleven rooms, and finally in 1960 brought the total number of rooms up to fifty, which is what he has today. The Hollywood film actors gave way over the years to a more cosmopolitan clientele that included the ex-King of Italy, the Archduke Otto of Hapsburg and Lord Mountbatten of Burma.

And over the years too, Monsieur Potfer has worked relentlessly to maintain and, where possible, improve the look of the hotel both inside and out. The result is unquestionably one of the most elegant hotels in the world.

He describes the style of the hotel as "Italian Renaissance with Louis XIII furniture, plus Florentine and Venetian, plus a bit of Spanish, plus quite a lot of local work—all of it adding to what might loosely be called Mediterranean."

The long dining room which looks out on one side onto a little formal garden and on the other onto the sea, is one of the prettiest I have ever seen. At the height of the season you will probably find between 150 and 200 people eating in it every day. "I have always tried to keep the place small and to keep the feeling of a private house," Potfer explains. "Quality and quantity do not mix. Some people say I have too many staff (a hundred to look after fifty rooms) but then to keep the quality you need a lot of staff. When I started in 1923 things were much easier, staff was easy to find. Now I have to be—not old-fashioned—but follow the old ways. If I don't I'm finished. It takes years to build a reputation and only weeks to lose it."

VILLA D'ESTE
CERNOBBIO, ITALY

IF YOU ARE coming down the stairs at the Villa d'Este and your mind is not too preoccupied with the prospect of lunch or a swim, your eye will almost certainly be caught by a large gray statue of a man who, at a casual glance, would seem to be sitting nonchalantly on the ground staring soulfully into space. Closer examination, however, reveals that his expression is one not so much of philosophical reflection as of pain verging on agony. Moreover, his hand is clutching fiercely at his abdomen. A wound perhaps from some barbarian sword? Or from Cupid's arrow? one wonders idly—until one looks more closely at the head. It is the moustache that finally reveals this classical poseur for the modern fraud he is. This is no Roman warrior, resting after heroic deeds on the field of battle; nor need he think that the removal of his clothes cuts any ice with the really observant guest. A cigarette in an elegant holder beneath that carefully trimmed moustache, a monocle in that soulful eye and a Homburg hat on those curly locks, and everything at once falls into place. The work is obviously modeled on a well-heeled guest who lost control of himself at the dinner table, ordered a third helping of *fettucini* with butter and anchovy sauce and suddenly, in the privacy of his room, began to regret his overweening greed.

My theory is borne out by the fact that at the other end of the long first-floor corridor is a statue of similar proportions of a woman in a suppliant posture wearing a similar air of despair. This, quite obviously, is the wife having a word with the manager upon discovering that her husband cannot pay the bill. As to the artist, no one I spoke to in the hotel seemed to have any idea of his identity, or of the date of the works, or of how they came to be where they are in the first place.

But then one of the delights of the Villa d'Este is that it is full of curious things. There's the Napoleon Room that was specially decorated by Count Domenico Pino, a Napoleonic general, in preparation for a visit by the Emperor that never happened. There are the extraordinary false fortifications set into the rocks up behind the hotel, built for the same general by his wife so that he could keep himself in practice during campaign breaks by beating off mock attacks from local inhabitants who had been roped in to impersonate enemy troops. Then there is the very odd statue, attributed to Canova, in the room just outside the bar, of Venus being crowned by Eros; and the great mosaic wall beyond which one can glimpse, at the top of a long avenue of cypress trees bordered by a series of artificial waterfalls, a statue of Hercules.

It is precisely because the hotel has evolved out of a much older building and because the history of that building is peopled with so many rich and extravagant eccentrics that the Villa d'Este is such a fascinating place to stay.

For a start, Lake Como itself is not just a pretty place. In Roman times it was known as *Lacus Larius* (Bellagio is often referred to still as "the pearl of Lario"). In 59 BC Julius Caesar sent five thousand

OPPOSITE Afternoon on Lake Como.

colonists there to establish "Novum Comum." Pliny, father and son, were born in the area, and Virgil almost certainly visited it.

In the fifteenth century where the hotel now stands was a convent known as the Cloister of Sant' Andrea, built by nuns who had fled there to escape the civil war. Some of the columns are still standing in the hotel grounds.

During the eighteenth century Como began to build up the reputation, which it still has today, as the center of the world's silk trade. One of the leading families in the area at that time was that of the Ottavio Gallios. They had three sons, two of whom became prominent in the government while the third, Tolomeo, went into the church and later returned as Cardinal of Como. The family meanwhile had acquired the cloister, and on his return Tolomeo decided to do the fashionable thing and build himself a villa in the grounds. The job of designing it was given to the famous architect Pellegrino Pellegrini of Valsolda.

The villa, named Garrovo after the mountain stream that flows into the lake, was completed in 1568. Tolomeo, as well as being a Cardinal, Secretary of State at the Vatican and Dean of the Sacred College, was also a great patron of the arts, and whenever he was in residence the villa hummed with life. He bought land as well as pictures and reliefs, and it was during his time that the great plane tree was planted beneath which lunch is now served on summer days.

After the Cardinal's death the villa became the property of his nephew, the Duke of Alvito, who continued his uncle's work by embellishing the grounds and the house, and such was the fame of the Villa Garrovo that in 1615 the Sultan of Morocco arrived with a huge retinue to see the place for himself.

For over two hundred years the Gallios reigned supreme at Cernobbio. But toward the end of the eighteenth century they began to lose interest in the villa.

For a while it was taken over by a Jesuit order and the villa and its grounds were virtually abandoned. In 1782 Carlo Tolomeo sold the estate to Count Ruggero Marliani, colonel to the Emperor of Austria and delegate to the Government of Lombardy, who left it two years later to his nephew, the Marquis of Calderara, an elderly Milanese playboy who had married Vittoria Peluso, a ballerina from La Scala, known familiarly as "Pelusina." Snubbed by Milan society, she moved to Cernobbio where she devoted all her time, and her husband's money, to restoring the villa to its former glory. She built the avenue of cypress trees that lead up to the statue of Hercules, as well as a reputation as a prodigious party-giver.

But undoubtedly the best known and most regal period of the Villa d'Este's history began on the day in 1814 when Caroline of Brunswick-Wolfenbuttel, wife of the Prince Regent of England, arrived at Lake Como, took one look at the view and decided she had at last found her spiritual home. Caroline had been so rebuked and reviled by the future king that she had virtually been forced into exile, and

Top left: The Grand Hotel Villa d'Este with the Reine d'Angleterre building to the right. *Top right:* The façade of the Reine d'Angleterre. *Above:* The female partner has been reconstituted after being smashed to smithereens by a falling tree. *Right:* Part of the gardens. *Far right:* The mosaic with the false fortifications above.

VILLA D'ESTE

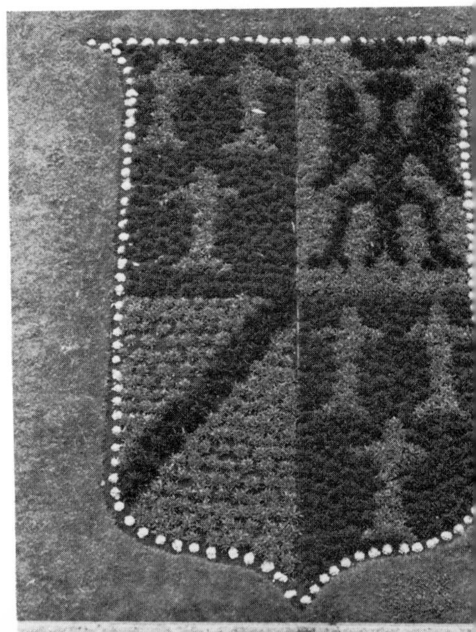

spent years wandering through Europe like a lost soul. The time she spent at Como was to prove the happiest period of her life. For a year she lived in a rented villa, but at last Donna Vittoria consented to the sale of the Villa Garrovo. It was at this point that the Villa Garrovo became the New Villa d'Este—the "New" being added to avoid confusion with the Villa d'Este near the Tivoli in Rome.

Legend has it that during the five years Caroline lived there the villa had never before witnessed such parties, such excesses, such gay abandon. The people of Cernobbio, unlike those in London, were very fond of Caroline, and she repaid their friendship with great generosity, which included among other things the road between Cernobbio and Como. Unfortunately, she was one of those people on whom the sun never shines for very long. So lavish was she in her generosity that she was soon deeply in debt—so much so that when she returned to England to take her place on the throne, she was forced to leave the deed of sale of the villa with her banker in Rome, on the understanding that when she paid off her debts it would be returned to her.

She was never to see her beloved Villa d'Este again. Not only did her husband order the doors of Westminster Abbey to be slammed in her face on his Coronation Day, but he then attempted to divorce her. The divorce never took place, but in 1821 Caroline, exhausted by the scandal, died. In her will she left the villa to her secretary Bartolomeo Pergami, but because of some legal tangle, nobody claimed the villa and it was abandoned until 1829.

For some forty years the place had a variety of owners and tenants, including the Empress Fedorovna of Russia. In 1873, a group of businessmen formed a limited company to buy the Villa d'Este and the adjoining building. Thus did the Grand Hotel Villa d'Este come into being.

To say that the first view the visitor has today of the Villa d'Este is the same one that Caroline had of it in 1814 would be something of an exaggeration, but not wildly so. A broad terrace has been built so that hotel guests can walk up and down or sit in the early evening sipping drinks and watching the sunset over the lake. Many new outbuildings have been put up over the years, and of course the huge first-floor rooms in which Caroline and the Czarina of Russia slept have long since made way for hotel bedrooms of less, though in some cases only slightly less, regal proportions.

One thing that almost certainly has altered very little over the years is the wonderful view across the lake and the sublime sense of peace that Lake Como manages to cast over everyone who has ever been there—from Longfellow, Goethe, Mark Twain, Shelley, Stendhal, Flaubert, and Franz Lizt, to the somewhat less serious names whose regular patronage gave the hotel its great reputation in the years up to the Second World War.

One man who remembers those days as though they were yesterday is Carlo Magni, surely one of the greatest concierges of

modern times. Magni has been with the hotel for forty-four years. He is a man whom I would travel many miles to see if I were in trouble and needed reassurance.

Magni attempts to hide his great gifts of memory, organizational skill and amateur psychology beneath the bushel of humility. ("You remember Carlo Magno?" he said the first time we met and I was having trouble with all Italian names, "Charlemagne in French? It is almost the same name. The only difference is that he was the Emperor of France and I am a concierge.")

Yet not for nothing is he known as "the concierge of the Iron Gate"; not a lot escapes his sharp eye.

"Once upon a time," he recalls sadly, "only presidents of big companies came here. Now you get general managers—and sometimes not even that. In the old days, they would never have dared to be seen in the same hotel as their boss."

Mr. Magni talks of such matters in kindly tones and yet one suspects he feels them deeply. Which is understandable when you think of some of the people he has seen in his time—heavies like Ribbentrop and Ciano, who met there in 1939 to sign their Iron Pact; Mussolini, and William Randolph Hearst; stars like Clark Gable, Garbo, Douglas Fairbanks and Mary Pickford, Robert Montgomery, Wallace Beery; scions of some of the oldest aristocratic houses in Italy—Torlonia, Sciarra, Aldobrandini, Colonna, de Robiland. He reels the names off with relish and regret. "Once upon a time, the name Villa d'Este was on everyone's lips. Top hoteliers would come here to try and discover our secret. The Palace Hotel at St. Moritz would try and get our staff. It is not quite so glamorous now as it was in those days."

But then nothing is as glamorous as it was, or as classy or extravagant or amusing, and certainly not to a perfectionist like Carlo Magni. But he need not fear. The Villa d'Este is still as great a hotel as ever it was in those golden days before the war. And as long as there are people like Carlo Magni to look after the guests, it will probably remain that way.

PRECEDING PAGE *Clockwise from upper left-hand corner:* The lake from the dining room; Venus being crowned by Cupid just outside the bar (attributed to Canova); Carlo Magni, one of the greatest concierges of modern times; the entrance hall and staircase; the entrance hall; the Villa d'Este's coat of arms, picked out in flowers near the front entrance; the terrace after drinks; the boathouse beside the Reine d'Angleterre building; "the greedy guest". THIS PAGE The end of a festive summer's night.

BROWNS HOTEL

COLLECTORS' ITEMS

BROWN'S
LONDON, ENGLAND

I HAVE HAD a soft spot for Brown's ever since the day I went there some five years ago to interview a young and talented actress by the name of Angharad Rees. My idea had been to let her decide where she would like to go for the interview, and she had plumped, without a moment's hesitation, for Brown's, adding that certain friends of her father (the Professor of Psychiatry at St. Bartholomew's Hospital) always stayed there.

We met on a cold, foggy Saturday in November in Harley Street and drove to Brown's in Dover Street through the gray gloom of the afternoon.

It was tea-time, and the wood paneling glowed with warmth and welcome as we walked along the soft carpeted corridor toward the hotel's other entrance in Albermarle Street and into the lounge. The little tables had been laid with white linen tablecloths and tea was already on the go as we entered—small square sandwiches, brown bread and butter, hot buttered scones, toasted tea cakes and little cakes whose icing sweated gently in the warmth that emanated from the two glowing open fires. Goodness knows what we talked about, but ever since that afternoon, Miss Rees has been one of my closest friends, and Brown's one of my favorite London hotels.

Rarely can a hotel have been quite so beautifully and aptly named as Brown's.

All the old-fashioned, friendly, down-to-earth Englishness that is conjured up by that particular combination of vowels and consonants is there in the hotel. Brown's. In a way, it tells you everything you need to know about the hotel and any attempt to describe it further seems almost superfluous. Yet so extraordinary an institution is Brown's Hotel that some sort of explanation is called for. Why, for instance, is it called Brown's in the first place?

Well, that part of it is simple enough. That was the name of the man who founded the hotel. James Brown, to be more precise. Not a great deal is known about him, apart from the fact that he had been a gentleman's servant, a position that no doubt enabled him to appreciate better than most what it was that travelers required in the way of food, comfort and service.

OPPOSITE The Albemarle Street entrance.

In 1836 Brown married one Sarah Willis who had been lady's

maid to Lady Byron, the widow of the poet Lord Byron. Sarah was, by all accounts, a woman who knew her own mind. She was also something of a businesswoman, and it seems likely that she was responsible for James's decision in 1837 (the year Queen Victoria came to the throne) to buy No. 23 Dover Street, one of a number of houses that had been built at the end of the seventeenth century by a couple of property tycoons of the day.

James Brown's neighbors at that time consisted of eight peers, three baronets, the Bishop of Ely and the Russian ambassador, all of whom would surely have been horrified had they suspected for a single moment that before long there would be a hotel in their exclusive street.

The following year Brown acquired the lease of the house next door, No. 22; in 1844 he bought No. 24 and the year after that, No. 21. This row of four terraced houses still makes up the front of the hotel on the Dover Street side.

Having acquired the four houses, the Browns were in a position to set about running the hotel they had been dreaming of for all those years. Of course in those days a hotel was a very different sort of establishment from its modern equivalent. Basically, it consisted of a number of separate suites in which guests lived and slept and ate all their meals. Apart from a reception hall, there were virtually no public rooms at all. The four houses together were perfect for such an establishment, comprising four floors, attics, basements and staircases, so that the place could be divided into sixteen family suites, each with a servant's room.

By the middle of the nineteenth century, more and more people began to travel to London by train from the English countryside; and when the Great Exhibition opened in 1851, bookings at Brown's, only a fifteen-minute walk away from the great glass and iron building in Hyde Park, were solid.

In 1859 Brown, his health deteriorating rapidly, decided to call it a day. He sent word to Mr. J. J. Ford, the owner of Ford's Hotel in Manchester Square, that Brown's was for sale, and that same evening Mr. Ford was round with the deposit. Mrs. Brown, who was away at the time, was furious when she heard what her husband had done. However, despite the use of practically every known business device, she was unable to have the transaction called off. The only thing she did manage to salvage was the valuable freehold of No. 23. The year after the sale of the hotel, James Brown was dead.

The new owner of Brown's Hotel, James John Ford, had begun life on a farm in Wiltshire and gone to London to seek his fortune. His first job consisted of holding people's horses while they went about their business, but soon he had acquired enough money to enable him to set up a highly profitable livery and stable business in Oxford Street, and later his own hotel.

The same year that he acquired Brown's, Ford also acquired a son, Henry, who, after leaving school, set off to Canada where he worked

Top: The lounge at tea time. *Other photographs:* The original Edwardian stained glass beside the staircase, and the original banisters.

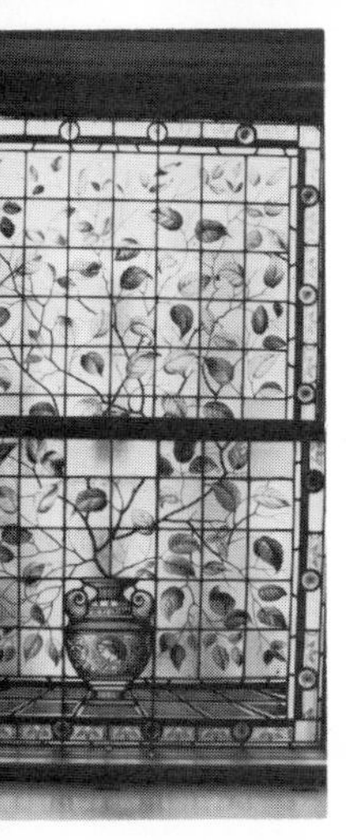

for the Canadian Pacific Railway, building wooden depots across the prairies. He would undoubtedly have stayed on there had his father not summoned him home in 1882 to take over the management of the hotel.

Up till then, very little had been done to the hotel in the way of improvements and modernization. However, Henry Ford's experience in the New World had not been wasted, and the moment he returned he set about introducing all sorts of revolutionary innovations. Within the first three years he had installed one of the very first elevators in London, "fixed baths," electricity—which came originally from the basement of a house in Holborn via a great number of wires laid across roads and people's roofs—and the telephone, to which he had been introduced by an obscure young Scotsman from America by the name of Alexander Graham Bell. It was J. P. Morgan, who had stayed at Brown's during the 1870's, who suggested to Bell that he stay there too when he went over in 1876 to try and interest the British government in his invention.

As it turned out, he could not have chosen a better place to stay, since the Fords had installed a private telegraph wire between the hotel and their own home at Ravenscourt Park, some four miles away. Using this wire, Bell fixed up his own instrument with himself at the hotel end and young Henry at the other. To begin with the experiment was a total disaster; all that could be heard was a great deal of very loud clicking and crackling caused by other telegraph subscribers on the line at the same time. They tried again at three o'clock the following morning when no one would be using the line, and this time the voices came through loud and clear. The first successful telephone call in Britain had been made from Brown's Hotel.

Other daring innovations during the last years of the nineteenth century included a men's smoking room and a public dining room—although a butler still went round to everyone's room during the morning in order to take their orders for the day's meals and find out at what hour they wanted them served.

In 1889 Henry Ford acquired the St. George's Hotel in Albermarle Street, which backed directly onto Brown's. It was an easy enough matter to join the two hotels together, since all that divided them was a small courtyard and a few walls. These were knocked down so that a passageway could be made right through from Dover Street to Albermarle Street. At the same time various structural alterations were made to both parts of the hotel. A fifth floor was added, and on the Albermarle Street side a new stucco front and portico were built and two mosaic panels announcing "Brown's and St. George's Hotel" were placed in the wall. They have remained there to this day.

The St. George part, named originally after St. George's Church in Hanover Square, was eventually dropped and now survives only in the name of the bar.

Finally, in 1906 the three adjacent houses in Albermarle Street

were bought, bringing the total number of houses of which Brown's is comprised to eleven.

Small wonder, then, that the corridors meander, the rooms are all different shapes and sizes, and the place is full of nooks and crannies and corners and unexpected recesses. After all, at one time there must have been at least twenty-two different staircases situated in different parts of the building, and the whole charm of the place today stems from the fact that it was never built as a hotel in the first place.

Eccentricity, when mixed with charm and kindness, is an irresistible quality, and I have no doubt that it is this air of nonconformity that has attracted so many extraordinary guests to the hotel.

In the 1880's Brown served for a while as a refuge for Don Carlos, Pretender to the Spanish throne, at the same time, although neither was aware of the fact, as one of King Alphonso XIII's staunchest supporters. It is believed that Napoleon III and the Empress Eugénie stayed there following the Franco-Prussian War, and the Comte de Paris, Pretender to the French throne, held court regularly in his suite there between 1886 and 1894. In 1886 Theodore Roosevelt arrived at Brown's, and walked from the hotel one morning to St. George's Church, Hanover Square, where he was married to a lady by the name of Edith Kermit Carow. A facsimile of their marriage certificate still hangs in the hotel.

In 1905 two other Roosevelts checked in to the hotel: Franklin and Eleanor, on their honeymoon.

"We went first to London," wrote Mrs. Roosevelt many years later in her autobiography, *The Lady of the White House*, "and were horrified to find that in some way we had been identified with Uncle Ted and were given the Royal Suite at Brown's Hotel, with a sitting room so large I could not find anything that I put down. We had to explain that our pocket book was not equal to such grandeur, but that made no difference. We lived in it for those first few days in London."

At the foot of the stairs just inside the Albermarle Street entrance there is a painting depicting the scene in Albermarle Street on May 12, 1895, when Queen Emma, Regent of the Netherlands, and the fourteen-year-old Queen Wilhelmina, who had been staying incognito at Brown's, departed in an open landau drawn by four horses with postillions and outriders laid on specially by Queen Victoria. In 1920 Wilhelmina, by then a widow herself, returned to stay at Brown's with the eight-year-old Princess (now Queen) Juliana, and it was in Room 36 of Brown's that the Dutch government in exile declared war on Japan.

During the First World War, Queen Elizabeth of the Belgians lived in the hotel with her children, where she was visited from time to time by King Albert, on leave from commanding his armies on the Western Front.

Another royal resident was King George II of Greece, who fled to Brown's in 1924 following the establishment of a republic by Venizelos. The room that is now the Hellenic Suite on the first floor

was the official court of the Greek Royal Family until 1935 when the monarchy was restored and King George was able to return to Athens.

The following year the Emperor Haile Selassie fled there from Mussolini's invading army, as did King Zog of Albania.

But of all the famous names who have occupied rooms at Brown's over the past 130 years, none evokes quite so many fond associations as Rudyard Kipling, who first went there in 1936. No one knows for certain whether it was at Brown's that he wrote *The Jungle Book* and the *Just-So Stories*, but on the walls of the Kipling Room, now a private dining room, hang a number of framed illustrations from both those books as well as from *Captains Courageous*, and by the window stands the green leather-topped writing desk at which he wrote.

Henry Ford finally retired in 1928, after forty-six years in charge of the hotel. Later Brown's was taken over by the Bon family, the famous Swiss hoteliers, and in 1948 it was bought by Trust Houses Forte, Ltd., who have over the years spent an enormous amount of money and effort in building new bathrooms, laying new carpets, redecorating walls, hanging new curtains, buying new furniture.

And yet for all that, I doubt if the feel, the atmosphere, even the look of the hotel has changed much in the last fifty years. The clientele may be a little more commercial in character than it was in the old days when Brown's was the recognized haunt of clergymen, doctors and nice English families up from Somerset; yet the hotel makes no more pretense at sophistication than it did when James Brown opened it early in Queen Victoria's reign. How could it possibly compete with Claridge's or the Berkeley for instant service when it was never built as a hotel in the first place and every order—trolley, waiter and all—has to be brought up from the kitchen or the bar? But then the sort of people who enjoy Brown's are not particularly concerned if the whisky and soda is not actually in their hand within seconds of being ordered, or if the breakfast trolley arrives *after* one has started shaving. They are there because they like the rather slow, old-world atmosphere of Edwardian furniture and hand-painted windows on the stairs; they like the clubby atmosphere of the St. George's Bar with its green leather banquettes and its open fire; they like the fact that the reception consists of two little tables halfway along the corridor between the two entrances, and the fact that there are two entrances; they like the smallness of the place and the comfy atmosphere of the lounge at tea-time and the friendliness of the staff.

Top: Edwardian comfort in one of the bedrooms. *Bottom left:* Theodore Roosevelt was staying at Brown's at the time of his marriage. *Bottom right:* The original sign outside the Albemarle Street entrance.

BYBLOS
ST. TROPEZ, FRANCE

ONE OF THE great advantages of having breakfast by the pool at the Byblos Hotel in St. Tropez is that, having ordered it, one has plenty of time to take in one's surroundings: the glitter of sunlight on the pool that laps the wall beneath the bar balcony; the curious angles and corners of the white-walled, red-tiled Provençal-style buildings that cluster around, peering surreptitiously down on the pool through half-open blue shutters as though in permanent hope of a glimpse of bare flesh; not to mention the owners of same—prosperous-looking men in early middle age carrying rather too much weight and not quite enough humility, accompanied by contented-looking girls in their late teens, carrying a great deal of gold jewelery and very little else; young men of Apollonian proportions, arranging towels and mattresses; middle-aged ladies, their unmadeup faces gleaming with sun-oil, having their toe-nails painted by girls in jeans from the hotel's hairdressers' shop; one rather more than middle-aged lady wearing nothing but a bikini bottom that might have been designed by Omar the Tentmaker, and waving around a pair of breasts that looked as though they had just been washed and she couldn't do a thing with them . . . nothing out of the ordinary, you know. Just the run-of-the-mill sort of sights and sounds any guest at the Byblos might expect to be confronted with while waiting for breakfast. . . .

Behind me, an English couple were wrestling with the knotty problem of whether or not he should try and get a Telex through to his office before or after they had had a swim—a dialogue brought to a brisk halt by the discovery that he couldn't remember the office Telex number and she had forgotten to bring it. A long silence ensued. And then, drawing on years of experience that had taught her that there's nothing like a change of subject to clear the air, she suddenly announced in ringing tones, "The great thing about this place is that you can wear things here you can't wear anywhere else. You know what I mean?" Another long pause. "I suppose," said the husband finally, "I *could* always give them a ring." They passed the remainder of breakfast in silence.

But of course she was quite right. You *can* wear things at the Byblos that you cannot, or at any rate probably *would* not wear, at any other place. The thing that struck me though, as a first-time visitor to St. Tropez, was just how self-conscious everyone down there seems to be about clothes—or more often than not, the lack of them. Having been made aware over a number of years now (and who hasn't?) that sartorially anything goes in St. Tropez, I had expected to find crumpled khaki denims, Tahitian sarongs, bared bosoms and bottoms being sported with much the same insouciance that stock-brokers carry rolled umbrellas in the City of London or ladies in Japanese tea-rooms wear kimonos. Not so, not so.

The vintage lady with the unwieldy bosoms removed her top (at every opportunity, I might add) with all the naturalness of a nun appearing first on the bill at a striptease show. The word "topless"

OPPOSITE All life revolves around the hotel swimming pool.

Top left: Everywhere there is wood. *Left and above:* The front door and the restaurant. *Top right:* A sudden view glimpsed through a window and the hotel's emblem picked out on a wall.

seemed to spring to everyone's lips at approximately three-minute intervals. And any normal healthy young man who tells you that he goes to St. Tropez because of its literary associations and fishing-village atmosphere is a downright liar.

On the other hand, it is perfectly true that before the war St. Tropez *was* nothing more than a little fishing village and it *was* a favorite holiday haunt of among others, Colette. Then in the late fifties, as everyone knows, Roger Vadim and Brigitte Bardot popped in for a fortnight's holiday and so did everyone else.

Suddenly St. Tropez was the St. Germain-des-Prés of the South of France, and it was on the crest of this huge wave of trendy enthusiasm that a Lebanese gentleman from Beirut called Prosper Gay-Para rode into town with plans for a hotel that would in its architecture, relaxed style of life, type of clientele and cost exactly complement this choicest of French seaside resorts. He called the hotel Byblos after the fishing town on the Lebanese coast north of Beirut, and in the hotel brochure there is a lot of rather pretentious stuff explaining the geographical and artistic affinity between Byblos and St. Tropez. What cannot be denied, however, is that Mr. Gay-Para's architect succeeded in producing a building that never fails to be interesting. Long corridors with sudden views glimpsed through windows; light, chintzy bedrooms, some with canopied four-posters; little studios with their terraces set inside the tiled roofs where you can sun every part of yourself in the utmost secrecy; a wide, airy entrance hall where you can sit on long, low sofas under a carved wooden ceiling, serenaded by the sounds of a tinkling fountain and businessmen at the reception desk busy trying to book air tickets to Los Angles or Teheran. And everywhere, everywhere, there is wood. Heavy old wooden beams, wood-paneled bathrooms, high wooden beds, open wooden galleries. . . .

The outbreak of the Arab-Israeli War prevented Mr. Gay-Para from seeing his dream realized, and it was left to his successor, Sylvain Floirat, the head of companies like the radio station Europe No. 1 and Matra engines, to complete the task and invest the hotel with the style that has attracted all the familiar names without whose patronage the Byblos just wouldn't be the place it is—whatever it is: Mireille Darc, Princess Ira Fürstenberg, Gunter Sachs, Aquelli, Heinecken, Polanski, George Hamilton, Jagger, Sacha Distel, Alain Delon. . . .

I'd like to be able to report that I spotted one of them in the bar or by the pool. But somehow there always seemed to be so many more interesting things to be looking out for.

CHÂTEAU DE ROCHEGUDE
ORANGE, FRANCE

I WAS AWAKENED shortly after eight by the loud, insistent clang of a church bell just outside my window. It poured through the narrow slits of the dark green shutter with the sunlight. I opened my eyes slowly and with some difficulty. It was a simple room, plain to the point of starkness: white walls, a chair, a table, a chest of drawers. Filled with the sound of the bell it had a vaguely monastic feeling that was pleasantly peaceful—though I daresay the unmonkishly comfortable Empire-style bed had something to do with that. Also the fact that the whole of the previous day had been, in contrast, noisy, packed with incident and worry, and one way or another absolutely exhausting.

We had left Paris in a gray drizzle late in the morning, wasted an hour in an inexplicably slow-moving jam on the *Periphérique*, got a flat tire just outside Lyon and had been obliged to go into the city to buy a new one, with the result that it was seven-thirty or eight before we finally found the sign to Bollène and another twenty minutes after that before we finally drew up outside the massive gates of the Château de Rochegude. By the time we had checked in, unpacked, and eaten dinner it was too late and too dark to do anything but collapse into bed, our minds filled with a jumble of images of medieval walls, stone passages, great staircases, ancient statues and eighteenth-century furniture, our stomachs with grilled *côtes d'agneau* and Cuvée du Château de Rochegude 1970, and our eyes with dust and sleep.

I flung open the shutters to be confronted with as breathtaking an early-morning view as I imagine I am ever likely to see. There, below the castle, stretching into the distance for as far as the eye could see, were fields and fields of vines, pale green in the warm June sunlight, fresh from the previous day's rain. To the right, wooded hills rose above the pinkish brown tiles of the church roof. The tones of the bell rang out patiently across the valley for a few more minutes and then stopped abruptly. For a while I could hear nothing for the ringing in my ears and then gradually I became aware of a sound that I had thought never to find again in such abundance in the South of France—the sound of bird song.

Breakfast was served on a terrace beneath a great wall which towered above us, pale gold in the sunshine, behind a row of cypresses that stood at its feet like little green sentries. Orange juice, coffee, and croissants; the butter started melting in the hot sun the moment it was set on the table. Sounds of village life floated up from below—the unmistakeable clatter of a van delivering something, a woman shouting at a small boy, water being drawn at a pump.

We were no longer tired, the journey was over and forgotten—left behind with the mist and rain in Paris and the ruined tire in Lyon. And yet we were still as bemused as we had been the night before.

What was this place exactly? A castle, to be sure. One of the most highly rated members of the Châteaux Hotels organization. *"Haut lieu des côtes du Rhône, l'immense château au confort inoubliable domine les vignobles du soleil,"* in the words of the guide. That much was clear.

OPPOSITE The château.

But many things still puzzled us. For instance, how did it come into being as a hotel in the first place? All those huge rooms, full of furniture and statues and carpets and pictures—of all styles and all periods: were they really as genuine as they seemed? By ten in the morning, all the other guests we had seen the night before in the dining room and at breakfast on the terrace seemed to have disappeared, leaving us with the whole place to ourselves. Had they gone out for the day? For good? Why should we have been so lucky? And the birds: knowing the Frenchman's passion, especially in the South, for killing and eating more or less anything that moves, why was it that so many of them had decided to find sanctuary on this great castle on the hill miles from anywhere?

It was not until we had made the acquaintance of Mr. Hubert Segura, the co-owner and director of the Château de Rochegude, that some of our queries were to be answered.

Monsieur Segura is exactly the sort of man I feel sure most new arrivals in a hotel hope their host is going to look like but very rarely does: substantial and moustachioed, dark-suited and dark-haired, exuding friendliness and enthusiasm and confidence. And mixed in is just a hint of worry that, comfortable and well-fed and happy though you may assure him you are, there is surely something more he can do to make your stay even more satisfying.

He had been an antique-dealer until 1963 when he had decided to buy the château, which had been in a state of considerable disrepair since the death of the last surviving Marquis de Rochegude in 1945.

PRECEDING PAGES *Left, top to bottom:* An eleventh-century parchment, the the twelfth-century dove of peace above the gateway, and statuary in the park. *Center:* The château dates from the twelfth-century. *Right, top to bottom:* A room off the entrance hall (the sideboard is Louis XIII); the pool and park with the château behind; the cellars, which include 450 casks of Cuvée de Rochegude. THIS PAGE *Top left:* A corner on the way to the dining room. The saddle is eighteenth-century Paraguayan. *Top center:* One of the bedrooms. *Right:* Hubert Segura. *Far right:* St. Francis of Assisi, Jeanne d'Arc, and Pope Benedict VI.

For three years he had labored night and day to restore the castle to something approaching its former glory. (One of the Marquis' stables, although it has been cleared out to make way for tables and chairs, has been left, at least as far as the floor, walls and ceiling are concerned, exactly as Monsieur Segura found it; and if it is any indication of the state the rest of the rooms were in when he first set to work on the château, then to have made it habitable at all must be counted something of an achievement in itself.) The castle had been in the hands of the Rochegude family since the twelfth century. Both it and the village were bisected by the frontier between the Kingdom of France and the Papal States during the period of the Avignon popes, so that one half of the castle was under the jurisdiction of the king and the other of the Holy Pontiff. The job of governing the two parts was placed in the hands of two priors—a task that must have been made curiously difficult by the fact that the frontier ran through the middle of the castle's kitchens!

During the seventeenth and eighteenth centuries much reconstruction work was carried out on the château, although the splendid medieval cellars, hewn out of the rocks at the time of the original building, remained as they were. And it was in the cool depths of the cellars that we began, appropriately enough, our guided tour of this most extraordinary hotel.

Rochegude used to be a great wine center, perhaps as famous as the Beaujolais is today. Some of the earliest vines in France were planted in the region by the Phoenicians. (A marble statue of Dionysus, found by Monsieur Segura *in situ* when he arrived, is now in the safe keeping of the Museum of Saint Germain-en-Laye, just outside Paris.) Sadly, the wine industry of the region was drastically curtailed by a disastrous disease which in 1893 killed off the large majority of the vines. Even so, the château is able to boast no fewer than 450 casks of Cuvée de Rochegude; the cellars of the château provide the setting for many a gathering of *Chevaliers de Tastevin* of the Côtes du Rhône; and the last marquis enjoyed the distinction of being the only sherry-producer in the whole of France. On a slightly more sinister note, you can still see in one dark corner of the cellar the original *oubliette*, the appallingly deep hole (not even in modern times has anyone succeeded in reaching the bottom) down which was shoved anyone unwise enough to displease the marquis of the day.

Back in the living light of day, we stood for a while in the castle courtyard. High above us, over the main gate, sits the bronze figure of a bird—the dove of peace—in a delicately wrought cage.

"Have you noticed the bird song?" Monsieur Segura asks us, and is delighted that we have. "That is because I never shoot birds here and never allow anyone else to. I love animals and I love people to bring their animals with them—dogs, cats, anything they like, within reason."

He points out the thirteenth-century well in the corner of the courtyard and the twelfth-century tower before we retire once more to the cool of the castle itself.

Monsieur Segura is justly proud of the way he has restored the interior of the building, and so much had he to show us that in the end he sounded more like a tour guide than the owner of a hotel.

In one room he shows us a seventh-century coffer with seven locks, all in perfect working order, and a Louis XIII sideboard. In the long vaulted gallery that runs along one side of the courtyard and is now separated from it by plate glass he shows us some authentic eleventh- and twelfth-century parchments, some rare sixteenth-century vases and statues of Benedict VI, Jeanne d'Arc and St. Francis of Assisi.

In a sort of intermediate room we admire an eighteenth-century Paraguayan saddle, and a pair of Renaissance doors and a column that have been strategically placed as a disguise for the elevator.

Through to two more smaller rooms, there to be shown a very rare shell-shaped armchair and an equally rare set of Beauvais furniture—chairs, settee and tapestry-covered table—and an eleventh-century kitchen chimney. And so it goes on, one antique collector's delight after another: a Louis XVI clock in blue enamel and ormolu on top of a Napoleon III chest of drawers, a Charles X desk which George Sand is said to have used. . . .

The bedrooms are equally splendid. They all have names. Laetitia is done entirely in Empire style; Chinon has an Aubusson screen depicting the four seasons. Our minds reeling, we head for the more mundane delights of the swimming pool, which is reached by crossing

Top left: A view from one of the corridors of the principal courtyard. *Top right:* The village and the château seen across the vines. The last Marquis de Rochegude produced the only sherry in France. *Bottom left:* The well is thirteenth-century. *Bottom right:* The front door. *Far right:* The desk on the right was used by George Sand.

a footbridge high above the village street and then following a path through a charming small park, past more pieces of antique stone statuary, until one is even farther from the maddening crowd than we were in the château itself. The really hearty can, if they wish, continue on up even higher through the woods to the very top of the hill behind. The view over the park and the château and the vineyards beyond is, I am told, extremely worthwhile. I preferred to work up my appetite for lunch in the bright blue coolness of the pool.

We ate salad and fruit and drank chilled rosé on the sun-baked terrace, lingering over it, not wishing to leave the peace and beauty of the place. But in the end it was time to pack up the car and move on. As we said goodbye, Monsieur Segura suddenly blurted out, "But this is ridiculous that you should be leaving now, just as you have begun to enjoy the place and we have got to know each other. This afternoon you should be making an excursion to some of the wonderful châteaux in the area, then coming back here for dinner. And after dinner we could have had some drinks and talked and then had more drinks and then done the same thing the next day. It is not enough that you stay only a day and a night. Next time you must stay a week—at least." Next time, Monsieur Segura, I will. I absolutely promise you.

Hotel
Eiſenhut

EISENHUT
ROTHENBURG OB DER TAUBER, GERMANY

THE STORY GOES that during the Thirty Years War, the Catholic Army of the Emperor Charles V, led by one General Tzerklas Tilly, laid seige to the little Protestant town of Rothenberg ob der Tauber in Franconia. Invasion seemed imminent and the townspeople were preparing for the worst when the mayor, knowing General Tilly to be something of a gambling man, suddenly came up with a plan to save Rothenburg. The plan was so brilliantly simple that the citizens must have wondered how nobody had thought of it before. He sent a messenger to the general with a proposal for a wager: whichever of them succeded in quaffing $3\frac{1}{2}$ litres of red wine in one go without a pause, could do as he wished with the town of Rothenburg. The wager was accepted, and on the Monday after Whit Sunday, the mayor—preceded by mounted guards, drummers and pipers—emerged through the main gates of the town and marched purposefully toward General Tilly's camp. The two shook hands, watched as a pair of enormous pitchers were filled to the brim with wine, then seizing the containers they both began to drink. The general drank quickly and had already consumed half his amount before the mayor, an older and wiser man, had reached a quarter of the way. From then on, the general's consumption slowed down rapidly; but the mayor continued to drink at the same slow, steady rate and, tortoise-like won the race by a good half liter from the rasher hare General Tilly. The general handed the remaining wine to his aide-de-camp, shook hands with the mayor, bowed slightly and returned to his tent. That same afternoon, the mayor stood with the citizens on the walls of Rothenberg and watched the imperial army march away down the Tauber Valley. It is rare to find such gentlemanly behavior in any conflict between Catholics and Protestants.

To this day, every Whit Monday, this historic event is commemorated by the citizens of Rothenberg in a spectacle called the *Meistertrunk*, or Master Drink. Soldiers, musicians and drummers in gorgeous costumes throng the streets; a procession is formed, and everyone marches out to the site of General Tilly's camp, where they celebrate the safe delivery of their town from the hands of their enemies over three hundred years ago.

As anyone who has ever visited Rothenberg will know, they have a great deal to be thankful for. This little town on the River Tauber has been preserved almost entirely in its original state; and when today's citizens march past the twelfth-century houses, through cobbled streets from which all but the most essential traffic signs are banned, and beneath which most of the telephone and electricity cables have been cunningly concealed, the scene they are reenacting cannot be very different from the original.

In these days when nothing that costs money is staged unless someone stands to profit from it, it is hard to believe that the *Meistertrunk* is not performed for the benefit of the tourists but for the enjoyment of the Rothenbergians. Similarly, the town is maintained in its authentic state first and foremost for the pleasure of being

OPPOSITE The hotel is made up of four ancient patrician houses.

able to live among beautiful surroundings that have remained untouched for nearly a thousand years. As one inhabitant put it, "The idea is to keep Rothenberg alive and real, not to turn it into a Disneyland."

But of course the sightseers and the tourists inevitably come. They wander up and down the streets and stare, and very welcome they are too. Some are able to devote little more than an hour or two to the place before it is time to return to the bus, and trundle on to the next stop on the itinerary. The lucky ones, with time and money on their side, can afford to put up for a night or two at the Hotel Eisenhut.

This extraordinary hotel is made up of four patrician houses, three of which stand next to each other on one side of the street, and the fourth of which stands opposite.

Eisenhut means "Iron Hat" (a splendid medieval example of which hangs over the front door) and it was also the name of the grandfather of the present owner, Mrs. Pirner. A hundred years ago, one of the houses was a Weinstube where the locals used to meet and drink, and it was to this Wine Cellar that Herr Eisenhut, a wine grower down in the Tauber Valley, used to sell much of his produce.

Toward the end of the nineteenth century, the town of Rothenberg, which had been more or less forgotten for four hundred years, began to be discovered by painters. In 1890 Herr Eisenhut, realizing that the time was not far off when Rothenberg would need a good hotel, bought two of the houses and set about converting them.

Had Eisenhut's granddaughter not had the good fortune to meet, fall in love with, and finally marry a thoroughly able hotelier by the name of Georg Pirner, there is no knowing what would have become of the place. As it was, by the 1920's the Hotel Eisenhut had begun to acquire a reputation that spread not only through Europe, but as far as the United States. Among the signatures of famous guests, kept under glass on one of the tables in the sitting room, I found those of Siegfried Wagner, the composer's son; Mr. and Mrs. Winston Churchill, their daughter Sarah, and Professor Lindemann—later to achieve fame as the government's chief scientific adviser; and William Randolph Hearst, his son, and Marion Davies.

Mr. Pirner, whose portrait hangs over one of the settees in the sitting room, died in 1959. Since then the hotel has been owned and managed, with great success, by his widow.

Both Mr. and Mrs. Pirner were avid collectors and amateurs of good furniture, fine paintings and wood carvings. Every room in the Eisenhut is filled with such an astonishing mixture of furniture, carvings, tables, statues, clocks, fireplaces, nooks and crannies. All are of different styles and periods, none really going with anything else, but they combine to produce an overall air of amiable eccentricity in which it is almost impossible not to feel at home.

Everywhere inside the hotel there is something extraordinary to catch the eye—starting with the entrance hall, the ceiling of which is supported not only by great wooden beams but by a massive octag-

Top left: Signatures of famous guests in a corner of the lounge. *Top right:* The Hofstube was once an interior courtyard. *Above:* The entrance hall and staircase.

onal column at the base of which, between two wicked-looking pikestaffs, sits a beautiful carved Madonna and Child. To the left of the hall is the old Weinstube; to the right is the old-fashioned Buergerstube in which we enjoyed a delicious lunch of pork, pancakes and light white wine from the region. From the center of the hall the wide, heavily-banistered staircase leads away upstairs, while at the far end, down some steps, is the sitting room. This in turn leads out onto the garden terrace with a marvelous view across the Tauber Valley.

Most spectacular of all the rooms downstairs is the Hofstube. This was once an interior courtyard between two of the houses, until the sixteenth-century oak galleries on either side were closed above and the whole thing was turned into one of the most unusual banquet rooms I have ever seen.

Upstairs, narrow corridors wind their way inconsequentially through the houses, changing levels and direction with such rapidity that a guest who has drunk rather too much wine at dinner stands a good chance of never finding his room at all. I should not be surprised to learn that the hotel is haunted by the ghost of a former guest, who wanders the corridors in a hopeless quest for Room 42.

Frau Pirner's choice of bedroom décor may not be to everybody's taste, but no one could possibly attack it on the grounds of dullness. Some of the rooms have been left as they were in the 1930's, with the bed enclosed modestly within its own hard-board partitions. Others are smothered from floor to ceiling with flower designs, which in one case had proliferated into the wash basin and the lavatory bowl. The Stork's Nest is on two levels—below, a sexy double room; above, a nursery with a Victorian cot.

Frau Pirner's love of the unusual and unexpected extends to every part of the hotel. When the German Agriculture Minister and his Spanish counterpart came to the Eisenhut for lunch one day, instead of finding their table decorated with flowers, they were astonished and touched to see that Frau Pirner had created an elaborate centerpiece out of apples, tomatoes, corn and all the fruits of the field. For the German Minister of Railways, it was toy trains.

But there is a serious side to the Eisenhut too. The hotel owns the largest private collection of pen-and-ink drawings of military costumes by the artist Anton Hoffman; on one wall there is a stone, designed by Dürer, which was once used by Alois Senefelder, the inventor of the lithograph; and the linden-wood figures in the sitting room by Ignatz Gunter are rare and of great value.

"It's really like staying in a museum," a friend told me when I said I would be going to the Eisenhut. I should have said it was more like staying with a generous and rather eccentric family. In the words of the family motto, printed inside the menu (and I assure you, this sounds a good deal better in German): "Where the same old family has drunk its wine, here in this room you are always welcome."

L'HOTEL LANCASTER
A
PARIS

LANCASTER
PARIS, FRANCE

OPPOSITE The ashtrays are made specially for the hotel at Limoges.

TIME WAS WHEN I would have stepped down from the boat train at the Gare du Nord to be confronted by a small crowd of *chasseurs* in uniforms of various hues, bearing the insignias of all the best hotels in Paris. My porter would probably have found the particular ones I was looking for—the six or so in blue from the Lancaster—and from that moment on my journey would have been over, my *ennuis de voyage* dispersed like an early-morning cloud in the warmth of the sun. Nowadays, unfortunately, the Gare du Nord seems less a final destination than a halfway point in an apparently endless journey into the interior of Paris. That day, certainly, there were no cheerful faces, no blue uniforms to disperse the cloud of gloom and despair that had, after some six hours of traveling, descended over me. Indeed, as I forced my way out into the station forecourt, staggering under the weight of a large suitcase, a heavy drizzle had started to descend from a dun-colored sky. A taxi was as difficult to catch as a chicken who knows it has been picked out specially for Sunday lunch, the driver might have been a deaf mute for all the reactions I had to my cheery cry, "au Lancaster!" and the rush-hour Parisians seemed even more bent on self-destruction than I had remembered. But then suddenly we were in the Champs-Elysées, heading up toward the ghostly shape of the Arc de Triomphe that loomed out of the evening murk. A moment later we scuttled sideways out of the six lanes of frustration and down the Rue de Berri, and drew up beneath the blue shutters of the Lancaster, and at last the journey was really over.

Anyone arriving at the Lancaster for the first time might be forgiven for supposing that the taxi driver was mistaken.

Through two pairs of heavy glass doors you go, passing a rather good table on your right and a massive arrangement of ferns and flowers in a stone urn on your left; thence into a salon with some nice chairs and a large table in the middle bearing yet another fine flower arrangement, and glass doors that look out onto one of the prettiest little courtyards in Paris, peopled with stone deer, chubby cherubs and a bust of Minerva. And still you haven't arrived at the reception desk.

By this stage you may have begun to wonder if you have stumbled unwittingly into someone's private home. And that's fine, because it is precisely what the general manager John Iversen would like you to think. True, you come to the concierge's desk eventually at the bottom of the stairs, and they do, contrary to expectation, even have a reception desk, tucked round the corner out of sight; but apart from these inevitable necessities, everything possible is done to make a guest feel he is *not* in a hotel.

It is a tradition that goes back to the end of the last century when the building was a *hotel particulier*, or private residence. In those days the entrance was strictly for the horses and the little courtyard was the stables. Later it became an apartment house, until in 1925 it was bought by Emil Wolf from Montreux, who proceeded to turn it into

one of the most elegant of all French hotels by filling the rooms with antique furniture, good paintings and fine fabrics. Perhaps his greatest inspiration was to call the hotel the Lancaster—a name that not only inspired confidence in those male members of the English aristocracy on the lookout for somewhere suitable for *le naughtee weekend*, but, perhaps more importantly, was pronounceable and understandable in both French and English.

And thus it was that the Lancaster began to build up the discerning, discreet and well-heeled clientele it still enjoys to this day.

Monsieur Wolf was, by all accounts, rather grand as hotel managers go. "I have no clients," he is reported to have announced on one particularly expansive occasion, "only friends." And very influential ones too, apparently, to judge by the fact that when Gestapo officers tried to take the hotel over during the war, he went over their heads and put a stop to any such ideas.

In May, 1970, Monsieur Wolf sold the Lancaster to the Savoy group in London (rather suitable really, when you think that the Savoy was built on the site of the palace of John of Gaunt, Duke of Lancaster).

The man chosen to be general manager was John Iversen, now thirty-seven, a protégé of the late Rudolph Richard who made the Connaught what it is today. They could not have found anyone more suited to the job if they had tried. Trained by the Savoy group (he worked in the Grill kitchen under the great Alban, the last of Escoffier's apprentices at the Carlton), he later worked at the Beau Rivage in Lausanne and then went as assistant manager to Reid's in Madeira for four years. It was there that he received the summons to the Lancaster.

His feelings must have been somewhat similar to those that Edward VII experienced following the death of Queen Victoria: namely, how on earth do you follow someone like that?

Iversen, however, was not the sort of man to let even a reputation as massive as Wolf's get the better of him. "The problem was that Monsieur Wolf had refused to make it commercial. I mean, some of his friends he'd charge nothing, and on top of that, he'd give them four times the cost of the room in flowers. My job was to make it commercial and at the same time try and perpetuate the sort of atmosphere that results from a complete lack of penny-pinching." And so it was that Iversen, with the full support of the Savoy group in London, set about creating a Parisian home for the sort of people who consider a particular room (they probably do not even know the number) to be *their* room.

It is easy to see why guests tend to take such a proprietorial attitude towards the hotel. It really is like being in a rather grand private home. Most of the furniture is either genuine Louis XIV, XV or XVI or very good nineteenth-century reproduction. The fabrics and the carpets are of the very best quality.

The delicate ashtrays, in the shape of leaves, are specially made

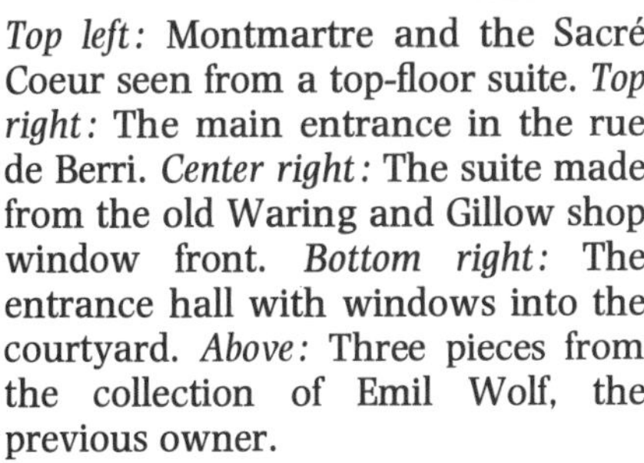

Top left: Montmartre and the Sacré Coeur seen from a top-floor suite. *Top right:* The main entrance in the rue de Berri. *Center right:* The suite made from the old Waring and Gillow shop window front. *Bottom right:* The entrance hall with windows into the courtyard. *Above:* Three pieces from the collection of Emil Wolf, the previous owner.

for the hotel at Limoges. There is not a single vitrine displaying handbags and jewelery. There is not even a bar. When you want a drink, you simply plump yourself down somewhere in one of the little salons and a waiter comes and asks you what you would like. You are never asked to sign for a thing. Every room is different, and if you don't like the little low-ceilinged suite on the top with the brick fireplace and the nooks and crannies that are faintly reminiscent of an English country cottage, then perhaps you'd prefer the one that has the sitting room created out of the old Waring and Gillow shop window front from the rue Faubourg St. Honoré.

The dining room seats only twenty guests, yet there are enough chairs in the two or three little public rooms to seat over fifty—and not many hotels anywhere can boast that. Service is impeccable but unobtrusive; no one ever fusses you in the dining room or anywhere else. As John Iversen put it, "Service should be remarkable by its absence."

And everywhere there are flowers—masses of them, in every room—not with a note saying "Compliments of the Manager" but just there, like all the other pretty things, to make you feel at home.

Naturally there is no travel desk or theater ticket office or anything like that. Instead, there is Alfred Larapidie, the chief concierge. Alfred has been confidant, friend and social secretary to Lancaster guests since 1945—people like Rex Harrison and Ella Fitzgerald, the Duke of Argyll and Duke Biddle, Noël Coward and Greta Garbo. He has had *cassoulet* sent by plane to Rome for Elizabeth Taylor, and red roses to a lady at the Hotel de la Tremoille for Curt Jurgens. He was matey with Dietrich when she lived there and with John Steinbeck, who later invited him to his flat in the Avenue Matignon. He remembers the party John Huston gave the day he won his first race at Longchamps and the cars guests would order to run them down to Spain and Italy. Perhaps more than anything else, he remembers the days when six *chasseurs* would go down to the Gare du Nord or St. Lazare to meet the boat train and return, laden with suitcases and cabin trunks . . . which is more or less where I came in.

OPPOSITE *Top:* One of the suites. The portraits are by Pastoukhoff. *Bottom:* A double bedroom. ABOVE The courtyard where guests dine in summer.

PORTMEIRION
PENRHYNDEUDRAETH, WALES

It must be a good ten years now since I quite suddenly grasped the fundamental principle of human life that it is never worth putting off anything for the sake of a TV program.

One of the rare cases in which I made an exception was a curious thriller series called *The Prisoner*. It starred Patrick McGoohan as a secret agent who, upon announcing to his chief that he was quitting the service, was promptly drugged and kidnapped and transported to a curious village consisting of a most extraordinary collection of houses, pavilions, domes and piazzas that tumbled down a wooded hillside to a tidal estuary. The place was peopled entirely by weirdly dressed eccentrics (other spies unwise enough to have announced their retirement, we were to suppose), who wandered about the little cobbled streets, through the houses, across the piazza, and on and off a mock sailing ship down by the sea.

Why our hero had been brought to this architectural limbo or what he was expected to do there was never quite revealed to us. All we knew for certain was that, try as he might, there was no escape. At the time, assuming it to be a high-budget production, I had supposed that the village was some kind of elaborate stage set, constructed by a designer with an enormous sense of style and humor who, given the chance to realize his wildest fantasies, had done so using all the skill and imagination and exuberant fun he could muster.

In a way, this is exactly what the place was and still is. But I was wrong about its being a stage set. It is a real village, fifty years old this year and situated on the northwest coast of Wales looking out onto Cardigan Bay. It is called Portmeirion, and it is the creation of a remarkable ninety-four-year-old architect by the name of Clough Williams-Ellis.

James Morris captured him marvelously in an article in *Horizon* magazine: "He looks like a figure from the Augustan or perhaps Arthurian past; a large, pointed, flamboyant man, who likes to wear knee-breeches, yellow stockings and bow ties and who strides through this Celtic landscape like a later Merlin."

As a young man Sir Clough had always nursed a conviction that it was possible to exploit the most beautiful place in the world and, far from ruining it, actually enhance its beauty. At the same time he realized only too well that whatever he finally created would have to pay its way. However, he saw no good reason that architectural good manners should not go together with good business.

For years he wandered round the coast of Britain in search of the perfect site. His first idea was to build it on an island where no speculator could get at it, but although he looked everywhere from the Scilly Isles to the Hebrides he was unable to find a site worthy of his design. At one point he even had a brief flirtation with an island off New Zealand.

And then suddenly one day in 1925, an uncle of his, Sir Osmond Williams, wrote to him asking if he would like to buy a place called Aber La which, although only five miles from his home, he had never

OPPOSITE: Sir Clough Williams-Ellis, the creator and architect of Portmeirion.

actually seen except from the sea. His tenant there for many years had been an eccentric and pious old lady who had resolutely refused to allow anyone to enter the grounds, let alone her old mansion down by the water.

She was deeply fond of dogs, preferring their company to that of human beings. The charming little gilt-and-mirrored dining room with the inlaid parquet floor was used exclusively as a kennel for her mongrels, while hidden away among the rhododendrons up on the peninsula is a little dog's cemetery the headstones of which bear such touching inscriptions as: "Mrs. Adelaide's Dear Dog Jim. Once a stray," and the following elegy:

My dear, dear dog, gone before
To that unknown and silent shore
Shall we not meet as heretofore
Some summer morning?

For reasons best known to herself she never, during the whole time she lived there, ever allowed a single bush, branch or tree to be

Above: Portmeirion.

cut down. As a result, by the time Clough arrived he was amazed to find himself in a total wilderness of, as he later described it, "beetling cliffs and craggy pinnacles, level plateaux and little valleys, a tumbling cascade, splendid old trees and exotic flowering shrubs; a coastline of rocky headlands, caves and sandy bays, and, on top of all, a sheltered harbor at the nearest possible point of the sea."

In fact so overgrown was it that when the old lady finally died, it took three days for the undertakers, with the help of a band of woodmen, to hack their way through the undergrowth and reach the house with the hearse.

But Clough Williams-Ellis knew, the moment he arrived, that this was the place he had been looking for. He at once bought as much of it as was available, including the house, and in the years that followed bought more and more of the peninsula, working his way slowly back from the sea, until the place was sufficiently enfolded by trees and fields that it would always be safe from any development that might take place in the vicinity. The first few months were

devoted entirely to clearing great areas of undergrowth, tangled trees, overgrown laurels and fallen branches in order to have some idea of possible views and vistas. At the same time, enormous care was taken not to destroy trees that were of obvious value or might help him in his design.

There is some confusion, certainly in Sir Clough's mind, as to the precise chronology of Portmeirion, which was what he renamed the place. All he knows for certain is that the next thing he tackled after the undergrowth had been cleared was the old house itself. This he converted into a hotel, and the stables and bothy he turned into annexes. The first new building was the Watch House, high on a hill above the hotel ("Just to show people something had happened"). There then followed two cottages a little lower down on the hill, which he called Angel and Neptune. Whether these buildings were in existence when the first guests arrived at the hotel, no one can quite remember. In any event, Portmeirion was launched with a house-party of about thirty people, friends of Sir Clough's, whom he invited down for a weekend to have a look at the place, enjoy themselves, and later to tell their friends about it, if they liked what they saw.

Wherever you look there is something to catch the eye.

Everything that could go wrong did go wrong that weekend. The water pump broke down, the electricity was cut off and the range blew up. But no one seemed unduly upset; how could they be in that setting? As a hotel, Portmeirion was an instant success. Over the years it has succeeded, not surprisingly, in capturing the imagination of many artists and writers, but never more so than in those early years before it was discovered by the *nouveau riche* and *nouveau cultivé*, and the Rollses and Jaguars began to get stuck in the narrow street and the rocks began to ring with the sound of voices complaining that their breakfast had arrived two minutes late and that someone had forgotten to clean their shoes. In the early days, before the war, the people who came to Portmeirion did so largely to get away from a world of increasing efficiency and uniformity. They enjoyed the eccentricity of it all and the fact that things went wrong merely added to the fun. It was twenty years before a single telephone was installed, and even then it was considered an unnecessary intrusion. The hotel's first manager was dismissed because she would insist on economizing—ironing the sheets herself and drying stale cigarettes in front of the fire. She was replaced by a remarkable figure named Jim Wylie, who understood from the beginning that Portmeirion was for the sort of people who had come there to get away from the dreariness of everyday life, not to be reminded of it constantly. Wylie stayed for thirty years, and it as much to see him as to see Portmeirion that so many guests returned over the years.

Shaw stayed there, and H. G. Wells; Noël Coward wrote *Blithe Spirit* in a week in the Watch House and John Osborne wrote *Luther* there; Rose Macaulay was a faithful guest for many years and particularly loved the swimming; Bertrand Russell went there often to write until be bought a house nearby; Richard Hughes was a neighbor;

Charles Laughton came there just before playing Lear at Stratford and was frequently to be found standing on a high cliff above the sea and calling on the winds to blow and crack their cheeks, rage and blow. . . .

Meanwhile, Clough Williams-Ellis continued to build his village.

The last building was completed only five years ago, and because Portmeirion was scheduled by the government in 1973 as a place of architectural and historical interest, it means that not even Sir Clough can alter any of it or interfere with it in any way without official approval. And so there it is, the realization of one man's wildest dream.

Were a modern developer to attempt to build another Portmeirion in one go, no matter how great his resources, he would not succeed. For Portmeirion had an organic growth; it developed bit by bit over the years, without any overall plan. Sir Clough put up buildings whenever and wherever it pleased him. Some of them are entirely his own creation; others have been transported lock, stock and barrel from all over the country; several are part original, part made-up from old buildings about to be demolished. The Hercules Hall, which is used for exhibitions, banquets and so on, is based on the ballroom and sculptured ceiling of a distinguished Flintshire mansion called Emral Hall. News of its imminent demolition reached Sir Clough by chance one day via the pages of *Country Life*. Horrified at the news, he immediately caught a train and arrived at the hall just as the sale was beginning. Really he only wanted the ceiling (which depicts the Labors of Hercules), and it was knocked down to him without any difficulty for just thirteen pounds. Having gone that far, however, it was impossible for him not to buy the rest of the room—mullioned windows, fire grate, oak cornices and all—not to mention a good deal more of the house as well. By the time he had dismantled the parts he needed, crated them, had them transported many miles across the mountains, stored them for several months in a warehouse in Portmadoc while he decided what to do with them, the cost of the enterprise had leaped from thirteen pounds to almost as many thousands. For a long time he contemplated the problem of what sort of building to make with these relics, and in the end solved the whole matter by simply knocking a couple of pegs into the ground—which is exactly where the front door stands today. When the building was finally up, the ceiling provided the room with such a degree of acoustic excellence that such distinguished musicians as Benjamin Britten, Sir Arthus Bliss, Ossian Ellis, Gerald Moore and Yvonne Arnaud have over the years been only too happy to come and perform in it.

Sir Clough refers to Portmeirion as "a home for fallen buildings." Perhaps the most notable is the elegant eighteenth-century colonnade, once the property of a Bristol copper smelter named William Reeve, which now dominates one side of the Piazza. At the far end is another handsome colonnade known as the Gloriette, which came from Hooton Hall in Cheshire. The Gothick Pavilion was a gift to Sir

Top left: Part of the ceiling in the Hercules Hall, depicting the Labors of Hercules. The Hall is based on a demolished Flintshire mansion. *Top center:* A view down one of the walks. *Top right:* The Dome above one of the cottages. *Left:* The fireplace in the hotel entrance hall. *Above:* The village seen across the estuary at low tide.

Clough from Nerquis Hall in Flintshire; the Norman Shaw façade fronting the green-domed Pantheon, high above the whole village, came from Dawpool, the great house he built in Cheshire in 1883; the oval grille in the Town Hall basement comes from the old Bank of England; the panels in the sitting room of the hotel itself were made specially for the 1831 exhibition; the dancing figures on top of the columns in the piazza are Siamese. And so it goes on. Domes, pinnacles, cottages, towers, grilles and gateways, charming corners and splendid vistas. Not surprisingly there are many people who find it all a bit too much; they say it is too contrived, too self-conscious. I have yet to meet one, however, who does not admit that it is all terrific fun.

Portmeirion was first put on the map, literally, by the German High Command; they pinpointed it as a possible invasion spot. Nowadays, the invading hordes tend to arrive from the back of the village in cars, their aim being to walk about, and take photographs, and eat picnics, and buy huge quantities of Portmeirion china designed by Sir Clough's daughter, Susan. They wander round the peninsula, along the narrow pathways which in May are overhung with rhododendrons and azaleas and all manner of flowering trees and shrubs, and hunt for the Ghost Garden, the Dancing Tree, the Old Gold Mine, and the Supreme Viewpoint high on some cliffs with views in both directions of Snowdon and Cardigan Bay. And later, I dare say, they return to the village and stand in the middle of the piazza and wonder, as I did when I saw it for that first time on television, what on earth it all means.

SCHLOSS LAUDON
VIENNA, AUSTRIA

FIELD MARSHAL ERNST Gideon Von Laudon had what must surely be one of the most unusual military careers of all time. After serving in the Russian *and* Prussian Armies, he was made a captain in the *Austrian* Army in 1742, and finally rose to become Generalissimus and Commander-in-Chief of the Austrian Forces.

In the year 1779, the Empress Maria Theresa handed over the castle that is now the Schloss Laudon to the Field Marshal by way of a thank-you present for services rendered to Austria in numerous successful campaigns (particularly that of 1789, when he snatched Belgrade from the Turks).

From all accounts, he seems to have represented for the Austrians a hero-figure at least as illustrious as the Duke of Marlborough in England. *"Laudon rucht an!"* ("Laudon rides on") was a well known folk song of the day. In 1756 Joseph Haydn composed the *Laudon-Marsch* in his honor, and a biography of the great man, written in 1789, includes an encomium by the philosopher Gallert (who designed the remarkable closed library which is still intact on the first floor of the hotel, and whose statue stands in the grounds).

Despite its distinctive seventeenth-century Austrian baroque appearance, its green shutters, and the *Schönbrunnergelp* of its walls (that yellow with which the period of Maria Theresa is so much associated), the Schloss Laudon's history stretches back a long way beyond that. The first written reference to the castle was in 1130. From 1385 it was the property of the dukes of Austria, one of whom, Wilhelm, transformed it in 1400 from a fort into a hunting lodge. In 1460 it was presented by the Emperor Frederick III as a wedding gift to his young bride Eleonore, Crown Princess of Portugal.

The next thing we know about the castle is that in 1677 the Emperor Leopold I gave it, again as a wedding gift, to Eleonore Magdalena Theresa, the grandmother of Maria Theresa. In 1708, Maria Theresa's mother, Elizabeth Christina, spent the two nights before her wedding there.

Maria Theresa herself seems to have taken a close personal interest in the castle, partly, perhaps, because of its close proximity to Schönbrunn. Not only was she responsible for Laudon becoming the owner, but soon after he had moved in she called on him for breakfast and, finding the road and bridge to nearby Hadersdorf in a bad state of repair, at once gave the Field Marshal six thousands guilders towards its repair.

The only other story of interest that we have relating to Laudon is that on July 27, 1785, while he was sleeping in his pavilion in the garden, the river Mauerbach rose and flooded the moat. If his favorite dog has not awoken him in the nick of time, the great man might easily have died in a thoroughly undignified manner.

When it did come finally, in 1790, his death upset the Emperor Leopold III to such an extent that he insisted that the messenger who had brought the news describe in full detail the Field Marshal's last hours. When the wretched courier had finally told him all he wished

OPPOSITE A token of appreciation from the Empress Maria Theresa.

to hear, the Emperor burst into tears and cried out: "I would rather have lost a decisive battle than this great general!"

In Hadersdorf Park there is a life-size statue of Laudon. It was erected at his request, before the conquest of Belgrade, and he would often visit the site and ponder upon the rather somber words inscribed on the plaque held in the statue's right hand: "Meditatio mortis optima philosophia".

Little is known of the history of the *schloss* from Laudon's death until the middle of the present century. Having been abandoned for a number of years, this lovely house had fallen into a state of terrible decay and disrepair. The Botanical Garden beyond the wrought-iron gate had run to seed, the tennis courts were a wilderness, the moat was thick with leaves and weed, the rooms were a mess. Today it would be nothing more than a ruin of mild historic interest had it not been bought in 1961 by a rich man named Alfred Weiss, who set about the massive task of restoration and modernization.

Fortunately, several of the castle's outstanding features survive: the charming vaulted hall where Laudon himself must have stepped many a time into his carriage before setting off through what is now the bar, across the garden and between the two stone lions that marked the start of the main road to the west; the enchanting fresco room on the first floor, today often used as a dining room, with walls completely covered by exuberant designs representing the four continents (the frescoes were taken from the Schloss Donaudorf and by some remarkable coincidence fit the Schloss Laudon Room almost exactly).

Although the address is Vienna, and although it is only half an hour's drive from the Opera (they run their own private car service to the center of town), the Schloss Laudon has all the atmosphere of a country hotel. It is situated in its own park, with its own farm adjoining, and surrounded by a large moat. Not only that, but the public rooms have a thoroughly rustic flavor. The sitting room is filled with huge tapestried armchairs and a big open fireplace, and the main dining room, with boars and bears rushing across the ceiling and antlered heads staring out blankly from the walls, is a reminder that ever since the fourteenth century, this has been a hunting lodge.

Alfred Weiss was a great collector of antiques and works of art. Not only does walking along a corridor to one's room seem like a visit to a rather good private museum, but the bedrooms themselves are a wonder to behold. On the ground floor is one of the most splendid collections of Empire furniture I have seen anywhere. The best suite on the first floor, with views across the moat and park contains the sort of rooms one normally walks through behind a thick rope on a guided tour. On the third floor, the rooms contain extraordinary examples of early nineteenth-century peasant baroque furniture in beds with raised sides like boxes, and wardrobes decorated all over with charming pastoral and religious scenes. Waking up in these rooms can convince you momentarily of having been transported back a hundred years to a peasant cottage in the depths of Austria.

Yet despite the beautiful furniture, the fine wall coverings, the good carpets; despite the constant upkeep required by the continued use of good antiques; and despite the time and effort and care that have gone into turning the Schloss Laudon from an abandoned wreck into one of the world's most charming hotels; despite all this, there are many guests who have the money to be able to afford to stay there.

Unfortunately, they do not have an appreciation of what this place once was, what it is today, and what has gone into making it so. As far as they are concerned it is a place to sleep and eat, rather expensive perhaps, and rather unusual, but still just a place to be used. And so they scrape their suitcases against the paintwork of the beds, thus removing a foot or so of a design that was put there over a hundred and fifty years ago. The present manager, Peter Laszlo, a gentle, cultivated Hungarian who bears an extraordinary resemblance to Alistair Cooke, showed me the silk-lined lobby of one of the biggest suites. "It cost me 19,000 schillings to re-cover just this small area," he said sadly. "Goodness knows what people did to it; knocked it with their luggage, I suppose. But they completely ruined it."

Ah well . . . times are hard. Gone are the days when men like Alfred Weiss could afford to run a place like the Schloss Laudon as though it were a large private house to which he welcomed the people he liked and discouraged those whom he felt were not quite up to it. Gone, too, is Mr. Weiss, leaving his beautiful hotel and his beloved possessions in the hands of Mr. Laszlo, who has the unenviable task not only of trying to carry on the tradition of hospitality and gracious living established fifteen years ago, but at the same time to make it pay. Shortly before becoming manager Mr. Laszlo stayed at the hotel for a conference; in an idle moment he found himself staring up at a particularly beautiful chandelier and thinking how glad he was that it was not his job to have to clean it. Within months, however, it was; his worst fears were realized, and, I daresay, continue to be realized daily.

But it is still a beautiful chandelier, and Schloss Laudon is still a beautiful hotel. How long it will remain that way depends entirely upon how much everyone concerned wishes it to. Mr. Laszlo is performing his part as best he can. The rest is up to the guests.

Top left: The Fresco Room. *Top center:* The dining room. *Top right:* Nineteenth-century peasant baroque furniture in one of the third-floor rooms. *Center left:* The entrance hall where the Field Marshal's carriage used to stop. *Center right:* The courtyard and main entrance. *Left:* The main staircase.

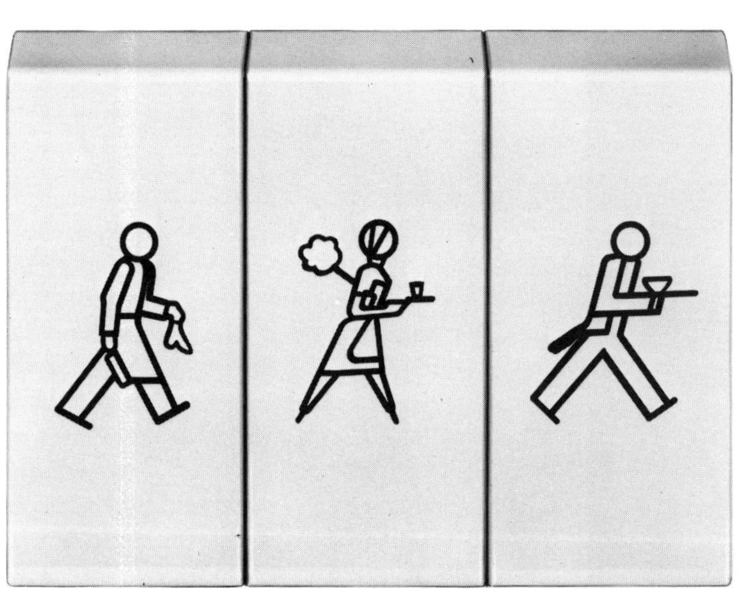